HALIFAX

THE FIRST 250 YEARS

JUDITH FINGARD · JANET GUILDFORD · DAVID SUTHERLAND

FORMAC PUBLISHING COMPANY LIMITED
HALIFAX

Formac Publishing Company Limited acknowledges the support of the Department of Canadian Heritage, the Canada Council and the Nova Scotia Department of Education and Culture in the development of writing and publishing in Canada

Canadian Cataloguing in Publication Data

Fingard, Judith, 1943-
    Halifax

    Includes index   ISBN 0-88780-490-X

1. Halifax (N.S.)--History. I. Guildford, Janet, 1946- II. Sutherland, David A., 1942- III. Title.

FC2346.4.F56 1999   971.6'225   F1039.5.H17F56 1999
C99-950217-4

Formac Publishing Company Limited
5502 Atlantic Street
Halifax, Nova Scotia B3H 1G4   Printed and bound in Canada.

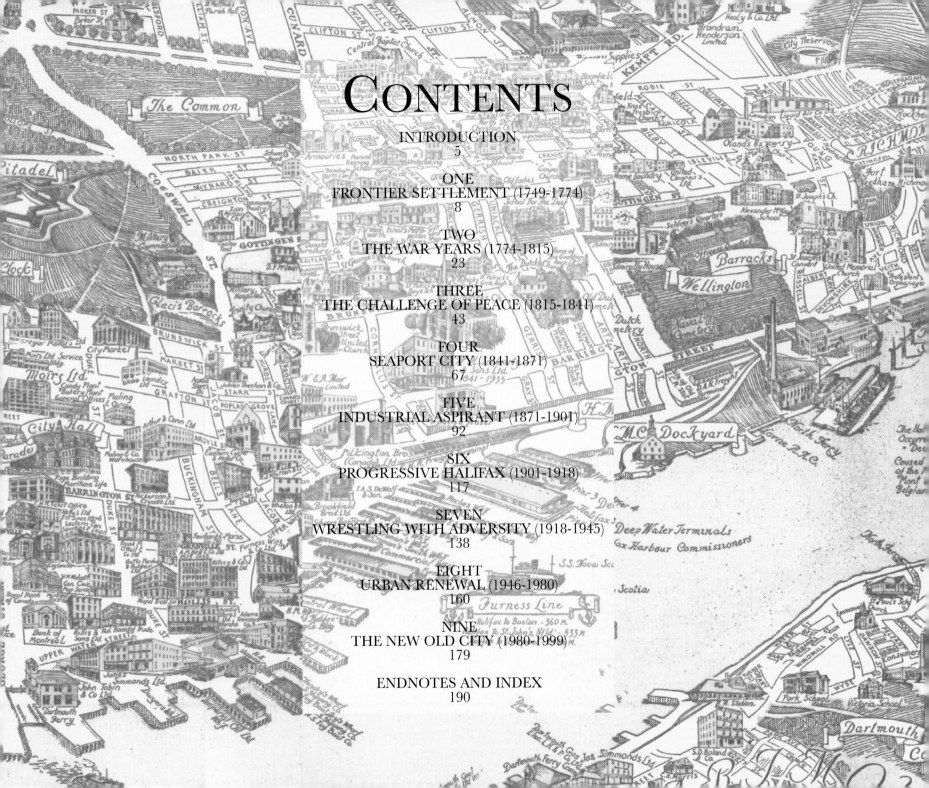

CONTENTS

INTRODUCTION
5

ONE
FRONTIER SETTLEMENT (1749-1774)
8

TWO
THE WAR YEARS (1774-1815)
23

THREE
THE CHALLENGE OF PEACE (1815-1841)
43

FOUR
SEAPORT CITY (1841-1871)
67

FIVE
INDUSTRIAL ASPIRANT (1871-1901)
92

SIX
PROGRESSIVE HALIFAX (1901-1918)
117

SEVEN
WRESTLING WITH ADVERSITY (1918-1945)
138

EIGHT
URBAN RENEWAL (1946-1980)
160

NINE
THE NEW OLD CITY (1980-1999)
179

ENDNOTES AND INDEX
190

ACKNOWLEDGEMENTS

The Halifax Citadel, as viewed from the Commons by A.C. Mercer, 1838. For 250 years, the downtown of Nova Scotia's capital has been dominated by this fortified elevation, a symbol of how state enterprise was imposed on a North American terrain.

We enjoyed a positive working relationship with all the institutions which assisted in finding evidence and illustrations for this book but special thanks are owed to the following people, who went out of their way to be helpful: Charles Armour (Dalhousie University Archives); Geraldine Beaton (Halifax Regional Tourism Department); Henry Bishop (Black Cultural Centre for Nova Scotia); Stephen Coutts (Nova Scotia Sports Hall of Fame); Michele Gallant (Dalhousie University Art Gallery); Marilyn Guerney (Maritime Command Museum); Philip Hartling (Nova Scotia Archives); Pauline Lafford (Parks Canada, Citadel); Ron MacDonald (Parks Canada, Citadel); Judy Pal (Halifax Regional Police); Anita Price (Dartmouth Heritage Museum); Lynn Richard (Maritime Museum of the Atlantic); Scott Robson (Nova Scotia Museum); Gary Shutlak (Nova Scotia Archives); Karen Smith (Dalhousie University, Killam Library, Special Collections); Karen White (Roman Catholic Archdiocese of Halifax, Pastoral Centre).

This book is dedicated to Betty, Clio, Emily, Iain, Peter.

INTRODUCTION

Founded in 1749, Halifax ranks as one of the oldest communities in Canada. The city's long and often dramatic story has been told and retold, in part or in whole, by way of scores of books, articles, novels, poems, drawings and songs. *Halifax: The First 250 Years*, attempts, through text and illustrations, to offer a revised overview of this city's history, in an account which challenges the standard portrait of Nova Scotia's capital. Today, recollection of Halifax's past is widely dominated by images of the *Bluenose*, Alexander Keith ("who made beer his way"), and the explosion of 1917. Besides salt water, suds and disaster, Halifax is usually thought of as place wedded so firmly to tradition that it cannot readily adapt to change. Echoing what by then had become a conventional wisdom, Isabella Lucy Bird, a sharp-tongued Englishwoman visiting in the 1850s, impatiently observed that Haligonians had "expunged the word *progress* from their dictionary."[1] While vivid, such an assessment is deceptive, in ways which this new study seeks to demonstrate, not in an effort to conceal Halifax's flaws but rather to put them into a broadened perspective. Here readers are led beyond episodes of success and failure to explore the roots of change in this mature but also dynamic east coast community.

In large measure, *Halifax: The First 250 Years*, has been designed as a successor to Thomas Raddall's, *Halifax, Warden of the North*.[2] Written half a century ago to help commemorate the city's two-hundredth birthday, Raddall's study presents Halifax as a place founded and sustained by war. Having begun as a military enterprise it evolved, according to Raddall, into a community with a garrison identity, a place where soldiers and sailors, rather than civilians, set the pace of life and defined urban values. Consequently, here was a city where peacetime served as little more than an interlude between episodes of military conflict. Without the stimulus of war, not much of significance happened. Moreover, Raddall suggested that, because of their garrison mentality, the locals learned to stoically accept their fate, becoming more watchmen than entrepreneurs. This was his explanation of why Halifax, which began life far ahead of other North American cities, ultimately fell behind in the quest for urban achievement.

Raddall's analysis aptly fitted the circumstances which prevailed when *Warden of the North* was written, late in the 1940s. World War Two, a devastating but for Canada ultimately victorious struggle, had ended. Once again, Halifax's strategic importance had been demonstrated but now peace loomed, threatening a repetition of the descent into hard times which had come after earlier wars against France, the United States, Napoleon and the Kaiser. Raddall's words offered a colourful but ultimately fatalistic reading of the past, suggesting that Halifax was locked into a single pattern of history, forever doomed to alternate between wartime bustle and peacetime stagnation.

As it turns out, Raddall's pessimism was not justified. The succeeding 50 years became, for Halifax, anything but an era of standing still. By the early 1950s the city had embarked on a sustained and dizzying array of change, in effect going through a process of reinvention. That upheaval, its links to the past and implications for the future, cannot be explained by way of the analysis found in *Warden of the North*. A new overview is required, one which transcends the old explanatory devices of war and peace, soldiers and civilians, and garrison identity.

We need to look more broadly for factors, both within and without, which shaped Halifax's destiny. For example, what legacy has been left by location and access to resources? How has Halifax been influenced by the origins of those who came to call it home? Did ideas about religion, respectability and democracy, play a major role in shaping community character? Which visions of development, ranging from trade through industrialization, worked best for Halifax? What has the city derived, in terms of both gains and losses, from its evolving links to Europe, the United States and the rest of Canada? How well have Haligonians done in coming to terms with the internal distinctions of class, gender, race, ethnicity and religion? When and why has discrimination flourished and what circumstances have allowed Halifax to move toward patterns of integration? These and related questions are under active review today by a host of scholars and in *Halifax: The First 250 Years*, we have attempted to draw together their insights.[3] The synthesis found here is less than definitive, largely because major segments of Halifax's past remain in shadow. Nevertheless, this book has been designed to offer a richer and more probing view of time past than what could be devised half a century ago.

Halifax: The First 250 Years, is a multi-authored book. Three historians have been assigned the task of writing an overview of the era closest to where they have done the bulk of their previous research and writing. Section one, written by David Sutherland, surveys the period from Halifax's founding to its incorporation as a city in 1841. As the population figures in Table One demonstrate, life in early Halifax was dominated by a pattern of boom and bust, triggered respectively by declarations of war and announcements of peace. While this tends to support Raddall's perspective, it is important to

Table One

	Halifax	Nova Scotia
1749	2,500*	15,000*
1758	6,000*	n/a
1767	3,685	8,104
1791	3,932	n/a
1802	8,532	n/a
1817	11,156	81,351
1827	14,439	123,630
1838	14,432	202,575

* Contemporary estimates or, in the case of post-Confederation totals, a calculation based on probably patterns with respect to suburbanization

note that subtle changes were under way, especially by the early years of the nineteenth century. The original vision articulated by Halifax's founders in 1749, that of establishing more than a military encampment, caught hold, such that the post-1815 era featured not a decline into peace-time apathy but rather vigorous self-assertion. Diversified trade, accelerated integration with its regional hinterland, surging immigration from the British Isles, and an eruption of cultural energy, transformed Halifax. By 1841 it had become not only a city but also a place dominated by its newly-emergent middle class, people driven by the ideals of moral virtue and material gain.

Section two, written by Judith Fingard, carries the story of Halifax forward from the 1840s to World War One, through what is generally thought of as the "Victorian Age." Here the dominant theme is the sustained effort to use science and technology, along with public and private enterprise, to establish Halifax as a modern community, one which emulated the success of other cities ranging from London, through Boston to Montreal and Toronto. The population figures in Table Two offer clues about what became of that dream. Nova Scotia's capital grew and acquired many expressions of modernization, such as railroads and factories, along with a network

	Table Two Halifax + Dartmouth	Nova Scotia
1851	19,165	276.9
1861	25,026	330.9
1871	31,773	387.8
1881	39,859	440.6
1891	44,688	450.4
1901	45,638	459.6
1911	51,677	492.3

of social and cultural institution, ranging from schools to hospitals. Nevertheless, Halifax could not keep pace with the rest of North America. Underachievement haunted Nova Scotia's capital but this problem became not so much a basis for despair as a stimulus for ever greater effort. By the early twentieth century Haligonians were actively experimenting with new-model ideas, what contemporaries called "progressivism," hoping that through yet bolder innovation they might catch up with the rest of Canada.

Part three of Halifax's story, told by Janet Guildford, begins with the great watershed of World War One. Haligonians, largely because of the optimism they had inherited from the Victorian era, thought this would be a war unlike other wars, one destined to advance rather than jeopardize their prospects. That self-confidence persisted, even after the disaster of 1917, since most Haligonians assumed that what rose from the ashes of the explosion would be a community even more fully engaged in "progressive" endeavour. Unfortunately, as the figures in Table Three show, those expectations were not immediately realized. The 1920s and 1930s came to feature a bitterly protracted slide into decay and obsolescence. Adversity became so acute as to prompt large-scale emigration, while many who persisted retreated into nostalgia and paranoia. World War Two brought ephemeral relief but ended amidst violence and anxiety, the latter primarily prompted by questions as to whether Halifax had the potential to become truly modern. The answer which has emerged since 1945 is decidedly in

the affirmative. Pushed both from without and within, by the 1960s Nova Scotia's capital became the pre-eminent growth centre on Canada's east coast. Challenges persist in this old/new city but most locals regard community difficulties as being more manageable than overwhelming. And in searching for a way forward, Haligonians are discovering that their past is an asset, not a liability.

The common focus throughout this volume is what might be termed the interaction between circumstance and character which, operating over a 250 year span, has come to define Halifax and its

	Table Three Halifax Metro	Nova Scotia
1921	67,726*	523.8
1931	79,352*	512.9
1941	96,636	578.0
1951	138,427	642.6
1961	193,353	737.0
1971	222,627	789.0
1981	277,727	847.4
1991	320,521	901.0
1996	332,518	909.3

people. The three authors all question traditional generalizations about this city being a "conservative" community, in love with tradition, hierarchy and deference. Those elements do exist and from time to time have prevailed but overall, Halifax has acquired a complex personality, one which includes hunger for innovation, a willingness to engage in protest, and a talent for creative reconstruction. The details of what that meant, ever since 1749, are found in the chapters which follow. A combination of words and images have been mustered to provide what we hope will be seen as a refreshing portrait of the Nova Scotian capital, from its origins to the near present.

Chapter One

FRONTIER SETTLEMENT
(1749-1774)

Chebucto Becomes Halifax

Late in 1749 George Hick, a blacksmith formerly of London, England, wrote to his wife back home describing his life as a pioneer in the frontier settlement at Chebucto, Nova Scotia. Hick spoke glowingly about the conditions he had encountered in North America:

> *My dear, I live as well as a man can desire, I want for no money nor clothes, I want for no victuals nor drink, nor lodging, I want for nothing but you and my dear children, and should be very glad that you would come in the fleet, the next spring in the year '50; you should be kindly welcome to enjoy my prosperous labour, as you may live an easy life, without labour to toil yourself.[1]*

As further encouragement for her to travel, George noted that he now combined his trade as blacksmith with the selling of rum. The two enterprises meant that he had become, overnight, a man of property, possessing £50 in ready cash, and would soon be given valuable real estate at the heart of what he was sure would emerge as the most prosperous town north of Boston.

It was an unusual letter, in the sense that mid-eighteenth century Englishmen rarely went to the New World. While America had attracted a few religious dissidents, along with a growing flood of

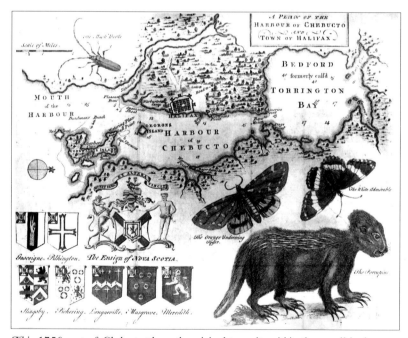

This 1750 map of Chebucto places the original townsite within the overall harbour context. The artist's peculiar rendering of a Nova Scotian porcupine suggests that most pioneers had only a vague understanding of frontier realities.

people from Britain's "celtic fringe," most of the King's subjects were content to stay at home. Moreover, those in power, both the government and Britain's landlord class, normally discouraged emigration overseas, fearing it might lead to labour shortages and a scarcity of military manpower. But there was George Hick, a man given Crown offers of free transport, land and supplies if he would participate in the building of a new town in the wilderness. This dramatic and costly departure from tradition, something destined to overwhelm the lives of many more than George Hick, derived from the harsh logic of imperial conflict.

In large measure, the occupation of Chebucto had been made necessary by Louisbourg, a French fortress located 302 kilometres up the coast on Cape Breton Island. Built in the aftermath of the 1713 Treaty of Utrecht, which ended an earlier bout of Anglo-French warfare, Louisbourg was designed to consolidate French control over the coastal approaches to the St. Lawrence heartland of New France. When first tested in battle Louisbourg failed, falling in 1745 to a siege force from New England. But that disaster for the French obscured a larger achievement. Prior to 1745 Louisbourg had attained remarkable success, as a base for trade and the fishery, and perhaps most importantly, as a device to give France close economic and diplomatic ties with those living in mainland Nova Scotia. This nominally British colony, established under the terms of the 1713 settlement, had a population which consisted mainly of "Acadians," French-speaking Roman Catholics, along with the Mi'kmaq, the First Nation people who saw themselves as being the true sovereign power in all of the present-day Maritimes. Even with Louisbourg in English hands

Duc d'Anville, commander of the French expeditionary force of 1746. He died of a stroke on board his flagship, shortly after sailing into Chebucto harbour.

through the later 1740s, British rule in Nova Scotia remained decidedly precarious.

Proof of that vulnerability came in 1746, when France despatched a massive fleet consisting of 61 vessels carrying 11,000 sailors and soldiers, to Nova Scotian waters in an effort to reverse the flow of war. Under the command of Duc d'Anville, this bold counter-stroke featured use of the Atlantic coastal location known to the French as Chibouctou (from the Mi'kmaq word "chebookt," meaning "chief harbour"). The site had much to offer, notably a large and secure anchorage, combined with relatively easy access, overland and by sea, to the then-Nova Scotian capital at Annapolis Royal, and beyond it to Boston. Storms and disease wreaked havoc in the French fleet, such that those who made port could do little but regroup for a humiliating return to Europe. But this demonstration of French sea power disturbed those in authority, both at Boston and in London. They realized that far from being beaten, France remained a potent enemy, capable

As this image suggests, when the English arrived at Chebucto they encountered a native population which had long been in contact with Europeans, a connection which enhanced Mi'kmaq capacity to assert their claims of sovereignty.

A Mi'kmaq domestic scene as portrayed by R. Petley in 1837. Despite the bloodshed associated with Halifax's founding, later Haligonians developed a fascination for native culture.

of waging war across the globe. The evenness of the prevailing balance of power was underscored by the treaty which, in 1748, ended four years of hostilities. Bolstered by victories in other theatres of conflict, France succeeded in winning back control of Louisbourg.

By mid-summer 1749, the fleur-de-lis flew over the ramparts of a fortress which once again posed a dire threat to British interests in North America.

Burdened with heavy debt incurred by war and distracted by the need to pacify the Scottish Highlands, which had recently risen in arms against Hanoverian rule, London might have been expected to neglect the North American colonies. However, imperial strategy, with its assumption that British security in Europe demanded possessions overseas, laid the basis for an initiative which would give George Hick a new life in America. Late in 1748 the cabinet in London received a document drafted by the Duke of Bedford, one of the inner circle of power, which called for construction of a "new" Nova Scotia, a colony which would be a source of strength, not vulnerability, if and when hostilities resumed with France. Inspired largely by ideas coming from an ever-assertive Governor William Shirley of Massachusetts, Bedford insisted that "the security of the northern colonies and the preservation of His Majesty's Dominions in America" demanded drastic British intervention in Nova Scotia.[2]

Bedford and Shirley had in mind change that went far beyond creation of a military strong point to offset the threat of Louisbourg. They called for a comprehensive program of settlement and resource development involving a series of new communities at key points around the coast. There settlers would be encouraged to farm, fish, lumber and trade, and in the process, function as agents of cultural and political transformation, assimilating the Acadians and Mi'kmaq so that Nova Scotia would acquire an identity which was essentially English-speaking, Protestant and white. Those in authority feared that without construction of this altered Nova Scotia, North America might be lost to the French, a reversal which could usher in defeat of British power in Europe.

Such a high-stakes game required bold and costly governmental intervention. The private sector, Bedford and Shirley insisted, lacked the will and the means to bring speedy and decisive change to Nova Scotia. The Crown must take the lead, beginning with an expedition to Chebucto, a place whose strategic importance had been demonstrated by the French. Such an initiative would be expensive and thus politically controversial but, as Bedford's memo noted, "economy neglectful of security is the most dangerous and destructive system that can be pursued."[3] In earlier times such logic would have been dismissed as scaremongering but in 1748, with intercontinental war a

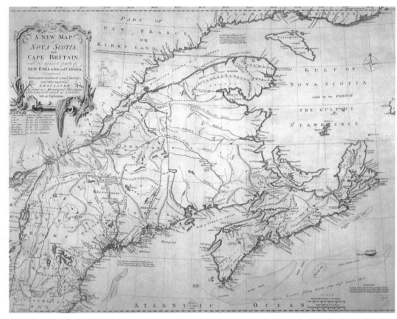

This map of the 1740s demonstrates how Chebucto stood strategically between English and French spheres of influence in eastern North America.

very likely prospect, it made sense to see Nova Scotia as being vital for the empire. Thus the London government set in motion the process for transforming Chebucto into an embodiment of British power.

Men like George Hick would first have learned of the government's intentions through handbills and tavern-talk circulating through London. The decision to go, in most cases, derived from the "push" of hard times at home, reinforced by the "pull" of opportunity in America, the latter brought into focus by the fact that migrants would have their way paid overseas and then be subsidized while putting down roots. A majority of those recruited had recently been mustered out of Britain's armed forces, while the remainder mainly came from the artisan section of English society. Carpenters particularly had been sought out for their ability to build structures in the wilderness. Similarly, a special welcome was extended to men with wives and children. Women, it was assumed, would help curb the debauchery likely to erupt on a male-dominated frontier. And children, it was hoped, would grow up to facilitate self-generating population growth.

Starting on 14 May 1749, after several weeks of frenzied activity in gathering together people, provisions and general supplies, a fleet of fourteen wooden, wind-powered vessels ventured down the Thames, en route to Chebucto, Nova Scotia. Opinions on shore about this venture were mixed. Optimists saw Nova Scotia as "a kind of Utopia where class distinctions dissolved, the common miseries of life faded from the memory, and riches abounded in vast expanses of land."[4] Pessimists poked fun at people like George Hick, satirizing his behaviour with lines of verse like the following:

> *There is nothing there [Chebucto] but Holidays*
> *With Music out of Measure;*
> *Who can forbear to speak the Praise*
> *Of such a Land of Pleasure;*
> *There you may lead a pleasant Life,*
> *Free from all Kind of Labour,*
> *And he that is without a Wife,*
> *may borrow of his Neighbour.*[5]

Despite such mockery George and most of his companions, initially at least, did very well. Their vessels escaped storms and crossed the North Atlantic with remarkable speed. First into port was the sloop of war *Sphinx*, which dropped anchor on 21 June 1749 (2 July by our modern calendar). The thirteen transports, carrying approximately 2500 settlers, followed over the next couple of weeks. Almost no one had died en route, thanks to good luck and the installation of devices which circulated fresh air to those crowded below deck. Thus the scene which unfolded at Chebucto, in the early

Edward Cornwallis, once viewed uncritically as the heroic "founder" of Halifax, is now seen as someone with a vision flawed by racial and class prejudice.

summer of 1749, provided a positive contrast to what had prevailed three years earlier when d'Anville's fleet had made its disastrous Nova Scotian rendezvous.

Command of the English settlement venture had been assigned to Edward Cornwallis, a thirty-seven-year-old army officer, a man determined to make this assignment a springboard for rapid career advancement. Once ashore Nova Scotia's new governor plunged enthusiastically into the enormously complex task of transforming a heavily-forested wilderness into a homestead for the likes of George Hick. The first problem Cornwallis faced involved selection of a town-site. After considering several options (and indeed making a false start at what has come to be known as Point Pleasant, near the open sea), it was decided to build on the eastern slopes of "Citadel Hill," an 85-metre high drumlin located astride the 1200-hectare peninsula which jutted into Chebucto harbour. This location, while it has forced generations of residents to move up and down a steep incline, offered several important advantages, including access to a sheltered, deep-water anchorage, close proximity to the ocean and a position which could be readily defended against attack overland or by sea.

By mid-summer 1749 work parties had cleared about eight hectares for a town which Cornwallis had decided would be named after George Dunk, Lord Halifax, president of the Board of Trade, the government agency responsible for coordinating creation of a new Nova Scotia. After a crude hewing down of the forest cover, effort shifted to building accommodations, which ranged from a relatively elegant two-storey wooden house for the governor, to scores of huts and even more primitive shelters, all laid out in a rough, seven by seven, grid of streets. At the centre was the

A modern artist's impression of land clearing on the slopes of Citadel Hill. It understates the bickering and confusion of which dominated the summer of 1749.

presumptuously named "Grand Parade," in reality a patch of rough ground littered with rocks and stumps, where only with difficulty could troops manoeuvre. The boundaries of Halifax that first year, were defined by five log forts, joined together by a hurriedly erected barricade of upturned trees. By the standards of contemporary London or even Boston, Halifax ranked as a place both primitive and precarious. But for George Hick and many of his associates, the town embodied promise.

A Town Under Siege

Nova Scotia's Mi'kmaq population viewed what was happening at Chebucto with considerable foreboding. Developments in neighbouring New England, where settlement had led to violent displacement of First Nation peoples, suggested that the founding of Halifax posed a dire threat to the Mi'kmaq, who cherished their

ability to avoid European conquest. Governor Cornwallis, however, insisted that the natives lacked sovereignty and thus did not have to be consulted over what was being done at Chebucto. Thus, while he was willing to meet with and offer presents to small groups of Mi'kmaq who came to observe, he at no time offered to negotiate the terms under which Chebucto might be transformed into Halifax. That arrogance set in motion a train of events which led to tragic violence, the memories of which would long complicate race relations in colonial Nova Scotia.

Exactly why conflict erupted between the Mi'kmaq and the English at Halifax remains a matter of debate. Some scholars insist that primary blame should be directed at Abbé Jean-Louis Le Loutre, a Roman Catholic missionary based in Nova Scotia during this critical era. Le Loutre did write in a letter, dated July 1749, saying that "we [the French] cannot do better than to incite the Indians to continue warring on the English."[6] While pressure to go to war likely was applied

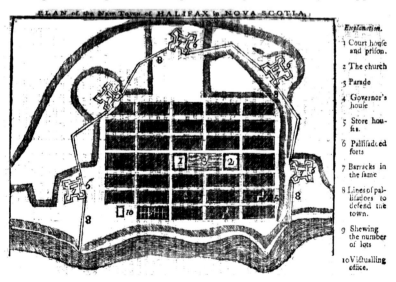

The orderly array of streets and fortifications shown in this early plan of Halifax reflected imperial ambitions which largely gave way to jumble and disorder as the town fought for survival.

by Le Loutre, the Mi'kmaq had not become so dependent on the French that they could be used as pawns in an imperial power struggle. Violence more likely arose out of a desperate attempt by a host people to persuade the English newcomers to make concessions which would give the Mi'kmaq continued rights to hunt and fish in what they regarded as their homeland.

The first of several violent incidents came in September 1749 at a mill-site located on the eastern side of Halifax harbour, that soon became Dartmouth. A small force of Mi'kmaq warriors attacked, killing several English wood cutters, possibly as a warning to Cornwallis that he must pay compensation for what amounted to a unilateral expropriation of First Nation lands. Unfortunately, the governor reacted by falling into a rage. Insisting that innocent civilians had been slaughtered by "savages," who were either rebels against English rule or mercenaries working for the French, Cornwallis opted for counter-violence rather than compromise. Rewards of £10 (later raised to £50) were offered for the

Too often overlooked or dismissed as lazy and drunken folk, the rank and file pioneers of 1749 played a key role in laying the foundations of Halifax.

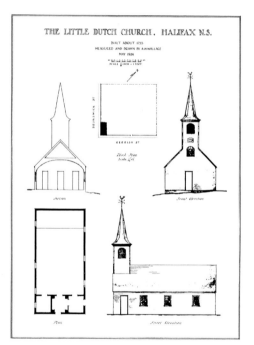

London's ambition to entice a flood of Protestant immigrants to Nova Scotia led to public works projects such as this, the "little Dutch Church," where Halifax's German-speaking settlers could pray.

scalp of any native brought in to Halifax. Then a force of colonial "Indian fighters," commanded by Captain John Gorham of New England, was mobilized to wage a campaign of terror through the interior of the colony.

The extreme measures Cornwallis employed against the Mi'kmaq in part grew out of the mounting frustration the governor felt about virtually every aspect of the job he was trying to accomplish in Halifax. That first summer ashore had brought him a host of problems. Most aggravating of all was the behaviour of the rank and file settlers who persistently defied official orders. When told to work on projects such as construction of fortifications, they refused, resorting to drink and desertion. Such behaviour has often been attributed to sheer laziness but it might be more accurate to say that pioneers such as George Hick were simply pursuing a personal agenda. Primarily that meant getting title to a plot of land which would be their own and on which they could begin building a shelter to ward off winter. Significantly, conflict between settlers and Cornwallis declined after a lottery had been held to allocate town and rural lots across the Halifax peninsula. As well, the stark reality of hostile Mi'kmaq operating around the edges of town made even feckless persons more willing to obey commands designed to protect them from capture and possible execution.

Nevertheless, Cornwallis's mood steadily soured as he slipped ever further into the morass of protracted Indian warfare. Never able to land a decisive blow against what became a most elusive enemy, the governor found himself bottled up in Halifax, largely unable to proceed with implementation of London's grand vision for establishing British hegemony across all of mainland Nova Scotia. An example of how badly things were going was provided by the presence in Halifax of several hundred "Foreign Protestants," immigrants brought out in the years 1750-1752 from Europe's upper Rhine valley, at heavy public expense. The intention had been to settle these Germans near the Acadians so that the newcomers might function as agents of cultural assimilation. Mi'kmaq resistance, however, prevented immigrants from venturing deep into the provincial interior. In the mid-1750s most of the Foreign Protestants were settled at Lunenburg, on the colony's south shore, while a few took up farming at places such as Dutch Village, on Halifax's extreme western boundary. Meanwhile, the bills continued to mount, such that Cornwallis came under ever more critical scrutiny from officials in London. In 1752, frustrated, increasingly disillusioned, and burdened by failing health, Cornwallis resigned as Nova Scotia's governor and went home to England.

It is unlikely that George Hick witnessed the departure of Halifax's founding father. He and many of his peers either died during their first winter in North America or moved on to greater opportunity in New England. Their places were filled by an influx of Yankees, mainly small businessmen and professionals, drawn north by the lure of government money. Representative of this influx was Malachy Salter, a young trader soon renowned for his skill in driving a hard bargain. Down on his luck and hotly pursued by creditors, Salter set up on "the beach" (Water Street) as a merchant, his fresh-start

Slave sales, such as the one portrayed in this modern cartoon, were a common feature of life in early Halifax. Slavery persisted in Nova Scotia's capital until the 1790s.

facilitated by the fact that Nova Scotian law prevented him from being sued for debts incurred prior to coming to the colony. This special protection for what some regarded as scoundrels had been established as an incentive to draw risk-takers to Nova Scotia. It persisted on the statute books until 1762.

Another new face was that of John Bushell, who came from Boston in 1752 to launch Canada's first newspaper, the *Halifax Gazette.* Surviving issues of this publication offer glimpses of groups rarely mentioned in official despatches. Here, for example, we find advertising by Elizabeth Render, who operated a reading school for children and also functioned as a cleaner specializing in gold and silver lace; nearby, Sarah Todd sold butter and linens, while Hannah Hutchinson combined needlework with instruction in "French and Country Dances." Black people also lived in early Halifax, usually working as servants, sometimes under the constraints of slavery. Explicit reference to bondage appears in an advertisement which offered for sale "several Negro slaves, viz. A very likely Negro Wench, of about thirty five Years of age, a Creole born, has been brought up in a Gentleman's Family, and capable of doing all sorts of Work," along with two young boys, a man of 18 and another aged 30. Far down Halifax's social hierarchy were the soldiers of the small garrison, men usually receiving mention only in the most dire of circumstances, such as in November 1752, when three came to the gallows after having been convicted of a capital offence, most likely theft. One, the *Gazette* reported, said little, a second protested his innocence, while the third "warn'd all People, especially his fellow Soldiers, to beware of those sins which had bro't him to that untimely End, to have a greater Regard for the Sabbath, and to spend more of their Time at the

By the end of the 1750s Halifax had matured into a small but bustling town. This scene, dominated by the governor's mansion, also shows how most Haligonians earned a meagre living through use of muscle power.

the Mi'kmaq but neither he nor his successors could stop the drift toward war between the empires of Britain and France. Hostilities began unofficially in 1754, with fighting along the western frontiers of colonies such as Virginia. Desperate to repulse what was widely perceived as French aggression, Governor Shirley of Massachusetts, acting jointly with Hopson's replacement, Charles Lawrence, mobilized for war on Nova Scotia's ill-defined frontier. Their immediate target was Fort Beausejour, an outpost of Louisbourg, located at the head of the Bay of Fundy. It fell in 1755, triggering the sequence of events which culminated in a mass expulsion of the Acadians from Nova Scotia. The decision to remove French Roman Catholics from Nova Scotia had been made in Halifax by Governor Lawrence and his council of advisors. It represented a fundamental departure from the original grand design of 1749. Instead of operating as an instrument for peaceful absorption of the Acadians into a British Nova Scotia, Halifax now became the agent for their being driven abroad. Lawrence justified this devastating depopulation of Nova Scotia as a military necessity, required because of the continuing threat of French invasion. Though surprised by what had taken place, the British government endorsed Lawrence's position, even though it meant that the colony's interior become virtually a

Church, and less at the Gin-Shops."[7] These executions reflected the mores of the mid-eighteenth century, a time when human life, especially for ordinary folk, was regarded being worthy of little consideration.

Militarization During the Seven Years War

The new governor, Peregrine Hopson, had the wit to seek peace with wasteland in terms of European settlement.

Largely shorn, for the moment, of its role for building a new Nova Scotia, Halifax concentrated on the challenges of war. In 1756 formal hostilities erupted between Britain and France. Conflict would rage worldwide for another seven years, with North America serving as a primary theatre of war. Since decision-makers assumed that the fate of empire turned on the tide of battle in America, London's purse strings were relaxed to provide payment for an unprecedented flood of military resources into North America. Halifax, being seen as a critically important forward base for waging war, received a huge share of imperial military spending.

Physical expressions of the changes brought to the Nova Scotian capital by war abounded. Perhaps most notable was His Majesty's Naval Yard, a sprawling complex of buildings and wharves which began to take shape in 1758 on the shores of Halifax harbour, about one mile north of the original town site. Engineers also redesigned the top of Citadel Hill, replacing the original small and ineffectual defence works with a large array of wooden walls and trenches designed primarily to defend the town from overland attack. Tucked beneath the walls were two massive barracks, built to house the thousands of soldiers who would wait in town for shipment to colonial battlefields. West of the Citadel, forest cover rapidly

Soldiers rather than sailors made up the bulk of Halifax's ongoing garrison presence but this naval yard, located just north of the original townsite, dominated the town's eighteenth-century waterfront.

disappeared as trees were converted to building material or used for fuel. Few people took up residence in this area, however, thanks in part to fear of the Mi'kmaq, who had allied themselves with the French. A longer term deterrent to expansion of the town was provided by Halifax's 100-hectare Common. Set up in 1760 as a pasture for locals, the Common quickly came to be regarded by the military as a space which must not be built on, lest structures there provide cover for an advancing enemy. Accordingly, as Halifax's population grew to some 6,000, almost all had to crowd into the original town-site of 1749.

The twin processes of expansion and compression gave wartime Halifax a distinct character dominated by noise, stench, and considerable disorder. One visitor, struck by the steep slopes of the town, said Halifax's houses, mostly wooden and jerry-built, hung "like seats in a theatre."[8] And as in a theatre, obtaining and providing entertainment seemed to dominate activity in town. Grog shops, both licensed and illicit, along with brothels, abounded, prompting the famous quip that in Halifax, "the business of one-half the town is to sell rum, and the other half to drink it."[9] The profits of war were never greater than in 1758 when some 22,000 military personnel crowded into Halifax in preparation for an assault on Halifax's old rival, Louisbourg. An American commentary on Halifax at this stage of its life read as follows:

Oh Halifax, the worst of God's creation,
Possest of the worst scoundrels of Each nation;
Whores, rogues and thieves, the dreg and skum of vice
Bred up to villainy, theft, Rags and Lice.[10]

The last word alluded to something more ominous than the mere presence of vermin. Lice carried typhus fever, which periodically swept through town, killing hundreds of Haligonians. Apart from inoculation for smallpox, local doctors could do little for the victims of disease, other than subject them to the torture of bleeding, blistering and purgation. When parents died, a common happening, their children went to an orphanage, which like the poor house, had been established by Halifax's founders. The fate of such children, if they physically survived, was to be put into the workforce as common labourers, starting at about age ten. For the most part, work in wartime Halifax derived from the garrison, which had swollen such that military personnel outnumbered civilians by a ratio of six to one. Acknowledging this militarization of the local economy, Governor Lawrence, in 1759, observed that without a large army and naval presence, "this Town and its environs ... must have sunk in misery."[11]

Lawrence's words contained a warning since, by 1760, the war which briefly had made Halifax's fortune was winding down. Louisbourg fell in 1758; Quebec followed in 1759 and a year later came the surrender of New France at Montreal. A peace treaty which formalized Britain's near unqualified triumph in North America would not come until 1763, but as early as 1760 demobilization had proceeded to the point of making Halifax little more than "a standby military and naval outpost of empire, to be held in readiness for war but as cheaply as possible."[12] Shrinking opportunity drove people away; the civilian population fell by fifty percent to under 3,000. Meanwhile, mainland Nova Scotia continued to wallow in the devastation of the Acadian expulsion, a reverse compounded in 1760 when Royal Engineers blew up the town of Louisbourg, thereby eliminating what had been a thriving centre for trade and the fishery. Halifax now faced the challenge of providing leadership in a colony which, outside the capital, had been devastated by war.

This critical juncture coincided with a significant shift in the colonial leadership. Governor Lawrence suddenly died in 1760 and his successors for the next thirty years were either second-rate personalities or men preoccupied with career prospects elsewhere. As the office of governor fell into eclipse, power migrated into the hands of a merchant clique led by Joshua Mauger. Born about 1725 on the island of Jersey, in the English Channel, Mauger had come to Halifax in 1749 to engage in trade. He stayed through the 1750s, gaining ever greater wealth and influence, mainly by way of the manufacture and sale of rum. Soon the distilleries controlled by Mauger were turning out a flood of liquor, most of which went to slake the thirst of the garrison. Despite confrontations with authority over alleged smuggling, Mauger ultimately prevailed. Retiring to London in 1760, he entered Parliament and quickly emerged as the imperial government's chief

Joshua Mauger (pronounced "major"), after whom Mauger's Beach at the harbour approaches is named, made a fortune in early Halifax, largely through the manufacture and sale of rum.

advisor on Nova Scotian affairs. Operating in conjunction with a network of agents in Halifax, Mauger, more than anyone else, presided over Halifax's tortuous transition from war to peace.

Two major innovations shaped Nova Scotian affairs through the 1760s. The first involved repopulation of the colony's interior, mainly by what were termed the "Planters," migrants from neighbouring New England, who settled both along Nova Scotia's south-western shores and up the Bay of Fundy, where they occupied lands taken from the Acadians. The second innovation featured creation of an elected House of Assembly, a legislative body largely brought into being to assure the incoming Planters that they would have those civil rights they had grown up with in New England. In practice, however, the Assembly served Halifax rather than outport interests. Nova Scotia's new rural communities, which took shape through the 1760s, found themselves persistently subordinated to the will of Joshua Mauger and his friends. The conflict which arose out of this unequal relationship between town and country laid the basis for Nova Scotia's ambivalent response to the next crisis of empire, the American Revolution.

From War to Peace

In Halifax, the 1760s opened on a positive note with the formal signing (in 1761) of a treaty of peace between the Crown, as represented by the acting governor, Jonathan Belcher, and leaders

Jonathan Belcher, one of the flood of New Englanders who sought their fortune in early Halifax, achieved considerable success. Named chief justice in 1754, he became a fixture in government for the next twenty years.

of several bands of the Mi'kmaq people. Deprived of French military support and enticed to the bargaining table by offers of supplies, as well as the major innovation of guarantees for their traditional rights to hunt and fish, the Mi'kmaq ended their resistance. Belcher's generosity, prompted by his desperate need to achieve peace in order to draw new settlers into Nova Scotia, though later repudiated by London, ultimately became the basis for native land claims in the late twentieth century. Ironically, in the short run the Planter influx created few rewards for Halifax, especially in terms of trade. Most settlers relied on Boston and neighbouring New England centres, both as a source of supply and a market for what they produced. Outport neglect of Halifax largely derived from its small size, economic backwardness and isolated location. Why should rural people bother with the Nova Scotian capital which held a small fraction of Boston's population, had virtually no commercial links with the all-important Caribbean, and lacked roads leading into the interior?

The inertia which became ever more characteristic of Halifax's existence in the aftermath of the Seven Years' War spawned considerable social tension within the community. Lack of money, both public and private, was the principal source of unrest. Halifax officials suffered from the virtual collapse of what had been their main source of revenue—money grants voted by the imperial parliament. By the mid-1760s this income had shrunk to less than £5000 per year, well under what it cost to govern the colony. Rather than experiment with risky investments, such as high seas shipping, Mauger's associates preferred to borrow, a policy which soon left Nova Scotia mired in debt. Cash grew so scarce that not even a public lottery could be operated at a profit. Meanwhile, Halifax's labouring poor, who made up the bulk of the town's population, increasingly fell into destitution, becoming dependent on relief for survival. Angered by rising welfare costs, Halifax's minuscule middle class launched a tax revolt, provoking town officials to deal ever more harshly with those unable to provide for themselves. Beggars, for example, faced whipping and then incarceration in the town's bridewell, a general-purpose prison designed to hold petty criminals, including debtors. In another effort to promote social order, laws were passed which required all persons over the age of twelve to attend divine service at least once every three months. Things got so bad that in 1771 Governor Campbell ordered the suppression of horse racing, declaring it to be an activity "tending to gambling and idleness."[13]

This is not to say that all was grim in the Nova Scotian capital. Halifax newspapers of the late 1760s and early 1770s do contain "good news" stories, such as when residents held their annual celebration of King George's birthday, in mid-September 1769. At dawn vessels in the harbour broke out in bunting, flags flew from the Citadel and volleys rang out from companies of soldiers drawn up on

Perched beside a sprawling, ice-free harbour, shown here from the vantage point of George's Island, early Halifax continually struggled to make itself into something more than a garrison town.

the Grand Parade. That evening the local gentry gathered at entertainment houses, particularly the Great Pontac, which offered facilities for dining (mutton pies a speciality), drinking and dancing, with lavishness reminiscent of London. Another expression of social achievement came in 1768 with formation of the North British Society, a mutual aid society which still exists. Members, mostly of Scottish extraction, gathered annually on St. Andrew's Day (30 November), for "harmony, joy and jollity and ancient Scots songs."[14] Higher culture also could be found in town, particularly at St. Paul's Anglican Church, which acquired an organ in the mid-1760s and allowed its facilities to be used for concerts of sacred and secular music. The emphasis Haligonians placed on the secular side of life proved shocking to Jonathan Scott, a Congregational cleric visiting from Yarmouth. Speaking of the capital, Scott observed,

The people here are much for visiting on the Sabbath at which my heart is grieved. Profaneness abounds ... I think I could not content myself to live in Halifax; I had rather live in a Cottage in the Wilderness than in the noise and confusion that attends the place.[15]

Life among the lower orders of town often featured a chronic struggle for survival, which some people lost. For example, in January of 1769 the press reported the fate of carpenter Robert Vowles, found

St. Paul's Anglican church, built by Halifax's founders in 1750 to instil deference and order within the local population, largely survived through sustained infusions of public money and patronage.

Mrs. John Bauer, "assaulted on the High Road [leading to the North West Arm], beat and dragged into the woods by William Lambert of the 65th Regt. and ... by him treated in a most barbarous manner."[16] Overall then, experiences differed in mid-eighteenth-century Halifax. A few lived in comfort but for the majority, life remained precarious.

A quarter-century after its founding, Nova Scotia's capital had the appearance of a small and essentially crude frontier village, which most visitors found repulsive. For example, a visiting Yankee, comparing Halifax to Boston, sarcastically commented, "The houses of Hallifax [sic] seem to have been sowed like mushrooms in a hot-bed, and to have decayed as fast; for although they have been many built but a few years, yet there are scarce any of them habitable."[17] Similarly, Messrs. Robinson and Rispin, from Yorkshire, warned folks back home that the cost of living in Halifax remained high, largely because most foodstuffs had to be imported. A few farms located on the peninsula, west of the Common, raised potatoes and hay but generally "the prospect appeared very discouraging and disagreeable; nothing but barren rocks and hills presented

frozen to death in a decrepit house on the waterfront, apparently because he lacked the fuel needed to ward off the bitter cold. Somewhat more adept at coping with adversity was a black woman, named Thursday, who ran away from her master, perhaps in search of freedom beyond Nova Scotia. Women out on their own, however, faced considerable danger, as was demonstrated by the case of

By the 1770s, much of the peninsula on which Halifax stood had been cleared for farming; small pockets of settlement existed further afield, such as around the windmill on the Dartmouth side of the harbour.

themselves." Having trudged along the boulder strewn path that led toward Windsor, on the Bay of Fundy, Robinson and Rispin informed would-be immigrants that the area around Halifax was "nothing but weary wastes, or forests of rocks and wood."[18]

A difficult terrain, the waxing and waning of support from home, native resistance and internal feuding had combined to make George Hick's boasts of 1749 an exercise in unfulfilled expectations.

Chapter Two

THE WAR YEARS
(1774-1815)

Revolutionaries and Loyalists

Left to its own devices, Halifax seemed destined for stagnation but then came the American Revolution, unleashing changes which ushered in a new era for Nova Scotia's capital. At first, the crisis of allegiance which built through the early 1770s across neighbouring parts of British North America simply aggravated the difficulties of life in Halifax. The local garrison fell to 100 as soldiers were transferred to Boston to intimidate would-be rebels. The resulting erosion of business and loss of policing power triggered unrest among those Haligonians who identified with the "patriot" cause in America. For example, Malachy Salter talked defiantly about boycotting imports of tea from Britain as a gesture of colonial solidarity. At night bolder spirits hung effigies and sabotaged army supplies as a statement of their anti-British point of view. Such

HMS Observer *battles the American rebel privateer* Jack *off Halifax harbour, 1782. Though never exposed to direct enemy attack, Halifax remained dominated by war for most of the late eighteenth and early nineteenth centuries.*

incidents, some thought, might carry Halifax and perhaps all of Nova Scotia into a state of insurrection.

Presiding over this growing tumult was Governor Francis Legge, a person described by his biographer as being "basically a stupid man."[1] Sent out by London, with a mandate to remedy the debt and underdevelopment which fuelled local disturbances, Legge quickly blundered into near-disaster. His single-greatest miscalculation came in December 1775 when he ordered outport militiamen to muster in arms at Halifax, to defend the town against an attack from New England, now largely in rebel hands. For the most part, the settlers refused to leave home, saying they had a right to remain neutral in the conflict between King and Congress. Worse news followed. In the autumn of 1776, Fort Cumberland, at the head of the Bay of Fundy, was placed under siege by Nova Scotia's small rebel minority.

Two factors saved Halifax for the Crown. First of all, Halifax merchants saw great opportunity for themselves if they backed Britain in this new crisis of empire. Fighting against rebel America could well restore the Nova Scotian capital to the vigour it had known during the conflict with New France. Moreover, war might sever the commercial ties between local outports and New England, creating a chance for Halifax to supplant Boston as the chief focus of Nova Scotia's trade and fisheries. Reinforcing such opportunistic calculations was the continuing influence of London-based Joshua Mauger. So great had his coercive power become that dissidents such as Malachy Salter abandoned resistance to become supporters of the British connection.

The second factor shaping local events was British sea power. The Royal Navy ranked as London's best instrument for smashing the forces of insurrection. For the navy to be effective it needed a forward base close to where fighting had erupted. Halifax, with its magnificent harbour and naval yard facilities, a mere two days' sail from Boston, was ideal for counter-revolutionary endeavour. Accordingly, by late 1775 imperial ships, men and munitions were mustering in the Nova Scotian capital. Bustle escalated into a true frenzy of activity in March 1776 when British forces and colonial Loyalists evacuated Boston. Refugees, such as Anglican cleric Jacob Bailey, found Halifax to be a somewhat dubious haven. Venturing north for the first time in his life, Bailey encountered a shore "inexpressibly rugged and broken," with trees "starving and misshapen," a sign of "the severity of the climate and the barrenness of the soil."[2] Ashore

Governor John Parr presided over the Loyalist influx which swept over Halifax at the close of the Revolutionary War; it was a development which made his job a misery.

he faced further aggravations, notably acute scarcities of housing and food, as well as terrifying stories about how rebel vessels were prowling the coasts and threatening any community which dared offer allegiance to King George. Outports such as Liverpool came under rebel attack, but Halifax remained secure, protected by its harbour defenses. Meanwhile local merchants generated enormous profits, basically by operating as war contractors, complemented by trading in prize goods brought to port mainly by ships of the Royal Navy.

As the revolution drew to a close Halifax, perhaps more than any other part of British America, had reason to celebrate. True, there had been problems, most dramatically periodic riots in the streets as civilians fought to escape the clutches of naval press gangs. But on balance, most had done well, particularly when they contrasted current conditions with what Halifax had known during the last bout of peace. John Parr, successor as governor to the disgraced Francis Legge, summed up Halifax's sense of achievement when he observed in 1782 that his new Nova Scotian appointment brought him:

a most excellent house and garden, a small farm close to the Town [a property located in Halifax's far North end] ... a snug little farm house upon it, a beautiful prospect, with good fishing, plenty of Provisions of all sorts ... with a very good French Cook to dress them, a Cellar well stock'd with Port, Claret, madeira, Rum, Brandy, Bowood strong beer, etc.[3]

Perhaps best of all was the salary. Parr would be earning £2200 a year at a time when an income of £500 enabled a gentlemen to live a life of self-indulgent leisure. Unfortunately the future boded ill for Parr, essentially because Britain had lost the revolutionary war. Out of that defeat came a volatile horde of refugees whose presence in Halifax would cause Nova Scotia's governor endless aggravation.

Controversy continues to swirl around the Loyalists, particularly with respect to their identity, motivation and impact on those North American colonies which remained within the British empire. A popular view, rooted in late-Victorian Canadian nationalism, holds that the typical refugee was someone from the Yankee upper classes who, as a matter of principle, fled the new United States to relocate in places such as Nova Scotia, there to become founders of a new nation, one committed to the values of "peace, order, and good government."[4] Such an analysis suggests that the Loyalist influx constituted a basic watershed in Halifax history. But close examination of what actually happened in Nova Scotia's capital through the 1780s reveals as much continuity as change. While the incoming Loyalists brought elements of innovation, in many ways they found themselves operating within structures and challenges inherited from the past.

The Loyalist "myth," which presents the newcomers as genteel folk who welcomed the challenges of pioneer life has at least have some basis in fact, as can be seen from the experiences of Penelope Winslow, the teenaged daughter of a Massachusetts family descended from those who arrived on the *Mayflower*. Her father's early and militant toryism had forced them from home, first to New York and then, in 1783, to Halifax. While Edward Winslow scrounged for land and position, a quest which ultimately took him to New Brunswick, a colony carved out of greater Nova Scotia in 1784, Penelope enjoyed herself in Halifax, taking in all the delights the town had to offer. Her letters to a friend brim with youthful excitement, such as when she commented:

The last Assembly [public ball] was amazingly brilliant, the Ladies Dress superb beyond what the New Englanders had seen before. Mrs. Wentworth stood first in fashion & magnificence. Her Gown and Petticoat of sylvan tissue trimmed with Italian Flowers & the finest blond lace, a train of four yards long, her hair and wrist ornamented with real Diamonds.[5]

A few months later parties continued to dominate Penelope's perspective. She wrote again to say that "Feasting, card playing & dancing is the great business of Life at Halifax, one eternal round."[6]

Everyone who counted played host to their peers, serving bounteous food and drink, dressing to make an elegant impression and boasting about how the Loyalist colonies were destined to become "the envy of the American states."[7] Penelope had a kindred spirit in Gregory Townsend who, at about this time, was writing back home to say that Halifax constituted a delightful place to live. Boastfully he noted,

We abound in the finest Strawberries, Sallad [sic], Cucumber, Green Peas etc. and are not wanting in Meat, Fish is almost nothing, the finest mackeril [sic] at 1/2 penny apiece ... Were your family and three or four more here, I could bid adieu to Boston without any great reluctance.[8]

The problem with the words of Penelope and her friends is that they ignored what life was like for most Loyalists. Typically the refugees were poor, desperate, and increasingly disillusioned with the prospects facing them in towns such as Halifax. Privately, in a letter to his wife, Jane, Edward Winslow admitted to what lay beyond the privileged world of the favoured few. "It is not possible for any pen or tongue," he wrote from Halifax, "to describe the variety of wretchedness that is ... exhibited in the streets of this place."[9] Paupers were everywhere, housing became almost impossible to secure, while hundreds resorted to a diet of fish, corn, and molasses, with the most desperate dining

Symbols of affluence, such as this locally made tall-case clock, shape our view of Loyalist-era Halifax but only a small minority of local people lived in comfort.

on dogs and cats. Crime flourished, as did draconian punishments. For example, in 1785 twenty men were hanged for miscellaneous offences, including one newly-arrived black man, convicted of stealing a bag of potatoes. As hunger, disease and despair crept even into the ranks of the once-respectable, Loyalists increasingly succumbed to intense bickering, both with old settlers and among themselves.

How many Loyalists came to Halifax will never be known. In 1784, Lieutenant-Governor (the title Governor disappeared after the Revolution) Parr estimated that the town held 1200 newcomers but many, like the Winslows, were sojourners, passing through in search of better prospects elsewhere. One element in the flow which stood out were those Loyalists of African descent, many of whom had gained freedom from slavery by fighting for Britain during the revolution. Having come to Nova Scotia to get the real estate needed to realize their dream of becoming yeomen in America, black refugees tended to congregate in urban places, such as the capital, while waiting for grants of land. As a result, by the mid-1780s perhaps one-tenth of Halifax's 4000 inhabitants were people of colour. Their share of the overall urban population gradually declined through the 1780s, as black Loyalists left to take up small land grants in the outlying rural districts of Preston and Hammonds Plains.

Parr and the other "pre-Loyalists" who dominated Halifax's power structure would have been delighted to see all the refugees depart, such were the chronic and loud complaints coming from these newcomers. Every action of the government, from distribution of land and provisions to adjudication of claims for compensation for losses in the revolution, seemed to generate nothing but hostile comment from the

War replenished the Halifax garrison. Shown here are troops stationed at Fort Needham, a height of land fortified to protect the naval yard from landward assault.

Loyalists. In large measure, unrest derived from newcomer desperation. Being people who most often had been driven unwillingly into exile, Loyalists yearned for a rapid return, either "home" or to the status and security they had known in the old colonies. One way to realize their ambition involved subverting the authority of officials like John Parr. Accordingly, the later 1780s witnessed a struggle between old and new elements in Halifax society, something which occasionally turned violent. For example, rival mobs clashed in the streets during a by-election held in 1788 to decide whether Halifax should be represented in the Assembly by pre-Loyalist or Loyalist. The former prevailed but only after three days of street fighting, complete with gunfire.

In the end, rivalry between early and later settlers was resolved more by a coup from above than a revolt from below. The key player

This woodcutter, with his "liberty cap," a symbol of having attained freedom from slavery, represents the multitude of black Loyalists who made Halifax and vicinity home during the 1780s.

in this episode was Mrs. Wentworth, the well-dressed lady alluded to in the gushing prose of Penelope Winslow. Fannie Wentworth and her husband, the pre-revolutionary governor of New Hampshire, had come as refugees to Halifax in 1783. There they wrestled with the classic Loyalist dilemma of trying to rebuild their lives, while depending on the rather meagre income John Wentworth earned in Nova Scotia as Surveyor General of the King's Woods. Fannie's diamonds, which had so impressed Penelope Winslow, concealed a

Lady Frances Wentworth, as she appeared at age twenty in 1765. Persistent beauty, combined with formidable ambition, gave her prominence in Halifax society throughout the late eighteenth century.

mounting array of debts. Conspicuous consumption, however, had the advantage of giving Fannie Wentworth a place in high society and more particularly access to young Prince William Henry, who paid several calls in Halifax late in the 1780s. Mrs. Wentworth's charms, the prince's fascination with elegant women, and John Wentworth's convenient absence from town combined to establish Mrs. Wentworth as a formidable figure in Halifax society. Given the relaxed code of morality then prevailing in aristocratic circles, her special relationship with the prince counted as an asset in the Wentworth campaign for self-advancement.

Precisely how Fannie Wentworth's royal connection factored into later developments cannot be established with certainty. What is known is that when John Parr died in 1791, John Wentworth, then conveniently located in London, was able to get himself named as Nova Scotia's new vice-regent. He retained this office until 1808, a remarkably long tenure during which Wentworth used his powers of appointment to fill Nova Scotia's administration with fellow Loyalists. Halifax's inner circle of power, now becoming ever more integrated through intermarriage, always included non-Loyalists. But increasingly, refugees from the American revolution would function as the dominant core of Halifax's oligarchy.

Wentworth Reigns while the Duke of Kent Builds

The single greatest challenge facing Wentworth and his associates was one all-too familiar to Halifax. Once again the town had to struggle with the rigours of a transition from war to peace. Nova Scotia now had more residents than ever before, thanks to a massive influx of Loyalists, but most of the new settlers, like the Planters before them, would spend years trying to overcome frontier poverty and isolation. Visions of moving quickly to make this colony a "new" New England, with Halifax as a latter-day Boston, faded in the face of persistently hard times. Curtailed transfer payments from London plus overwhelming competition from New England, especially in the vital fisheries and West Indies trade, meant that Nova Scotia's economy entered the 1790s in a stagnant condition. Circumstances were so bad that more people were drifting out than coming in. The most celebrated exodus involved some 1200 black Nova Scotians, mostly drawn from communities in and around Halifax who, in 1792, departed for Sierra Leone, in Africa.

Ever an optimist, Wentworth persistently bombarded London with despatches boasting about how, under his leadership, public spending on roads, canals, mills, farming, and the fisheries was making things better. Unfortunately, intentions were rarely matched by performance. In essence, Nova Scotia lacked the public and private capital needed to launch major economic development. Outside investment remained a dubious likelihood so long as Nova Scotia ranked as a minor fragment of empire, overshadowed by the greater importance of places such as the West Indies, Canada and even Newfoundland. Then in 1793 came war, as Britain and Europe's other conservative powers attempted to crush the upstart French republic. Fighting against first Jacobin and

The most enduring of the fortifications commissioned by Prince Edward, this massive stone tower stands today in Point Pleasant Park, overlooking the ocean approaches to Halifax.

Prince Edward erected a "Rotunda" on his estate on Bedford Basin for the performance of musical concerts. Seen here as sketched by William Eager in 1839, it has survived into modern times.

then Napoleonic France would persist for the better part of the next twenty years, during which time Halifax would finally begin to achieve significant economic and social development.

Initially, Halifax's role in the war against France involved serving as a base for British forces operating in the Caribbean. Thus, once again the harbour bustled with naval shipping; the naval yard hummed with the activity of vessels being refitted for action; and hundreds of military personnel passed through the local barracks en route to and from the zone of strife. More than anything else what made the mid-1790s something beyond business-as-usual was the arrival, in 1794, of another royal prince, twenty-seven-year-old Edward Augustus, fourth in succession to the British throne. Coming fresh from the conquest of Martinique and St. Lucia, the prince

settled in for a six-year stay in Nova Scotia's capital.

Driven by a compulsion for action designed in part to restore him to the King's favour, Edward launched into a bold program of harbour refortification. Once again the existing but now ramshackle defence works atop Citadel Hill were torn down, to be replaced by a vast array of wooden walls and trenches. Even more impressive were the five stone towers erected at strategic points overlooking the harbour's seaward approaches. To facilitate coordination of defence efforts in the event of enemy attack, Edward had built a series of semaphore towers which, using flags by day and lamps by night, could quickly relay messages from outer fortifications, such as York Redoubt, to the Citadel. This bristling mass of military hardware, while never actually tested by a foreign foe, proved crucial for overcoming local poverty. Demand for construction labour, rising wages, a swollen garrison market and the opportunity for profit offered at auctions held to dispose of goods seized from the enemy, combined to make Halifax a scene of economic bustle.

Meanwhile Edward, elevated to the rank of Duke of Kent in 1799, diversified into more domestic forms of building activity. On the shores of Bedford Basin about five miles outside town, he erected a rambling wooden mansion (Prince's Lodge), complete with assembly rooms, an adjacent round music pavilion, meandering walkways, artificial ponds and miniature Chinese temples. The retreat was designed to offer an escape from urban tumult and also provide a romantic abode for Edward's French mistress, the mysterious Julie St. Laurent. Supposedly the walkways through the estate had been laid out in such a way that they spelled out her first name. Back in town, Edward gave further vent to his mania for architectural innovation. In April 1800 he

Madame St. Laurent, companion to Prince Edward. Prevented by British law from getting married, they lived together in Halifax as man and wife, behaviour which shocked puritanical elements within local society.

Wartime population growth, mainly along streets laid out north of the Citadel led to construction St. George's Anglican church, whose round centre was inspired by Prince Edward.

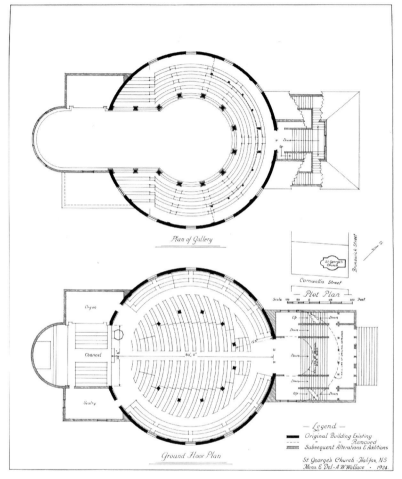

laid the foundations for what would become a gem of Halifax architecture, the magnificent St. George's Anglican church, built in the round. That same year, he presided at the ground breaking ceremony for Mason's Hall, a large waterfront facility which served as the main site for meetings and entertainments for half a century. Edward's final legacy involved a garrison (later known as the Old Town) clock. Erected on the eastern slopes of Citadel Hill and

Visible from most points in the old downtown, this clock derived from Prince Edward's mania for punctuality. Today is stands as Halifax's most celebrated piece of early-colonial architecture.

operational by 1803, the machine's four faces become an enduring reminder of "the Duke's time" in Halifax. [10]

Community Character in the Age of Revolution

The quality of life in Halifax during the 1790s attracted comment from several visitors, one of whom was the French traveller, Monsieur de Saint-Mesmin. He liked both the town and its resident gentry, praising, for example, the harbour for being "one of the prettiest, best and safest in the whole continent of America." Moreover, he noted that Halifax had the advantage of being close to New England, providing "great opportunities of carrying on illicit trade" with the Yankees, an observation which signified the importance of smuggling in the local economy. As for social conventions, Saint-Mesmin insisted that Haligonians emulated London styles but avoided preoccupation with politics. Colonial gentlemen, he observed, "pay more attention to women and value their company more." As for the ladies, they were "generally dressed with scrupulous cleanliness and those who are in fairly good circumstances ... have carriages."[11]

Dining out, Saint-Mesmin observed, dominated Halifax's social agenda, built around formal meals which ran from five to eight in the evening. Attentive hosts strove to see that "wines of all kinds" covered the table. Liquor featured in a protracted ritual of salutes (toasts) to everything from the health of the King to the fair breezes of summer. Interspersed with dining and drinking came amusing conversation, spiced liberally with gossip and jokes. After about two hours the ladies departed, leaving their male companions for an hour of talk, tobacco and stronger drink. Then both sexes reconvened in a drawing room for coffee and tea, and flirtation.[12] Saint-Mesmin's insistence that gentlemen never got "befuddled" on these occasions clashes with oral tradition which argues that this was an era when leaders of society did not face censure for becoming drunk in public. As for fidelity in marriage, a shocked observer from stricter times complained that in late-eighteenth-century Halifax "the greatest laxity of conduct had sprung up," such that "men learned to smile and applaud the most unhallowed scenes of dissipation."[13]

Times were changing, however, as can be seen from the career of Joshua Marsden, a twenty-three-year-old Englishman. Inspired by religious zeal, he had converted from Anglicanism to Methodism and then, in the autumn of 1800 emigrated to Nova Scotia to wage war on sin. Like many other folk who dared cross the vast North Atlantic before the age of steam, the initiative almost cost this missionary his life. Describing conditions on board a small and leaky wooden ship,

Alicia Uniacke, third daughter of Attorney-General Richard John Uniacke, shown here as painted by Robert Field, embodied the elegance of Halifax high society early in the nineteenth century.

Marsden observed:

> [T]he ominous sound of the pump, combined with the whistling of wind, the dash of waves, and often the stentorian voice of the captain, created a chillness of soul that nothing but the warmpth of faith and devotion could beguile.[14]

On the ocean for six weeks, suffering frequent bouts of sea sickness, continually drenched as water poured down the hatches, and finally terrified by the need to run from a French warship, Marsden arrived at Halifax in a state of shock.

Immediately he was swept into the company of fellow Methodists, a zealous assembly whose growing presence in Halifax had led, in 1792, to construction of Zoar Chapel, located north of the Citadel. Huge by the standards of the day, with seating for 900, this "converting furnace" for the faithful, Marsden noted, was "well attended, and on the Lord's day in the evening[,] always crowded."[15] Most of those at service were not full-members of the Methodist community but rather nominal Anglicans, people classified by one activist as "a great swarm of infidels."[16] Through its free pews, passionate preaching and zestful hymn tunes, accompanied by the sounds of violin, flute and clarinet, Zoar Chapel struggled to popularize christian faith.

Methodist self-assertion clashed with the social design laid down by Halifax's founders. In the beginning great care had been taken to provide the new town with an infrastructure which included organized religion. Within a year after Cornwallis's arrival, the Anglican, or Church of England, presence was established in St. Paul's, erected at public expense on the Grand Parade. State subsidies also helped pay

Anglican bishop Charles Inglis, portrayed by Robert Field in his robes of office, endeavoured in vain to smother the forces of religious dissent across Nova Scotia.

for a pastor at Mather's Church, a facility for the miscellaneous array of Protestant Dissenters resident in Halifax. Non-Anglicans (though not Roman Catholics) had extensive civil rights in early Halifax, but Anglicans would long claim privileged status as a semi-official "established" church. Their ascendancy became even more pronounced following the American Revolution when an Anglican bishopric was established in Nova Scotia. By strengthening the presence of well-educated, genteel and conservative clergymen, London hoped it could undermine religious dissent and thereby consolidate Nova Scotia's allegiance to the empire. But neither Bishop Charles Inglis nor his early successors had the physical or intellectual energy needed to cope with frontier adversity. Thus Nova Scotian Anglicanism was on the defensive by the time Joshua Marsden arrived in Halifax.

Dissenter ferment extended beyond the ranks of Halifax's Methodists. By the 1790s the growing ambitions of Halifax's small Scottish community, mainly made up of Lowland-born business men and professionals, led to their transforming the old, interdenominational Mather's Church, such that it became St. Matthew's, complete with a Church of Scotland minister recruited from the Old Country. An even bolder break with founding principles came in the early 1780s when Halifax Roman Catholics, drawn primarily from the "servant" class, sought repeal of the law passed in the aftermath of the Acadian expulsion which criminalized their faith. Now that "popery" was no longer identified with French power, officials yielded to demands for toleration. Accordingly, in 1784, Roman Catholics received permission to build a chapel and a year later they brought in from Ireland their first priest.

This modern painting showing Maroons from Jamaica working on Halifax's fortifications makes the point that black labour played an essential role in the economy of wartime Halifax.

The spirit of emancipation also extended to Nova Scotia's black community. Despite the exodus to Sierra Leone in 1792, which took away the core of the colony's black leadership, along with a high percentage of those already freed from slavery, people of colour did not lapse into apathy. An example of what could be accomplished, even among those living in slavery, was provided by an individual known to posterity only as "Jack." Late in the 1790s he ran from his master in rural Annapolis Royal, coming to Halifax in search of work in the free labour market. Eventually the master traced Jack to the capital and brought suit in court to have him returned. At that point certain white leaders, most notably Attorney-General Richard John Uniacke, intervened in an effort to have slavery declared illegal in Nova Scotia. Uniacke and others were here echoing the new fashions

of the British "enlightenment," which by the 1790s had begun to make anti-slavery "an emblem of national virtue."[17] Enthusiasm for new notions of what it meant to be "British" were not universally shared by those in power, with the result that Jack's case dragged indecisively through the courts, ending only when his former master died (some say having been poisoned by a black female servant). But this man's example inspired other slaves to escape, almost invariably to Halifax, a town where in practice slavery had died by the beginning of the nineteenth century.

One group of black immigrants who contributed, albeit briefly, to Nova Scotian history were the Maroons, 600 of whom came to Halifax from Jamaica in the summer of 1796. Exiled from their homeland by a colonial regime convinced that the freedom for any black people was incompatible with the slavery demanded by island sugar planters, these newcomers faced a cruel welcome in Nova Scotia's capital. Prince Edward immediately tried to conscript them into the labour pool needed for his construction agenda. Governor Wentworth sought to use the Maroons as a captive labour force on his estates east of the harbour and also made certain of their women his mistresses. Maroon resistance to exploitation, combined with exhaustion of the funds coming from Jamaica for their settlement in Nova Scotia, put a speedy and tragic end to this experiment in black colonization. In 1800 virtually all the Maroons departed to join other former-Nova Scotians in Sierra Leone.

Those, both black and white, who persisted in Halifax shared certain problems, including a climate which, by English standards, proved most uncongenial. In an all-too typical complaint, a garrison officer observed in March 1788 that the "cold nasty weather" had left him trapped indoors, with nothing to do but eat, drink, and play cards. April brought a thaw and in May mild temperatures reminiscent of home briefly appeared. But then Arctic air swept down on the town, bringing twelve centimetres of snow, followed by chronic fog. Summing it up, he muttered, "It is impossible to depend on the weather for four-and-twenty hours in this country."[18] Generations of Haligonians crippled by aches and pains induced by winter cold and dampness would yearn for an early spring but then face disappointment, sometimes persisting into June.

Of course poor weather had not been the main reason why black people left Nova Scotia for Africa. Their departure amounted to an act of protest, a refusal to stay in a place which denied them an equal share of real estate and civil rights. The slow withering away of slavery, while insufficient to satisfy more restless souls, nevertheless could be regarded as a significant expression of a pattern of intellectual and social change in Halifax. By 1800 this little colonial town had begun to develop expressions of some maturity and self-consciousness.

One sign of improvement involved the theatre. Plays had been performed in Halifax as early as 1768 but over twenty years passed before locals built a proper playhouse. The New Grand Theatre, located near the central waterfront, opened in February 1789 and for about a decade offered performances by all-male casts of both comedies and tragedies. Parallel innovation of an even more lasting character occurred in the realm of education. Loyalist ambitions, reinforced by fear of the neighbouring republic, led in 1789 to the establishment of a university, King's College, strategically located in the genteel rural satellite community of Windsor, so as to prevent its young male students from being corrupted by urban vices. A parallel venture involved creation of the Halifax Grammar School, a facility which, in 1879, would evolve into a public high school.

Clerical-educators like the Rev. William Cochran provided orthodox but energetic leadership in the communication of ideas, pioneering with ventures such as the *Nova Scotia Magazine and Comprehensive Review of Literature, Politics and News*. That publication lasted only from 1789 to 1792 but it stimulated others to think, talk

John Howe's simple style of dress reflected the mood of moral earnestness ascendant within early nineteenth-century Halifax.

and write. For example, Andrew Brown, when called to the pulpit of St. Matthew's in 1787, brought with him Scottish intellectual energies, which led to research into what was intended as a history of Nova Scotia. Brown's project never achieved completion but a few authors, concentrating on less ambitious ventures such as sermons and pamphlets, made it into print. These ventures owed much to John Howe, a Loyalist printer from Boston whose family monopolized the publishing scene in Halifax into the second decade of the nineteenth century.

Howe's career points to another vital aspect of change in Halifax at the end of the eighteenth century, namely, the emergence of a growing sense of moral stewardship. Howe came to town in 1780 and remained until his death in 1835, at age 81. By then he had become "the most respected man in the Halifax of his day."[19] Patriarch to a huge blended family (he married twice), John Howe would always be haunted by money problems, but he insisted on seeing public office, ranging from King's Printer, to Deputy Postmaster General, as an obligation to serve, rather than an opportunity to profit. Though

Judge Alexander Croke, shown here in his court regalia, became notorious for the poetic satire he wrote to reveal the foibles of his social peers.

The Halifax dock yard concentrated on maintenance of navy vessels. This image, from the 1770s, shows a vessel tipped on its side to allow for the removal of barnacles, using burning tar.

Society, along with new organizations such as the Charitable Irish Society, formed in 1786. Such activity gave participants a measure of status and power but it also entailed considerable sacrifice of time and money, the latter mainly being required to pay for the food and drink served at banquets held to foster camaraderie. On occasion these affairs reached flamboyant extremes. For example, in 1794 the North British Society invited Prince Edward and Governor Wentworth to their annual dinner. After three weeks of costly preparation some 200 members and guests, accompanied by two military bands, sat down for a meal and toasts which persisted until one in the morning. In the aftermath, delighted society leaders declared this to have been "the greatest public dinner ever given by a charitable institution" in Halifax's history.[20] Tellingly, a majority of the rank and file rebelled, insisting that such conspicuous consumption discriminated against men of lesser means and also clashed with the new, more fastidious spirit of the age. As a result, the North British Society suspended its annual dinner for the next twelve years. "Old" Halifax had not died. Self-indulgent debauchery would prevail among the local gentry for another generation. But John Howe and his kind, a new "middle element" in the community, were beginning to make their presence a force to be reckoned with.

passive in politics and fatalistic about government's ability to effect social change, Howe vigorously asserted himself to help others. For example, he was the kind of person who left the comfort of home on Sunday to visit those incarcerated in the bridewell, bringing scripture and food. Similarly, Howe insisted he had a moral obligation to reach out to the prisoners of war lodged in primitive facilities scattered around the periphery of town.

Significantly, Howe was not alone. A core of others came forward to offer long-term, unpaid service to the community, becoming magistrates, overseers of the poor, firewards, commissioners of streets, etc. They and others also joined Freemason lodges, the North British

By 1804, the date of this image, Halifax's Naval Yard had grown into a massive complex, employing hundreds of artisans skilled in everything from hull repair to manufacture of sails.

Working-class behaviour and attitudes are harder to discern. Labourers and servants, although they constituted the majority of Halifax's civilian population, rarely appear in the record and when they do, usually it involves complaint over how the "lower orders" were addicted to criminality. But on occasion, we receive a glimpse of something more positive. For example, in November 1797 Halifax suffered its first notable disaster when HMS *La Tribune* sank at the harbour approaches. More than 250 drowned but twelve survived, thanks largely to the daring of a Herring Cove youth, an orphan, apprentice fisherman, known both as Joseph Shortt and Joe Cracker. Asked by Prince Edward to name his reward, Cracker thought only of asking for a new pair of trousers and a return to his humble life by the sea. Joe's altruism made him legendary.[21]

Meanwhile the lives of most common folk in Halifax remained steeped in deprivation. Among the worst off were the sailors serving on board the vessels running in and out of Halifax harbour. These men, growing in number as Halifax trade with the British West Indies expanded through the 1790s, faced numerous hazards, ranging from shipwreck to "yellow jack," a fever which haunted the tropics. Wartime conditions added to the perils they faced. At sea and in port, press gangs could carry them off to the horrors of service in the Royal Navy. French vessels also posed a dire threat, primarily involving imprisonment in some Caribbean island, there to face

Halifax from George's Island, as portrayed by G. I. Parkyns in 1801. The prominence assigned by the artist to gun emplacements makes the point that Halifax was then a town dominated by war.

malnutrition and disease. Such victims had little in common with the dandies who had dazzled M. de Saint-Mesmin with their mannered self-indulgence.

Alarms and Rewards as War Persists

The opening years of the nineteenth century proved particularly difficult for Halifax. In 1802 news of a European peace settlement stirred up fears of an all-too-likely return to hard times, should there be a slump in the town's military business. That anxiety died a year later, to be replaced by even greater concern when hostilities resumed between Britain and France. Napoleon proved to be a most formidable foe, at sea as well as on land. French privateers so harried colonial shipping in Caribbean waters that Nova Scotian trade with the sugar islands virtually collapsed. Rumours of a possible French invasion circulated through Halifax, reducing residents to near panic. Confidence began to return in 1805 following Admiral Nelson's heroic victory over the combined French and Spanish fleets at Trafalgar, but British naval power failed to prevent Napoleon's armies from sweeping across Europe. Military conflict escalated, becoming the dominant fact of life in Halifax for another decade.

Fortunately, this era brought rewards to eastern British North America as the colonies became ever more integrated into the imperial

Government House, as drawn by J. E. Woolford in 1819. The building reflects a combination of John Wentworth's ego and the prosperity Halifax enjoyed early in the nineteenth century.

war effort. For example, Newfoundland underwent a decisive transformation, once European hostilities drove up the price paid for cod and prompted thousands to settle year-round along the island's coastline. Similarly, the forested valleys of New Brunswick filled up with people when Britain turned overseas for timber, in response to French threats to cut off supplies from the Baltic. St. John's, Newfoundland and Saint John, New Brunswick both boomed as a result of these developments but benefits also flowed to Halifax, which by 1810 had emerged as the region's leading commercial port. In contrast to the past, when Water Street merchants thought of little beyond the garrison market, now they actively explored business opportunity through the surrounding hinterland. Thus an expanding flow of European manufactures, American foodstuffs, Caribbean produce and colonial staples (mainly fish and timber) passed over Halifax's docks, to be carried away in a growing fleet of wooden, sail-powered craft.

The bustle generated by economic diversification drew an increasing number of people to Halifax. By 1801 the town had a population estimated at 8500. The single-largest group of newcomers consisted of Irish Roman Catholic labourers who negotiated cheap transatlantic passage on westbound vessels employed in the timber trade. Fewer in number but often better endowed in terms of money and skills were people drifting in from the United States and communities across Nova Scotia. Among all those who gambled on making Halifax their new home, none did better than Enos Collins. Born into a merchant family in the Planter outport of Liverpool, Collins honed his business skills as a captain in command of vessels engaged in the West Indies trade. Then in 1811, at age 37, he moved to Halifax, drawn by the opportunities available there for ambitious young entrepreneurs. Collins and his partner Joseph Allison acquired Water Street premises where they soon built an impressive array of wooden docks and ironstone warehouses. Speculative buying and selling, combined with shrewd investment in shipping and real estate, along with insurance and banking transactions, enabled Collins to move ahead, laying the basis for the fortune which eventually would make him (tradition insists) the richest man in all eastern British North America.

Halifax's emergence beyond a military base into a dynamic centre for trade and home to entrepreneurs such as Enos Collins marked a crucial stage in the town's overall development. It was a process, however, which through most of the war years remained overshadowed by expressions of an older, more official and military-oriented Halifax. Linkages to the past were perhaps best personified by John Wentworth. His closing years in office became steeped in controversy, particularly over the massive amount of public money being spent to build a vice-regal palace in what was then the city's far

Nova Scotia's war at sea during the Napoleonic era was waged primarily by vessels of the Royal Navy. Here we see HMS Bonne Citoyenne *towing the French warship* Furieuse *into Halifax in 1809. Both vessels show the effects of heavy cannon fire.*

south end, lower Hollis Street. Government House, as it came to be called, was finally finished in 1808 at a cost of £22,000. Destined to become a lasting feature of Halifax public architecture, the building constituted a last hurrah for the age of Loyalism in Nova Scotia's capital. Besieged by critics and suffering the debilities of old age, Wentworth never got to occupy his intended new residence, essentially because London feared this "earthy little man" could not meet the dire new challenges approaching over the horizon.[22]

Dealing with "Cousin Jonathan"

Imperial anxiety primarily involved growing tension between Britain and the United States of America. Trouble was brewing on two fronts, one inland and the other at sea. Far off in the valleys of the Ohio and upper Mississippi valleys, Americans faced ferocious Indian resistance to the westward expansion of settlement, behaviour which 'war-hawks' in Congress blamed on British collusion with the natives. On the North Atlantic American merchant vessels seeking access to French-controlled European ports encountered a British blockade. Even more provocative were the Royal Navy's seizure of sailors from American vessels, action deriving from the sometimes justifiable argument that these men had deserted from service to the Crown. Conflict steadily built as the government in Washington became ever more desperate to protect American vital interests.

A worried London, fearful that Wentworth could not cope with rising danger, abruptly replaced him as lieutenant-governor with a British military officer, Sir George Prevost.

After four years of futile diplomatic manoeuvring, the government in Washington declared war on the British empire. Halifax learned what had happened in June 1812, when HMS *Belvidera* entered port having been mauled by an American naval squadron cruising off New England. Immediately near-panic gripped Nova Scotia's capital since most residents realized that war with the neighbouring republic could spell ruin. The most immediate threat involved American sea power. The narrow escape of the *Belvidera*, followed by a series of single ship-on-ship encounters, all of them ending with American victories, suggested that the Royal Navy was incapable of protecting Halifax from republican assault. But even before a foreign fleet came knocking, Halifax might be devastated by an American-imposed trade embargo. The town could not survive without large-scale imports from the United States, especially of food. Prevost's successor as Nova Scotia's lieutenant-governor, Sir John Sherbrooke, made desperate efforts to shore up harbour defenses and mobilize the town's rag-tag militia force for attack, either by sea or by land. Simultaneously, he began issuing licenses, authorizing continued trade between Nova Scotia and the United States in either locally registered or even American-owned craft. The gamble worked, essentially because most New Englanders did not want to engage in total warfare against the British empire. Shrewd self-interest and the lure of profit meant that Yankee merchants were willing to trade with the "enemy," coming to Halifax to exchange goods such as flour for imports of European manufactures and Caribbean produce.

Popular folklore, kept alive by the lyrics of modern songs, argues that Nova Scotia's fate during the War of 1812 was largely decided by privateers, privately-owned vessels of war, licensed by the Crown and operating under strict rules (meaning they were not pirates). These vessels, it has been suggested, engaged in a quest for "American gold," thereby saving the colony from invasion and generating the prosperity which ushered in Nova Scotia's "golden age." That heroic image has some basis in fact, especially for outports such as Liverpool, where privateering became a mainstay of the local economy. But in Halifax things were substantially different.

Enos Collins's actions through the course of hostilities demonstrate how and why the war meant different things for different places. Early in the conflict Collins made a bold foray into

Halifax's harbour fortifications now stretched seaward as far as York Redoubt but urban development remained confined to a small part of the peninsula dominated by Citadel Hill.

privateering, becoming part owner of several vessels commissioned to stop and seize enemy merchantmen. Collins's most successful privateer, the *Liverpool Packet*, brought him major profit but by the end of 1813, he had begun to retreat from privateering. In large measure Collins did so because his base of operations in Halifax gave him other and better ways to make money. One involved the auction of goods and vessels seized from the enemy by the Royal Navy.

Throughout the war, most of the damage done to American shipping was inflicted by His Majesty's ships, something made possible by a shift in the tide of battle at sea. Despite initial unpreparedness, and the losses which resulted, British sea power quickly reasserted itself in the western North Atlantic as better ships with superior crews began to come on station. An early sign of what was taking place occurred in June 1813 when HMS *Shannon* fought and seized the USS *Chesapeake*, off Boston harbour. The unexpected arrival in Halifax harbour of the *Shannon*, with the *Chesapeake* following in her wake, triggered mass euphoria.

Follow-up British naval victories soon forced most American warships off the high seas, leaving the few merchantmen which ventured offshore ready prey for Royal Navy capture. Almost all those captures were brought into Halifax for adjudication before the Court of Vice Admiralty to determine whether they were subject to confiscation. The resulting steady flow of goods and vessels into the Halifax marketplace meant that entrepreneurs such as Enos Collins had no need to employ their own resources in the risky game of privateering. Instead, they could concentrate on making Halifax a commercial linchpin between the United States and the British empire. Summing up the local pattern which emerged at the height of

HMS Shannon *towing the American frigate* Chesapeake *into Halifax harbour, 1813. This two-vessel battle fought off Boston marked the beginning of the collapse of United States sea power during the War of 1812.*

the War of 1812, one Halifax editor commented, "Happy state of Nova Scotia! Amongst all this tumult we have lived in peace and security; invaded only by a numerous host of American doubloons and dollars."[23]

In the summer of 1814 British forces went on the offensive along the American coasts in ways which had a major impact on Halifax. First of all, north-eastern Maine was occupied with minimal fighting, thanks to New England's ambivalent attitude toward waging war.

Seizure of the Penobscot area and particularly the port of Castine, gave Halifax merchants a lucrative forward base for trade into the United States. Later that same year, the Royal Navy entered the Chesapeake Bay region of Virginia and Maryland, briefly occupying Washington, where they set fire to the presidential mansion. Encountering stiff military resistance, the British withdrew but took with them several hundred black American slaves who were promised freedom in Nova Scotia. Brought to Halifax where they received shelter, supplies and work on the town's fortifications, these new immigrants became the core of a permanent black community living in and around Nova Scotia's capital.

By 1815 Halifax exuded an atmosphere reminiscent of the conditions which had prevailed during the Seven Years War against New France. Soldiers and sailors were everywhere and the service enterprises which catered to their needs had a dramatically high profile. In a recollection based on oral tradition, an early-Victorian observer recalled, "The upper streets were full of brothels; grog shops and dancing halls were to be seen in almost every part of town."[24] That section of present-day Brunswick Street, which ran in front of the town clock acquired the nickname Knock Him Down Row, thanks to the frequency with which brawls and worse occurred at almost any time of day. Cheap liquor and easy access to illicit sex made "the hill" a place celebrated in folk songs warning honest sailor lads about how they would be "left naked in the bed" if they tarried there for wine, women and song.[25] Looking back at what he saw as the bad old days, pioneer Halifax historian T.B. Akins complained about how this part of town "presented continually the disgusting sight of abandoned females of the lowest class in a state of drunkenness, bare headed, without shoes, and in the most filthy and abominable condition."[26]

Paradoxically, the frenzy of war also produced enduring expressions of extravagant gentility, no more so than at Mount Uniacke, a 4500-hectare rural estate owned by Nova Scotia's attorney-general, Richard John Uniacke. Built from a fortune largely earned from Vice Admiralty Court fees collected in wartime, Uniacke's estate house, with its sumptuous mahogany furniture, carpets, and oil paintings, along with liveried servants, a library,

No Haligonian did better during the war than Richard John Uniacke, who accumulated a fortune and established a family dynasty, through shrewd use of income and connections gained from public office.

Halifax gentlemen, as part of their drive for prestige, often acquired country estates, where they led a lifestyle emulating the English aristocracy. Shown here is "Mount Uniacke," the rural retreat owned by R.J. Uniacke. The mansion house still stands.

away from the Crown. The Nova Scotian capital then had been little more than a stagnant colonial backwater, but an enduring military struggle against a series of enemies, the French republic, Napoleon, and finally the United States, had brought major rewards to both Uniacke and Halifax.

Rescued from treason charges by family influence, Uniacke rose within the ruling oligarchy and then used office and contacts to harvest the opportunities which flowed from Halifax's successful integration into Britain's imperial war machine. Not all locals did as well as Uniacke but overall, their community had benefitted from this protracted episode of worldwide hostilities. Cornwallis's original vision of integrating garrison functions with trade and resource development finally seemed to be emerging as an accomplished reality. Halifax, it could be argued, now ranked as a good place to live for those with ambitions.

billiards room, and wine cellar, made a fashion statement to all British America. Gazing out his front windows as of 1815, Uniacke could reflect on what had been accomplished both by himself and the town he had come to call home over the past 40 years. For both things had begun badly. In 1776 Uniacke arrived in Halifax as a prisoner, accused of having joined with rebels in an effort to wrest Nova Scotia

THE CHALLENGES OF PEACE
(1815-1841)

Prospects in Jeopardy

Late in the War of 1812, the question of what would happen when hostilities ended preoccupied all Haligonians. Many feared the worst, namely that the town would lapse in the doldrums it had known during earlier episodes of peace. Such pessimism seemed fully warranted, in light of what happened through the years 1815-22. The triumph of Waterloo, Napoleon's final exile to St. Helena and the end of conflict between Britain and the United States brought considerable distress to Halifax. Left with a drastically shrunken garrison and moth-balled naval yard, as well as being deprived of its role as a central conduit of trade between Europe and the United States, Halifax suffered major losses of economic vitality. One newly-arrived Scot, who had come to Halifax to make his fortune, now commented glumly, "The rejoicings of

humanity are checked in my bosom by the whispers of self-interest as I know not what new direction trade may take ... This peace has blasted all our prospects."[1]

A symptom of the hard times experienced by Halifax after the Napoleonic wars is provided by the stillborn condition of Dalhousie College. Launched in 1818 at the prompting of Lieutenant-Governor Lord Dalhousie and endowed with money collected from the custom house at Castine, Maine, this institution began with a flourish of construction activity. By 1821 the college possessed an impressive building on the north side of Halifax's Grand Parade. But

George Ramsay, ninth Earl of Dalhousie. As lieutenant-governor from 1816 to 1820, he embarked on a bold program of innovation, including settlement of black war refugees at Hammonds Plains and Preston, near Halifax.

Dalhousie College, incorporated in 1818, quickly fell prey to the poverty and factional bickering which swept over Halifax at the end of the Napoleonic wars.

typified the immediate postwar period in Nova Scotia's capital.

Frustration over Halifax's inability to cope with the demands of peace came to be felt even by men such as Enos Collins, who began talking bluntly about the need to move to New England where his money and talent could better be put to use than in stagnant little Halifax. Many residents did move away, often to more dynamic neighbouring communities such as Saint John, New Brunswick. But in the end Enos Collins stayed, persuaded in large measure, by promotion to a seat in Nova Scotia's combined Executive/ Legislative Council, followed in 1825 by

then Lord Dalhousie's departure to Quebec, denominational bickering and lack of operating funds brought progress to a halt. Instead of emerging as a facility of higher education, the "college" remained a phantom, its premises surrendered for use as everything from a post office to a brewery. Dalhousie's unfulfilled expectations

marriage to the daughter of Justice Brenton Halliburton. Persistence paid off, since by the mid-1820s things were looking up as Halifax began to benefit from the growth spawned by Britain's industrial revolution and America's expansion across the North American continent.

A Halifax street-scene of 1819, dominated by Nova Scotia's new Province House. In the foreground are people wearing the latest European fashions but also present are two women dressed in traditional Mi'kmaq attire.

Expressions of Recovery

When opened in 1819 Nova Scotia's Province House, which housed the legislature and supreme court, had cost £52,000, an enormous amount by the standards of the day. At the time it seemed absurd to place such a magnificent structure in a minor colony like Nova Scotia. However, a decade later the building fitted Halifax's altered circumstances. Economic adversity had been replaced by mounting signs of recovery, which together suggested that Halifax could thrive without the stimulus of war. One optimistic sign of the times which came in the form of a newspaper advertisement by an aspiring immigrant manufacturer. It read as follows:

Alexander Keith, begs leave to inform his friends and the public in general that he has commenced in the Brewing Business ... opposite Dalhousie College, where he intends to Brew Strong Ales ... and hopes by strictest attention to his

business, added to his long experience in the above line ... to merit a share of the public patronage and support.[2]

Keith, who had come to town as a poor immigrant at war's end, was now setting out in business on his own. Though fraught with risk, his gamble paid off and through the next two decades Alexander Keith rose from obscurity to become a pillar of community life, in possession of wealth, prestige and power. Today Halifax is littered with Keith memorabilia, including his massive stone brewery on Water Street, an adjacent mansion house on Hollis Street, and a gigantic tombstone, found in Camp Hill cemetery. Together these structures conjure up the elements of economic growth found in Halifax during the second quarter of the nineteenth century.

In part Alexander Keith's success derived from the decision by the British government to launch a massive and costly public works program focused on reconstruction of the fortifications spread in and around Nova Scotia's capital. Despite having vitually shut down the naval yard, imperial military planners remained acutely conscious of Halifax's strategic importance should war again erupt. By the 1820s much of what had been built by the Duke of Kent had fallen into ruins, especially the Citadel at

Among the many Scottish people who poured into postwar Halifax was the young brewer, Alexander Keith. Besides success as a brewer, Keith gained fame through involvement with community organizations, especially the Freemasons.

Halifax, looking south from the naval yard in 1827. Government buildings dominate the foreground but south of the naval yard lay an expanding array of wharves and warehouses, the emerging heart of the port.

of prosperity, plus the fever for canal construction then sweeping neighbouring parts of North America, investors recruited from the local merchant community brought over from Britain an engineer and several hundred stoneworkers to build a waterway designed to link Halifax harbour with the Bay of Fundy. Efficient overland access to the farms and forests of Nova Scotia's hinterland, contemporaries believed, would allow Halifax to eclipse Saint John, its main competitor for regional trade. Construction began in the summer of 1826 and continued with great diligence over the next five years, until spring freshets damaged key locks in the system. Then began a sustained campaign to raise the additional capital needed to bring the project to successful completion. Thirty years would pass before traffic began on the waterway, by which time local boosters had been persuaded that a railroad would serve their ambitions better than a canal. Nevertheless, this project left a positive legacy, one found mainly on the eastern shores of Halifax harbour.

the top of the town-site. To correct this situation engineers arrived in 1828 with plans to cut down the hill by six metres and then use the enlarged surface to build a star-shaped array of walls and ditches capable of defying virtually any enemy. Unlike past efforts, this new complex, to be named Fort George in honour of the king, would feature extensive use of stone in order to achieve durability. Design flaws, unstable soil and Halifax's volatile weather all played havoc with construction such that completion did not come until the 1850s, by which time improvements in military technology had made the fortifications largely obsolete. Their construction, however, did much to sustain Halifax's garrison identity while simultaneously giving an enormous boost to the local civilian economy. As for Alexander Keith, his India Pale Ale had became a staple commodity for slaking the thirst of those stationed at or working on Halifax's harbour fortifications.

The other great public work launched in the 1820s involved construction of the Shubenacadie canal. Inspired by mounting signs

Until the 1820s, Dartmouth had been little better than a rural annex to Halifax's urban core. Settled in 1750, early developers had made several attempts to establish Dartmouth as a centre for

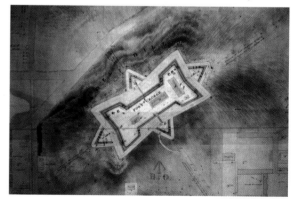

London's insistence that Halifax must not be allowed to slide into military obsolescence led to a thirty-year refortification effort, focused on the citadel but including other sites, such as George's Island.

manufacturing, using mills powered by both water and wind power. In the 1780s Loyalists from Nantucket, in Massachusetts, set up a deep-sea whaling station at Dartmouth. But that venture failed, thanks to British intervention and for the next thirty years the eastern side of the

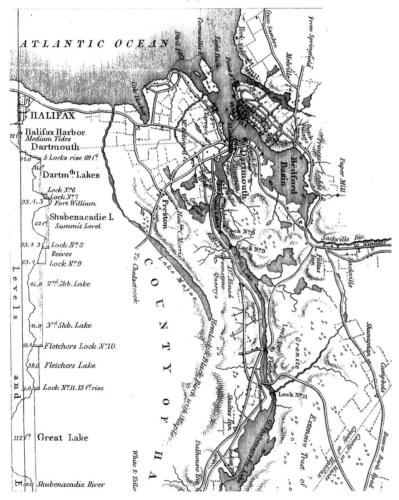

This map, published in 1832, shows the greater Halifax area, oriented around the harbour and leading inland, along the route of the projected Shubenacadie canal.

harbour languished. Finally, in the 1820s, labour and capital began a substantial migration into Dartmouth, drawn largely to the area where the Shubenacadie Canal emptied into the harbour. Here developers had access to the most powerful mill race in all of greater Halifax, energy which could be used to drive an array of mills, foundries, and related works. Eventually, tanneries and shipyards sprang up around a series of waterfront locations to make Dartmouth the focal point for industry in the early-Victorian period. Also about this time Dartmouth's lakes became a hive of winter activity as crews using large saws harvested blocks of ice destined to be used as summer refrigeration both locally and in the far-off Caribbean. By 1838 some 1200 people (about 10 percent of the urban total) lived on the eastern side of the harbour.

Another major technological innovation, one which contributed significantly to urban expansion, came in 1830. After over a decade of experimentation with a cross-harbour ferry driven by a horse-driven propulsion system, local investors commissioned construction of the *Sir Charles Ogle*, Halifax's first steam-powered vessel. Despite frequent breakdowns, this little craft, joined in 1838 by another steamer, the *Boxer*, revolutionized Halifax public transport. Stage-coaches, in operation as of 1816, now routed their eastbound runs through

This horse-driven "team boat," launched in 1816, pioneered in providing Haligonians with mechanized transportation across the harbour, a service which became ever more essential as Dartmouth grew in terms of people and industry.

The inner reaches of Halifax harbour, such as Bedford Basin, shown in this 1839 lithograph, began to be used as summer recreation sites. once they were made accessible by steam-powered ferries.

Dartmouth, since harbour steamers considerably shortened the distance to Truro and beyond. The new-model ferries drew people, as both commuters and excursionists, to parts of the harbour they had previously neglected. By the late 1830s a highlight of summer

Halifax's ferry landing and the adjacent public market, shown here as they existed in 1838, daily drew scores of people from outlying rural areas bringing everything from berries to baskets to sell to urban dwellers. This was also a favoured site for mass election rallies during the drive for "responsible government."

recreational life involved chartering a ferry to venture away to McNab's Island, Prince's Lodge or Bedford for a group picnic, complete with dancing and games.

Notable as a strident participant in and promoter of innovation was John Howe's son, Joseph. Born in 1804, Joe came of age just as Halifax made the transition from recession to recovery. Opting for a career in publishing, young Howe acquired a newspaper, the aptly named *Novascotian*, and soon made it a vigorous advocate of all forms of contemporary progress. Forever preaching the message that country and urban folk shared a common potential for material and moral achievement, Howe delighted in reporting good news, such as the establishment of Halifax's first bank (1825), inauguration of direct trade with the East Indies (1826), and construction of the *Royal William*, the vessel which pioneered steam service between Halifax and ports on the St. Lawrence River (1831). By the middle of the 1830s Howe saw himself and in large measure was seen by others as chief exponent of colonial enterprise.

Joseph Howe, publisher of the Novascotian, *champion of Nova Scotian economic development and advocate of political reform, made Halifax his home base for a career which lasted almost half a century.*

The Ambiguity of Urban Character

Word portraits of Halifax on the threshold of the Victorian age often contain flattering comments about the town. For example, T.C. Haliburton, then a young lawyer and aspiring writer, said of the Nova Scotian capital:

Few places present so pleasing an aspect as Halifax, when viewed from the harbour. Its streets are laid out with regularity, its spires have a picturesque and even magnificent effect, and the trees which are scattered throughout ... give it an appearance softened and refreshing.[3]

Commenting on the scenes found along Water Street, in spring and autumn as new goods poured in from abroad, British army officer William S. Moorsom observed:

The wharves are then crowded with vessels ... Signals are constantly flying at the citadel for vessels coming in; merchants are running about, in anticipation of their freights; officers of the garrison are seen striding down with a determined

Ironstone building, housing an extensive array of waterfront offices and warehouses, inspired "boosters" like Joe Howe to predict that Halifax was destined for greatness. When greatness proved slow in coming, locals insisted that railroads would be a cure-all for the place they called home.

pace to welcome a detachment from the depot, or a pipe of Sneyd's claret for the mess; and ladies, tripping along on a tiptoe of expectation, flock into two or three soi-disant bazaars for the latest à-la-mode bonnets.[4]

Similarly, John McGregor, a touring Scot, bubbled enthusiastically about the high society which swirled around Government House. The presence of military officers and high functionaries in the imperial bureaucracy, most of whom were "gentlemen of respectability and education" from the Old Country, imparted "to the first class of society in Halifax, more refinement, more elegance and fashion, than is to be met with probably in any town in America."[5] As another sojourner put it, "the British visitor at a convivial party almost forgets that he is not at home."[6]

Such charming images did not tell the whole truth. For example,

This 1842 sketch of backyards in Halifax hints at the overcrowding and poverty found in the slums which lurked within a stone's throw of the public buildings and private homes frequented by the gentry.

J. J. Audubon, the celebrated American naturalist, arrived at Halifax in August 1833, exhausted from the travails of life in the wilderness of Labrador. Instead of the comfort and convenience he had been looking forward to, Nova Scotia's capital presented Audubon with an exercise in frustration. "Halifax," he muttered "has not one good hotel." Boarding houses, the better ones run by women, offered service which Audubon categorized as being "miserable." Worst of all, on Sunday the town shut down in business terms, so much so that Audubon had enormous difficulty in finding a barber to shave the beard he had grown during his northern adventures.[7]

An even darker side of life, one steeped in poverty, dirt, and disease lurked in Halifax. This squalor leapt forth with a vengeance in the summer of 1834 when cholera, a mysterious new illness coming through Europe from Asia, arrived in port. Halifax's overcrowding, pervasive filth and polluted water made the town ripe for a disastrous outbreak of infection. Spreading from the docks into the barracks, the poor house and the jail, cholera quickly became a mass killer, fostering panic and flight among people high and low. By early September Halifax had the appearance of a "City of the Plague," complete with bonfires lit to drive off "noxious vapours" and death carts rumbling through the streets to collect a multiplying array of corpses.[8] Municipal leaders made clumsy efforts to impose quarantine regulations and then turned the crisis over to local doctors. Unfortunately, the latter had no effective remedy to offer, other than offer early versions of patent medicines, laced with alcohol and morphine. Cold weather finally ended the calamity, leaving in its wake growing public criticism about how the town was

Peter Toney, a Mi'kmaq resident in the Dartmouth area, is show here as sketched about 1840. While marginalized, native people occasionally featured in Halifax society. Toney gained fame as a champion canoeist, winning races on regatta day.

being managed, a problem which some insisted required incorporation as a city.

A parallel source of disquiet involved the influx of people from overseas which reshaped all parts of Nova Scotia through the postwar era. Residents of the British Isles poured across the ocean, their passage facilitated by cheap fares charged to cross the Atlantic on vessels in the continuing timber trade. In the case of Halifax, a high percentage of the newcomers were Irish Roman Catholics, whose leaders vigorously asserted their distinct cultural identity in the New World. The result was a proliferation of church and secular institutions which increasingly undermined traditional assumptions about Halifax being destined to function as a bastion of English and Protestant values. Viewed from the self-serving perspective of the old host population, this influx of "aliens"

St. Mary's Cathedral, the adjacent glebe house and St. Mary's school, shown in this 1838 sketch, constituted the heart of Roman Catholic institutional life in early-Victorian Halifax.

William Walsh, came to Halifax from Ireland in 1842. Over the next sixteen years he presided over a dramatic strengthening of the city's Roman Catholic presence, an achievement acknowledged in 1852, when he was named archbishop of Halifax.

was unwelcome. Newcomers were accused of competing for jobs, being diseased and prone to drunken violence. Such hostile stereotyping obscured the extent to which most immigrants made strenuous efforts to acquire property and respectability. For example, by 1840 the largest and most militant of Halifax's temperance societies were run by Irish Roman Catholics. Nevertheless, those "from away," especially if they did not belong to "charter" ethnic and sectarian groups, continued to be looked upon with disfavour.

A more subtle reordering of Halifax social fabric involved expansion of the town's middle class. A small and deferential segment of town society, Halifax's "bourgeoisie," made up largely of master craftsmen and retail shopkeepers, began to be transformed during the second quarter of the nineteenth century. Prosperity increased

their numbers and also allowed individual members to acquire substantial amounts of real estate, education, and leisure time. Rising affluence and expanded intellectual horizons gradually fostered ambitions within this section of the community towards a greater role in civic affairs. Accommodation of these demands proved relatively easy in the case of the informal sector of Halifax institutional life. For example, middle-class infiltration of voluntary philanthropic organizations, such as the North British Society, provoked little controversy. But the formal components of Halifax's power structure, those involved with the exercise of political authority, persistently remained the exclusive possession of what might be called the town gentry, a grouping dominated by wholesale merchants, high colonial officials and leading members of the learned professions.

The boundaries between middle class and gentry often were blurred, notably by the factors of kinship and religion. Moreover, those in rapidly expanding occupations such as medicine, the law and journalism, defied easy categorization. Under such circumstances, middle-class "consciousness" remained nebulous, with "new" men all too likely to emulate rather than challenge those deemed by custom to be their "betters." Persistent deference among the middle class also derived from anxieties they felt about the labouring elements of Halifax society. The poor remained the majority in town and were widely, if unfairly, viewed as being inherently dangerous. Periodic riots, often provoked by clashes between soldiers and slum dwellers, fed middle-class fears and long made them hesitant to campaign for liberalization of Halifax's formal power structure. Nevertheless, by the

Harbour races, such as shown in this 1838 lithograph, featured competition among officers from the garrison and leading members of civilian society. Lesser folk participated as spectators and sometimes as gamblers.

Genteel recreation in winter was dominated by horse and sleigh riding. Shown here is the Tandem Club gathering in front of Dalhousie College for a ride into the country by young men and their lady friends.

mid-1830s talk of "reform" was coming to dominate public affairs in Nova Scotia's capital.

The Quest for Improvement

Those Haligonians of the 1830s who led the drive to transform their town into a better place usually began at home, which for many functioned as both residence and work place. The nuclear family of parents and children, it was believed, constituted the key building block for improvement. Mutual affection, self-discipline, and humanitarian concern for others had come to be regarded, especially by those in the

middle class, as being essential for comfort and self-fulfilment. That meant a retreat from old traditions such as marital infidelity, gambling, and blood sports, in favour of a new morality, the components of which were alluded to by a Halifax publication, *Belcher's Farmer's Almanack*, as it told its readers:

Drink neither too much hot rum, or cold water. Make not haying and harvest an excuse for intemperance, but eat and drink in order to live, and not merely to eat and drink. Rise before the sun, and mow before the dew is on; mow morning and evening, and make hay and get it in while the sun shines. Be regular, temperate, industrious, but not violent—and your harvest will be gathered earlier and better than your neighbour Thirsty's.[9]

Similar advice was offered by Margaret Stairs, wife of a struggling shopkeeper, when she wrote her son, then a student at Horton Academy (later Acadia University, in Wolfville), to say:

The present season of suffering will impress your mind with the necessity of keeping out of debt. If men would be satisfied with small things and regulate their house expenses accordingly, it would be much better for us all ... I hope

This scene, painted by William Eager in 1839, shows Halifax in transition. St Paul's represents tradition but innovation is embodied in the new fire station to the right of the church.

you will commence [business] with a firm determination to be proud of industry. Some men in this town have been ruined by their son's indolence and pride.[10]

Traditional community leaders made diligent efforts to identify themselves in the public mind with the quest for earnestness. For example, John Inglis, enthroned as the Anglican bishop of Nova Scotia in 1825, engaged in an energetic routine of fund raising, visitation, and clerical recruitment, as he sought to popularize his denomination. In Halifax that meant bold innovation, such as evening church services on the sabbath and Sunday schools offering everything from literacy to picnics by the sea. Undermining such initiatives was the fact that Inglis and his peers faced growing competition for the hearts and minds of the public. An early expression of that rivalry was provided by Walter Bromley, a retired army officer, who, on arrival in Halifax about 1813, threw himself into a series of good causes, particularly in realm of mass education. Bromley's "egotistical arrogance and cussed determination," especially his insistence that middle-class people like himself possessed more "sense and virtue" than their nominal betters, made him a target for severe censure.[11]

By 1825 Bromley had left Halifax but others took his place. Perhaps the most impassioned of the new voices clamouring to be heard was William Jackson, a sometime Wesleyan (later Baptist) cleric who burst onto the Halifax scene in the autumn of 1832. A superb orator given to outdoor preaching complemented by indoor services where his wife and children played assisting roles, this flamboyant newcomer drew in huge crowds of ordinary folk. As Jackson explained it, the common people were eager for conversion and thus crowded his hall (Ebenezer Church, in Halifax's north end) "almost to suffocation," asking "what must we do to be saved."[12] Despite being arrested for disturbing the peace, denounced as a "witch," assaulted by thugs and having his house set on fire, Jackson persisted, sustained by support especially from the lower echelons of Halifax society. Significantly, women and young adults, two groups marginalized by social convention, stood out among those drawn to the fervent call for moral regeneration.

Another group demanding to be heard

Protestant dissenters in Halifax became ever more self-assertive through the early nineteenth century, building large facilities such as St. Andrew's Presbyterian church, shown here in a pre-Confederation photograph.

were the members of Halifax's black community. Many of the people of colour seen in town actually lived in nearby rural settlements, coming to the capital from time to time to sell country produce and crafts. Their colourful clothes and distinctive dialect captured the attention of visitors to Halifax but usually this led to demeaning comments about how black poverty proved that Africans could not cope with Nova Scotia's northern climate. However Captain William Moorsom was perceptive enough to note that local blacks possessed an inner pride and liked to insist that as British subjects in a colony now free of slavery, they were better off than their American counterparts. This sense of being a people with potential for improvement received reinforcement in 1833 when Britain abolished slavery throughout its empire.

Black self-assertion during the 1830s derived primarily from among the approximately 500 people of African descent who dwelt in Halifax's urban core, mainly in homes clustered a few blocks north of the Citadel. Most worked as labourers, servants and sailors but a few operated small businesses. In the 1830s, black leadership came to be embodied by Richard Preston, a former Virginian slave who had bought his freedom and then come, about 1820, to Halifax in search of relations who had fled north during the War of 1812. Talent and ambition eventually carried Preston to London and involvement with the British campaign for abolition of slavery through the empire. In 1832 he returned to Halifax, having been ordained as a Baptist cleric and carrying an endowment which made possible erection of the town's first all-black church. The Cornwallis Street African Baptist

Richard Preston, a dynamic refugee from slavery in the American South, emerged in the 1830s as the most prominent of several black leaders who used religion and politics to challenge racism in Halifax society.

congregation, with Preston as its pastor, quickly became a focal point for male and female black activism which strove for racial equality. One of those won over was Joe Howe who by 1840 had committed himself to a program of granting full civil rights to all Nova Scotians of African descent.

Jackson, Preston, and occasionally Howe dared to invoke a confrontational approach to the pursuit of change. Others proceeded in a more deferential manner, although in the end they too played a crucial role in carrying Halifax toward a more liberal order. Here one might cite the career of Beamish Murdoch, a young Halifax-born lawyer who, in the decade 1825-35, dedicated himself to the cause of improvement. Murdoch read widely, wrote for the press, did charity work, urged the establishment of public libraries, published a major treatise on the origins of Nova Scotian law, while also promoting abstention from alcohol, abolition of debtor imprisonment, and championed equality for Roman Catholics. Murdoch's dedication to public service climaxed in 1826 with his being elected to the Nova Scotian Assembly, winning over an aged incumbent seemingly devoid of new ideas.

There Murdoch joined forces with another young lawyer, T.C. Haliburton, whose facile tongue and clever pen made him a cautious but sometimes trenchant critic of what he saw as the inertia of tradition. For example, Haliburton's literary creation, "Sam Slick," responding to the question "what do you think of the present state and future prospects of Halifax," said "If you will tell me when the folks there will wake up, then I can answer you; but they are fast asleep."[13] What Haliburton and

Thomas Chandler Haliburton, lawyer, politician and most notably author of Nova Scotian history and fiction, inspired a rising generation of Haligonians to think critically about their community and its prospects.

Murdoch were really saying is not that Halifax remained inert but that it must become committed to yet more ambitious innovation in order to realize its potential for joining the nineteenth-century's march of progress.

Reform Encounters Opposition

Initial hope that reform might come readily to Halifax were shattered in the 1830s as Halifax's gentry, sensing danger, rallied to defend its privileged grip on political office. Beamish Murdoch became an early casualty of this process, losing his legislative seat in 1830. In large part Murdoch's offence had been to appeal directly to the "middle and humble class" of Halifax, telling them to look beyond "the smile or the nod of the rich man" at election time.[14] Murdoch had been easy to purge but Halifax's old guard encountered far more difficulty when it sought to stifle complaint over the administration of municipal affairs in the town. Here generations of tradition came into direct collision with the belief, festering among middle-class ratepayers, that their town had fallen under the control of men prone to ineptitude and even graft.

Municipal government in Halifax followed conventions which dated from the 1750s. Unlike Saint John which early on had received a city charter that provided for rule by elected officials, Nova Scotia's capital continued to be governed by appointed magistrates who held office at the pleasure of the Crown. Virtually without exception these officials were chosen from among the gentry element of town society which meant that, over time, they became ever less representative of the community at large. In practice, the Crown, that is, Nova Scotia's lieutenant-governor, rarely interfered in the day-to-day operations of local government in Halifax. Lack of any effective external check on official behaviour fostered a host of abuses, ranging from nepotism to irregular bookkeeping. Cruelty also flourished, especially at the town jail where inmates lacked proper food and clothing, were denied proper medical attention, nearly froze in winter and in summer lay in beds "infested with vermin."[15] By the mid-1830s talk of reform had begun to focus on the then radical idea of selecting magistrates through a process of election, rather than appointment.

A potent combination of rising taxes, a business recession, and proliferating incidents of scandal finally provoked a confrontation. Middle-class ratepayers, aroused by press reports of neglect, waste, and possible criminal behaviour, petitioned for remedial action. Then, when these complaints achieved nothing, critics took to writing letters of protest to local editors. One particularly vehement diatribe, signed

This stern-looking matron, painted by local artist William Valentine, was the kind of woman who, by the 1830s, was emerging to demand a role in the reshaping of Halifax society through enterprises such as the temperance movement.

As part of the drive for "responsible government," in 1841 Halifax became incorporated as a city, complete with elected mayor and such trappings of civic authority as the city seal, shown here.

"The People," appeared in Joseph Howe's *Novascotian*. It directed allegations of fraud and corruption against certain of the magistrates, who responded by demanding that Howe tell them who had so slandered their reputation. When Howe refused to identify the culprit, he found himself hauled before the Supreme Court on a charge of criminal libel.

That set the stage for perhaps the most celebrated trial in Halifax's history. Sustained by a belief that both the facts and public opinion were on his side, Howe went into court early in 1835 to argue that broad justice should prevail over the narrow technicalities of the law. The presiding judge was not persuaded but Howe won over the jury (mostly drawn from Halifax's middle class) who declared him innocent, and beyond that free to speak his mind on the issues of the day. Left to his own devices, Howe might have said relatively little, since he remained more interested in economic development than constitutional change. But others intervened, in effect conscripting the editor of the *Novascotian* to lead what quickly grew into a province-wide movement for political change. Characterized as "responsible government," the new system meant, in the case of Halifax, that the old gentry would now have to share power with the new middle class.

In 1840 Howe and his allies moved from control of Nova Scotia's House of Assembly into the seats of government. It would take another eight years to complete the drive for constitutional change but, for Halifax, the process moved decisively forward in 1841 when the province passed an act of incorporation establishing Halifax as a city, to be run by an elected mayor and council. Initially democracy remained highly diluted. Only adult men with extensive real-estate holdings could vote and office holding was confined to the richest ten percent of the population. But exclusive rule by the gentry had ended and on the horizon stood the possibility of reaching across the distinctions of race, ethnicity, and religion to forge a common sense of citizenship among Haligonians.

The chief priority facing the new municipal administration involved regulation of space within the six wards which constituted Halifax city. Residents, who now numbered over 14,000, lived east and north of the Citadel, in an urban zone so compact that few people were more than a half-hour walk from one another. The most

Hollis Street as portrayed by Wm. Eager in 1840. The institutions of state and church provide a background for promenading citizens, complete with cane and carriage. But note the loungers by the wall, who suggest popular resistance to the new city's quest for order.

densely populated part of town remained the tenement-dominated streets between the North and South barracks, located on the edge of Citadel Hill. Here, along streets such as Albemarle (later renamed Market Street) one found not only many residents but also multiple forms of land use, as homes coexisted with a jumble of shops and craft enterprises. The result was a volatile combination of noise, smells and lurking danger, all the way from fire to disease. By the 1840s, Halifax slums were beginning to move downhill, encroaching into once genteel neighbourhoods, such as that along Argyle Street. In response notables began to desert the downtown core, moving south

William Eagar's 1837 drawing from across the harbour. Sails and steeples dominate the scene but smokestacks, harbingers of industrialization, begin to appear.

This bucolic scene, drawn by William Eager, shows the upper reaches of the North West Arm, which constitutes the city's western boundary. Sites such as this drew crods of picnickers, a new fashion in the 1840s.

Maynard. Beyond lay farms, interspersed with the occasional villa, such as Enos Collins's magnificent property, Gorsebrook, situated in the far south end, on the road leading toward Point Pleasant.

Overcrowding and the lack of town planning under the old municipal regime left a legacy of challenges. Perhaps the most notorious involved the almost total absence of utility services. A few sewers had been built before 1841 but most human and animal waste continued to be dumped into cess pools scattered all over town. A small number of public wells, notorious for going dry in summer, could be found downtown but much of the population relied on shallow backyard wells as a water source. As a result, typhoid remained a chronic source of illness and, for many, death.

to homes near Government House or west along Spring Garden Road. Among the affluent, stone was becoming the building material of choice but most could afford only wooden structures. Fortunately the town's appearance began to brighten in the 1840s as slate-coloured paint began to be replaced with white or pastel shades. Middle-class folk tended to concentrate in the north end, along Brunswick Street and into adjacent streets such as Creighton and

The corpses of those who passed on generally ended up in burial grounds such as that operated by St. Paul's, at the corner of Barrington Street and Spring Garden Road. By 1840, ninety years of interments had created a scene of ooze and stench so bad as to offend even jaundiced contemporaries.

Proponents of municipal incorporation viewed such problems with an optimistic eye, being convinced that order could be brought out of chaos through vigorous regulation, combined with technological innovation. Reform began with a rush, featuring innovations such as a five-shilling tax on dogs, a ban on bathing in the city reservoir and heavy penalties for dumping manure on the Common. Over the next few years much would be accomplished including construction of a water works, the laying of gas lines, establishment of new public ceme-teries and enactment of the beginnings of a municipal building code. Controversy over the cost of all these initiatives and the prospect of chronic public debt would make Haligonians disillusioned with municipal reform. Indeed the farm folk of ward six, on the western side of the peninsula, would eventually attempt to secede from the city, arguing that their rural way of life should not be subordinated to urban values. Such protests proved unavailing, however.

Thomas McCulloch, longtime resident of Pictou where he gained notoriety as a cleric and social commentator, came to Halifax in 1838 as part of an abortive effort to revive Dalhousie College. McCulloch played a major role in spawning Nova Scotia's "intellectual awakening."

By the 1830s, mayflowers, such as these painted by local artist Maria M. Morris, had begun to be used as a patriotic symbol, appearing on flags and banners, along with the new city seal.

A City Celebrates

The creed of civic activism embodied by the newly elected municipal councillors, men such as Alexander Keith (elected mayor in 1843), drew strength from the prosperity which had returned to Halifax after a brief economic slump in the mid-1830s. Trade recovered, employment rebounded and property values soared to

William Eager's portrayal of Haligonians celebrating Queen Victoria's coronation is dominated by members of the social elite. But note the presence of three Mi'kmaq people at the bottom right of the picture.

1830s the institute met weekly through the autumn and winter to hear papers delivered by interested amateurs on virtually all topics of the day, excluding only the sensitive issues of sectarian religion and partisan politics. Although women did not function as speakers, they attended in significant numbers and their presence became a matter of pride for executive officers of the institute, who boasted that "ladies" imparted an extra tone of refinement to the evening's proceedings.

Unlike earlier relatively short-lived eruptions of interest in higher culture, by the 1830s Halifax possessed a more durable interest in the arts, thanks largely to institutional development in the town. For example, now many churches integrated choirs and organ playing into their services, a development which encouraged performers and teachers of music to locate in Halifax. Similarly, familiarity with the written word was promoted by a network of bookstores, reading rooms and libraries (three of which had emerged by 1840, one being linked to the Mechanics' Institute). Publishers had also proliferated, specializing in almanacs, school texts and especially newspapers. By the early 1840s Haligonians could choose from among a dozen local papers, several of which appeared

levels never before experienced. Out of this came new-found energy and confidence which carried Nova Scotia's "intellectual awakening" to higher levels of achievement. Perhaps the most significant expression of Halifax's swelling interest in literature, science, music, and art involved the Mechanics' Institute. Formed in 1831 as an echo of developments in Britain, the institute quickly became a major success story, acquiring a membership of over 100 recruited mainly from among the town's middle class. By the late more than once a week. Local editors, many of whom were highly flamboyant characters, continually enlarged the definition of what constituted news, combining vigorous editorial commentary with reportage of foreign and local events, along with imaginative forays into poetry, music and serialized novels.

While much of what appeared originated abroad (Dickens proved enormously popular), a few local authors emerged in this era, building on the precedent established by T.C. Haliburton. One of the most interesting was Maria Morris who in 1839 illustrated and had published (with supporting text written by local pioneer naturalist, Titus Smith) *Wildflowers of Nova Scotia*, an attractive study on the province's flora. Enthusiasm for self-discovery became a feature of cultural activity during these years. The reason, as explained by Joseph Howe, was to "make the race growing up upon her soil familiar with the beauties and resources of Nova Scotia, to make them feel that they had a country beneath their feet worthy of being loved and improved."[16]

The urge to find events and symbols which could be used to create a common sense of citizenship led, in 1834, to formation in Halifax of the Nova Scotian Philanthropic Society, an organization for locally-born men who wanted to assert their patriotism. On 8 June 1838 members held their first outdoor rally which took the form of a picnic, with catered food, followed by sports and other amusements. The date had been chosen to commemorate the day Cornwallis landed at Chebucto. Organizers

Samuel Cunard, born in Halifax in 1787, built a fortune after 1815 by investing in such diverse ventures as whaling, coal mining, and the timber trade. But his fame mostly derives from work in launching a transatlantic steamer service.

were early by almost a month but such was Halifax's poor collective memory that no one complained. On 28 June the Philanthropists were again out in public, this time as part of mammoth celebrations in honour of Queen Victoria's coronation. Processing 300 strong through town at noon, behind a blue banner carried by Mi'kmaq natives emblazoned with mayflowers and the words "We bloom amidst the snow," members attempted to steal the show by being first into the streets.[17]

Event organizers, conscious of the sensitive issue of rank and precedence, countered by insisting that the "real" parade did not begin until 1:30 in the afternoon. Mobilized by the firing of a gun, over 1000 enthusiastic Haligonians sallied into the downtown streets. Fraternal orders, friendly societies, militia units, and citizenry, ranging from local notables and to mere truckmen, all dressed in their finest, many with ritualistic regalia and carrying banners, passed over the cobblestones to the cheers of an audience thought to number 10,000. Three military bands played patriotic airs while from balcony windows, ladies waved handkerchiefs as praise for their men-folk. Proceeding out to the Common, marchers saluted the lieutenant-governor and then dispersed for refreshments. Genteel folk went to tents serving caviar and champagne while humbler folk made do with roast beef and beer. As evening set in, the sky lit up with fireworks, "a chaotic but eminently beautiful mass of sparks." The next morning, in a display of somewhat selective reporting, all local papers insisted that the affair had been played out amidst "perfect peace." Readers were told to

Shown here is the Britannia, *the first of Cunard's wooden-hulled, coal-burning side-wheelers. Though small and prone to roll in rough weather, vessels such as this could make the run from Liverpool to Halifax in under two weeks.*

ignore reports of drunkenness, theft, and assault and instead appreciate how "loyalty to the Queen, and fraternal greetings to one another, marked all the proceedings of the day."[18]

This emphasis on decorum and allegiance to a higher authority reflected the yearning found especially within Halifax's middle class for a community disciplined not through police repression but rather by moral ideals. The early-Victorian quest for an elevation of human character can be seen in what took place in May of 1840, at the monthly meeting of the Halifax Temperance Society. After lively entertainment, provided by an orchestra and choir, society president Beamish Murdoch introduced the evening's speaker, the Reverend William Cogswell, the thirty-one-year-old curate of St. Paul's and leading spokesman for an evangelical strain of Anglicanism then taking hold in Halifax. Cogswell had a blunt message for the mixed company of men and women sitting before him. Drinking intoxicants, he insisted, had once been considered proof of one's manhood, but in this modern era, with its emphasis on moral reform, religion and science were united in saying "the habit, instead of being MANLY, was BESTIAL, DEGRADING and in every way injurious" to the well-being of family and community life.[19]

Cogswell's argument, which earlier might have generated ridicule, now evoked ecstatic applause. Halifax's new-style "Victorian" people saw it as both a duty and an opportunity to strive for moral self-improvement. Moreover, they believed that the exercise would be enjoyable. The mood of the meeting, as reported by the *Colonial Pearl*, a new journal dedicated to destruction of the liquor trade, was more

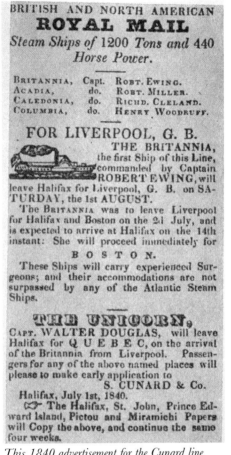

This 1840 advertisement for the Cunard line makes no mention of fares, which were extremely high. That and the need to cram the holds with coal for fuel meant these vessels, unlike later steamers, did not carry "steerage" passengers.

jubilant than ponderous. Cogswell's lecture had been followed by the singing of a series of lively hymns, all new compositions crafted by an unnamed local musician. Participants departed having had fun, while being bolstered in the belief that they were building a new civic order, one being weaned from strife and degradation by the power of moral persuasion.

The sense among early-Victorian Haligonians of living in an era of creative transformation received perhaps its most powerful boost in the summer of 1840 when transatlantic steamers began running into Halifax harbour. Early experiments with the *Royal William* had proven disappointing but then came the electrifying news that Samuel Cunard, successor to Enos Collins as the embodiment of local entrepreneurial daring, had won the contract to inaugurate scheduled steam-packet service from Liverpool to Boston, by way of Halifax. The first of Cunard's vessels, the paddle-wheeler *Unicorn*, powered by a coal-fuelled engine, was sighted off the harbour mouth shortly after dawn, on Monday, 1 June 1840. Signal flags ran up the masts on the Citadel triggering a rush of people toward the docks. There they cheered madly as the *Unicorn* "glided up the harbour in gallant style." Once the vessel tied up, Haligonians poured over the rails to gawk at this "floating palace" which, as a local paper put it, had "opened a new era in Provincial History," one which would be characterized by "excitement and change."[20]

Change often invites controversy and a demonstration of what that meant for early-Victorian Halifax was provided by an incident which took place on 14 March 1840. Near the Martello Tower at Point Pleasant journalist Joseph Howe met lawyer John C. Halliburton for an exchange of

"Three Mile House" at Bedford Basin was one of a series of inns found on the outskirts of Halifax. The better of these facilities acquired a reputation for good food and drink. Others were commemorated for their fleas, watered-down liquor, and lewd servants.

pistol fire. This "affair of honour" arose out of the bitterness spawned by the drive for political reform. Halliburton missed and Howe fired into the air, a gesture designed to demonstrate courage and thereby earn him the moral right to reject future challenges. The incident could be taken as a symbol of where Halifax had come from and where it was going by the early 1840s. Inherited institutions and ideals, including the gentlemanly ritual of duelling, were increasingly giving way to middle-class values which stressed devotion to work, family, and community stewardship. This is not to say that Halifax suddenly became a town steeped in virtue, but the goal of making it such a place would come to dominate the public mind as the new city entered the middle-decades of the nineteenth-century.

Chapter Four

SEAPORT CITY

(1841-1871)

The Halifax Club, an Italianate building on Hollis Street, epitomized the flowering of the merchant class of nineteenth-century Halifax. Designed by leading architect David Stirling, constructed in 1862-63 by George Lang, the city's most prolific master builder, and still standing in 1999, it attracted as its members élite male citizens who needed a dining club in which to transact business and discuss current events. One of its advocates was William Murdoch, a successful businessman who branched out beyond his initial dry goods import firm to pursue shipping and banking and such local ventures as the Halifax Water Company and Inland Navigation Company, which revived the Shubenacadie Canal project. Like many of Halifax's entrepreneurs and one-sixth of the city's civilian population, Murdoch was an immigrant from the British Isles—in his particular case Scotland. Although over two-thirds of the

Cronan's Wharf and warehouse complex Upper Water Street near the foot of Jacob Street where the dock labourers are weighing hogsheads of fish. Daniel Cronan was one of the leading Roman Catholic merchants in Halifax in the second half of the nineteenth century. He was reputed to be the city's richest man on his death in 1892. The church in the background is Trinity Anglican on Argyle Street (1855-1907), formerly Salem Chapel.

This 1840s map identifies the military forts in greater Halifax at a time when the city itself was confined to the area marked in red. Similarly the settled part of Dartmouth is indicated.

Pictured with their teacher in 1893 are some of the children who benefitted from the concern of Murdoch and others for the handicapped.

citizens of Halifax in 1871 had been born in Nova Scotia, the first federal census identified the major ethnic origins of the population as Irish (38.9 percent), English (32.4 percent), Scottish (16 percent), German (4.9 percent), African (3.2 percent), and French (1.6 percent).

Unlike the mass of the population, Murdoch had the money and time to contribute to the improvement of the city. His voluntary interests were typical of a man of his prominence. As a good citizen he took his turn as fireward and city alderman. In the 1850s his varied activities included patron of the Halifax Curling Club, president of the Highland Society, president of the Halifax Visiting Dispensary, treasurer of the Royal Acadian School Society, governor of the Protestant Orphans' Asylum, director of the Nova Scotia Horticultural Society and life member of the Young Men's Christian Association. Murdoch was a member of the first generation of Nova Scotians to practise a public stewardship of their wealth. Believing that everybody should contribute to good causes "according to their

several ability,"[1] he made donations to most charitable ventures, and bequeathed in his will gifts, with suitably prudent conditions, for St. Matthew's Church, the public hospital he had promoted for many years, and a residential school for the hearing impaired, known as the Institution for the Deaf and Dumb. He also left a legacy to establish a similar specialized home for the education of the visually impaired.

At a time when reformers called for responsible government at both the provincial and civic levels, Murdoch provided an example of the responsible entrepreneur. Or did he? Late in life Murdoch took most of his immense, Halifax-earned wealth to England, contributing to a trend in the export of local capital which the fledgling city could ill afford as it struggled to develop a diversified economic base and provide its citizens with modern amenities.

While Haligonians like Murdoch made impressive fortunes and joined forces to build handsome edifices like the Halifax Club, they were also engaged in international trade and developed an urban infrastructure for the new city. Despite the challenges posed by

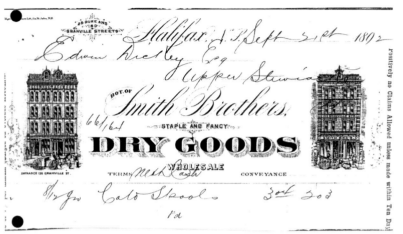

Left: *The Halifax Club as portrayed* Illustrated London News, *14 November 1863. The building on Hollis Street still serves as a club but it is now open to women as well as men.* Above: *Invoices often included a sketch of the firm's premises. The Smith Brothers of Granville Street were supplying J.E. Dickie's store in Upper Stewiacke.*

economic instability and the novelty of city status, mid-Victorian citizens pursued a program of institution building unparalleled in the history of Halifax. Some changes occurred at too slow a pace to please everyone, but the results nonetheless encouraged pride in the city, confidence in the potential of its middle class and concern for its less fortunate residents.

The Age of Sail

The mid-nineteenth century witnessed the apogee of the Maritime "age of sail" when a regionally owned fleet of wooden-hulled sailing vessels prowled the oceans of the world. Halifax, unlike Saint John and many Nova Scotian outports, was not a major ship-building port. An occasional vessel was launched from various yards on the harbour's shoreline but most of the substantial tonnage owned in Halifax, amounting to about half the province's merchant shipping, was built elsewhere. Halifax businessmen specialized in shipping and trade. This transport of goods included local products, imported goods, and the cargo of other jurisdictions carried in vessels owned both locally and externally. As an entrepôt or centre for trade, the port required facilities for warehousing, repairs, outfitting, and the local carriage of goods. Insurance and banking were a natural outgrowth of this activity. Since it was not heavily dependent on the timber trade, Halifax was not as disrupted by the loss of British

The Stag, *a barque of 209 tons, was built at La Have by Ebenezer Moseley in 1854. It was owned successively by several Halifax businessmen until it was lost in 1863. The painter was John O'Brien, Halifax's best known marine artist of the century.*

protectionism as were the resource-dependent ports of Saint John and Quebec. Elsewhere, Britain's shift to free trade in the 1840s and 1850s meant the end of protective tariffs and most-favoured shipping status but change did not diminish the large military presence in Halifax, which sustained a vital portion of the business life of the city. In any event, trade continued to be determined more by supply and demand than by legislation designed to regulate commerce for political or

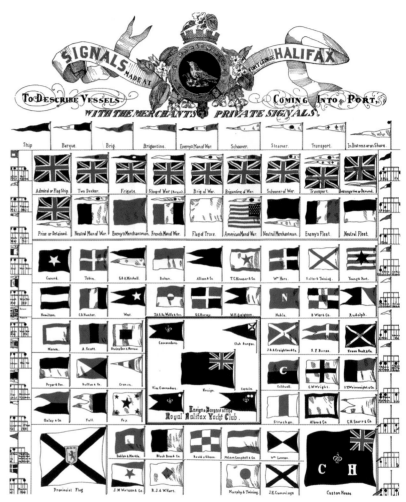

Signal flags that were flown from the masts on Citadel Hill which served as Halifax's signal hill.

fiscal reasons. This applied to the demands of British trade and industry for raw materials and the needs of the Caribbean population for foodstuffs. Combined with new markets and opportunities, these

Racing boat crew, HMS Pert, *November 1878. The Naval Yard, dominated by the Commissioner's house, can be seen in the background. The British navy participated in the city's water sports, both rowing, which was also very popular with fishers and artisans, and the more elitist sailing competitions, especially after the establishment of the Halifax Yacht Club in 1857.*

The first Halifax Railway Terminal located in Richmond near the foot of Duffus Street.

commercial activities created a mid-century boom in Halifax.

What Halifax could not avoid suffering, however, were the effects of being part of a larger whole. Its businesses were adversely affected when the commerce of its trading partners and the international firms for which it supplied local shipping agents contracted. For example, the traditional British West Indies sugar trade collapsed in the two decades following the abolition of slavery in the 1830s. Although similar markets were thereafter developed in foreign Caribbean possessions, the period of adjustment resulted in occasional business failures, bankruptcies and family hardship.

The port of Halifax was also open to the influx of newcomers during the tumultuous middle decades of the nineteenth century. Although circumstances were never as dire in Halifax as in the major immigrant ports, the city nonetheless experienced the trauma associated with the famine immigration of the late 1840s. The persistent threat of disease—cholera, smallpox,

typhus—occasioned the establishment from time to time of quarantine regulations and infectious diseases hospitals. Disease control remained superficial, however, and three health officers, William B. Almon (1840), Matthias Hoffman (1851) and John Slayter (1866), died from infection. The distress of new arrivals, mostly from Ireland, mobilized the fraternal societies, churches, and individuals to provide relief, particularly during the season of winter unemployment.

Halifax enjoyed a number of economic opportunities in the 1850s and 1860s which related to its relationship with the United States. A reciprocity treaty which lasted from 1854 until 1866 increased trade. Then in 1861 the American Civil War erupted, leading to an expansion of the British military presence in the city. Simultaneously, as Confederate raiders devastated Union shipping, the American carrying trade increasingly fell into the hands of Halifax shipowners who were delighted

Left: *Notice advertising railway fares, 1855* Above: *One of many nineteenth-century views of Halifax from Dartmouth, this one by the prolific British scene painter, William Bartlett, captures the steamboat which served as a ferry between Halifax and Dartmouth and enabled many farmers, gatherers, and craftspeople on the eastern side of the harbour to travel regularly to the city market.*

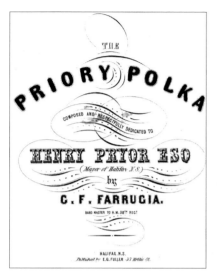

Conservative Henry Pryor served as mayor for five one-year terms in the 1840s and 1850s, much to the disgust of the Liberals, who lampooned him at every opportunity. Not only did he inspire the composition of a polka but also in 1867 he became the city's first stipendiary magistrate (equivalent to a 1999 provincial court judge). His inconsistencies in sentencing and generally erratic behaviour as he aged in the job exposed him to the same kind of ridicule he had endured as mayor.

to do business with both sides in this fratricidal combat.

Another opportunity—this time for long-term, reliable development—involved railway construction. Dreams of extending the traditional shipping economy from sea to land and tapping the trade of the interior of British North America preoccupied Halifax civic boosters through the 1850s and 1860s. Everyone wanted a railroad: not everyone wanted the state to pay for it. The high cost of the venture divided politicians and contributed significantly to creating a city fragmented on the major question of Confederation. While the role of government in economic development remained contentious, the modernization of Halifax came to depend on the expansion of state power because of the high debt load imposed by the construction of the short railway lines in the 1850s and 1860s. The prospect of an intercolonial railway, funded by a larger political entity, proved to be a powerful incentive for favouring Confederation.

The Urban Infrastructure

In 1841 such innovations as railways and political union were not even on the horizon. The key constitutional change for Halifax in the

1840s involved the introduction of elective municipal government, desired by reformers because it would give the middle class control over local affairs. The growing pains, personality clashes and political manoeuvres during the first decade or so invigorated the urban scene. For example, the first mayor, Stephen Binney, a merchant and member of the local élite, harboured grandiose notions about his office. He thought the mayor should take precedence over the lieutenant-governor in functions welcoming foreign royalty to the city and represent the city in dealings with the Crown.

For the first few years after 1841 the civic elections commanded considerable attention but the political stripe of the mayor and majority

The new Market House painted by L.J. Cranstone in 1860. It was largely a meat market and disliked by the country and native folk who preferred a "curbstone" market on Hollis, Cheapside, and Bedford Row.

of the council seems to have had little effect on the nature of improvements. The agonizingly slow pace with which changes materialized—for example, a new market house, mud-free sidewalks, a clean and tidy Grand Parade, a general hospital—soon generated indifference and scepticism. Establishment figures such as Binney gave way to "new" men as the Liberals gained control of the council in the

The destruction of the North Barracks in December 1850 resulted in the construction of the Wellington Barracks. Until the new barracks were completed, British officers were housed in the Halifax Hotel which was rented by the War Office. This put the one decent inn in Halifax out of commission to visitors for almost a decade.

drunkenness, they did not expel him, content instead to see him die in a fortuitous industrial accident a couple of months later. While most municipal politicians shared a middle-class vision for the orderly development of the city, the committee structure tended to encourage ward politics and patronage in such matters as road repairs and the provision of municipal services.

Some of the more routine difficulties encountered by the council related to the very limited powers of taxation and borrowing which the law allowed. As a result voluntarism remained a vital element in the provision of urban services. A prime example of voluntary civic

The volunteers of Union Engine Co. No.5 (Mayflower) outside the Spring Garden Road Engine House, ready for the carnival, 10 August 1886.

late 1840s. In 1849 they objected to the election of John Willis, the city's erstwhile road-tax collector, as councillor for ward one after he had been dismissed for the misappropriation of funds. Because of the accountability clause in the city charter, Willis was not permitted to take his seat.

Public interest in the annual elections revived in 1862 with the return, on the basis of an expanded franchise, of Thomas Spence, a leading ship caulker, as alderman in ward five. Spence epitomized the worst fears of upholders of the status quo because of his working-class vulgarity and inability to hold either his liquor or his tongue. Once more the council refused an alderman his seat. After Spence's rights were sustained by the supreme court, the revised city charter of 1864 provided a new mechanism for getting rid of miscreants by a two-thirds vote. Although the council found Spence guilty of public

services was the firefighting brigade. The various companies—the Union Engine, Axe, Ladder, Hand in Hand, and Phoenix Companies—attracted members out of a sense of responsibility, or a desire for social intercourse—club features prevailed—or as a way of securing exemption from onerous civic responsibilities, like militia duty and jury service. It would not be until the mid-1890s that the city adopted a salaried fire department.

Although Halifax did not burn down in the second half of the nineteenth century as frequently or as catastrophically as did Quebec, Saint John, and St. John's, it had its share of major conflagrations. On such occasions, the proficiency of the firefighters, who relied on hand-powered pumps, received mixed reviews. After the Hollis Street fire of New Year's Day,

Right: *Granville Street after the fire of 1859.* Left: *After it was rebuilt uniformly with freestone and cast iron. The church in Cranstone's painting is Chalmers Presbyterian on Barrington Street, built in 1849 as a part of the Free Church movement.*

1857, their efforts were universally applauded and their injuries deplored; any inefficiencies were attributed to the inadequate supply of piped water made available by the Halifax Water Company, formed in

1844 as a private enterprise. On the other hand, in 1858 during another Hollis Street fire, criticism focused on the tardiness of the Ladder Company and the lack of direction within the ranks of the Union Engine Company. Costly property losses in the Granville Street fire of 1859 prompted demands for a dedicated water supply and modern firefighting equipment, under threat of withdrawal of fire insurance coverage. After another serious fire in 1861, the council purchased steam-powered engines, expropriated the water service and passed regulations to create a brick and stone district in the downtown core.

Other priorities for the city included some of the most basic services which the old town had lacked. Sewers, waste removal, sidewalks, street cleaning (or at any rate watering the streets to lay the dust), and improvement of public spaces often generated controversy. For example, the council's attempt, in the mid-1850s, to restrict by ordinance access to the Common by impounding cattle found at large disadvantaged those

Halifax's first hotel, the Halifax, was run by Henry Hesslein and his wife, and later their sons, for many years.

A royal occasion on the Common: review of the troops by the Duke of York (future George V) in 1901.

who customarily used the common land to pasture their animals.

Arguments with the military over the use of the Common also ensued. They came to a head in 1859 when the troops knocked down city fences on the western half of the North Common, claiming it as

their property. The city recognized military rights to some 20 hectares adjacent to the Citadel for an exercising ground, 5 hectares surrendered in 1830 for extension of the glacis of the Citadel, and about 3 hectares on Camp Hill, which had been exchanged in the early 1840s for a portion of the military's Fort Massey land, needed to create Holy Cross Cemetery, but the council baulked at the garrison's claim to the rest of the North Common, an area about as large again as the total of the three uncontested parcels of military land. Since the town magistrates of 1800 had apparently agreed to the arrangement, the memorandum of agreement signed with the War Office in 1860 resolved the problem largely in the military's favour and perhaps, by preventing enclosure, in the public's favour.

Halifax City Council itself was busy alienating the South Common, beginning with the establishment of the Protestant cemetery of Camp Hill in 1844, followed by leases for building lots along Spring Garden Road (including Sacred Heart Convent) and for the gardens of the Horticultural Society. The first public building on the Common was the hospital, erected in 1859, the next being the

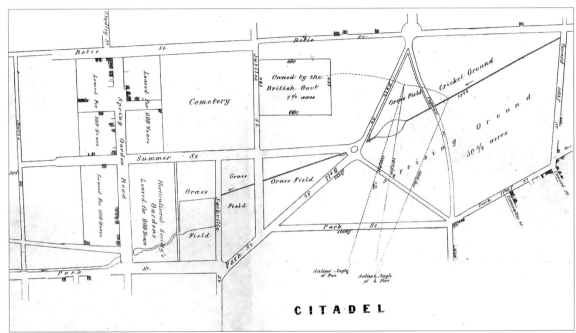

Map of the Common in 1859 at the time of the dispute between the city and the military. Below: *Cows grazed on the lower reaches of the Citadel in the 1890s as they had formerly done on the Common, seen to the left. In the distance on the far left (north west) is the domed roof of the new exhibition building on Windsor Street.*

were a bridewell and cells in the 1810 brick court house at the foot of George Street. The city had no system of publicly funded schools. A range of private schools existed but only a few endured. These included the Royal Acadian, National and St. Mary's schools which were variously supported by individual churches, societies of citizens, and annual legislative grants, and provided subsidized education for some children. However, funding, standards, equipment, and facilities remained inconsistent. Worst of all, a majority of children received no formal education and grew up illiterate. Only a tiny minority, mostly male, attended educational institutions offering secondary and collegiate education. At the Halifax Grammar School and St. Mary's College, for example, the sons of the well-to-do received preparatory training for professional careers in the church, law, and medicine.

The health of the citizens was even more neglected, with only the

new poorhouse (usually called the poor's asylum), accommodated on South Street west of the hospital in 1867 and completed two years later. By the time the next encroachment occurred, with the appropriation in 1868 of a lot for the School for the Blind, a group of concerned citizens had formed a society for the preservation of the Common, the city's first conservationist movement.

New Public Institutions

Early-Victorian Haligonians recognized the need for improved facilities for the punishment, education, health, and welfare of the city's population. At the time of incorporation in 1841 the only jails

This westerly view on George Street pictures the city hall (built 1810) on the right, which served also as a police lock-up and magistrate's court until 1890. The market place on the left is outside the market house. To its west is the federal building used as the customs house and post office.

of new institutions aimed at disciplining and elevating community character. The council's top priority was law and order. Until the 1860s the mayor served as chief magistrate and he or one of his aldermanic colleagues presided daily as judge in the police court and several times a week in the city (civil) court. These elected judges, though often lacking formal legal training, discerningly assessed the needs of the city with respect to by-laws, policing, sentencing, and jail accommodation. Three new correctional institutions opened in the two decades following incorporation—a provincial penitentiary for serious offenders, located in the south end, on the North West Arm near Point Pleasant (replaced by Dorchester Penitentiary after Confederation), a county jail on Spring Garden Road adjacent to the new court house, and, for short sentences, a city prison at Rockhead Farm in the north end, successor to the bridewell. The police lock-up was located in the old court house, now reconstituted as the city hall. So many prisons in the infant city, together with the British prisons for military offences, reflected the contemporary belief that crime could be virtually eradicated through jail sentences.

Changes occurred in how Halifax was policed. A permanent twelve-man volunteer night watch, initiated in 1846, served alongside a dozen paid daytime constables. In 1864, the two services were combined to create a modern law-enforcement agency. Reflecting a trend

North End City Mission: Mission school children and female mission workers, with missionary, Adam Logan, probably in the 1870s.

poorhouse to function as a totally inadequate hospital and maternity home. Public welfare and geriatric care were also restricted to the poorhouse which persistently could not admit all those in need. The churches and ethnic societies sponsored some winter charity and the city occasionally dealt with winter unemployment by paying poor men to break stone for road making. The spiritual welfare of the population was more secure since sin, salvation and the sacraments remained priorities and identity within the city was largely church-based. By 1841 Halifax possessed two congregations each of the Church of England, Church of Scotland, Methodist, Baptist and Roman Catholic faiths.

The first generation after incorporation saw a veritable explosion toward increased professionalization, a salaried (stipendiary) magistrate with legal training was appointed in 1867. Until 1870 he had control of the police, but then police authority passed back to the mayor. The mayor, however, never again presided in court, a change which Mayor Matthew Richey believed placed the council "in a much more advantageous position for conducting the general business of the city."[2]

Schools received a lower priority than jails. A modern school system had many advocates but cost, as well as the denominational character of most schools, delayed reform. During the 1840s and 1850s churches and interest groups opened additional schools, usually part fee-paying, part charity. A teachers' association for Halifax and Dartmouth was formed in 1862 which advocated "free" schools supported by property taxes, combined with supervision to promote higher standards and improved pay scales. Although the council opposed assessments for the support of schools, the provincial government was determined to introduce mass education as a step toward modernization. In 1865 Halifax came under the operation of Nova Scotia's Free School Act, which meant that henceforth public schools would be the norm.

The inclusion of the Roman Catholic schools in the new system reflected the accommodation possible in a city with only occasional Catholic-Protestant conflict, elsewhere widespread at the time. Despite separate Catholic and Protestant schools, one integrated board supervised all facilities, a compromise which endured into the mid-twentieth century. In 1868 the city gained some control over the Halifax Board of School Commissioners when the council acquired from the Province the right to name half of the board members. The revamped schools of Halifax, free but not compulsory, provided a basic primary education. They were graded by level and, for the moment,

Rockhead Prison on north Gottingen Street.

usually segregated by gender, except for separate black schools, which persisted in the inner city until 1902 and in Africville until 1953.

Just as the school teachers were a pressure group on behalf of free public schooling, Halifax physicians mobilized to promote a public health-care system focused on a hospital. Citizens demanded emergency measures to combat epidemics and early on they endorsed the establishment of facilities for the care of persons with psychiatric disorders as a service as necessary as jails. Thus a provincial mental hospital, initially known as Mount Hope Asylum and later the Nova Scotia Hospital, opened in a rural setting in Dartmouth in 1859. Almost another decade passed before a modern public hospital for medical and surgical ailments was established in the city. Cost delayed action by the council on the hospital. In addition, public suspicion of the medical profession's hunger for cadavers (needed for teaching purposes) blocked progress on erecting a hospital.

The Halifax Medical Society emerged in 1854 to sustain the pressure for the establishment of modern clinical and educational facilities. In 1859 a hospital was finally built on the Common but remained empty amidst wrangling over money and control. After the provincial government agreed to cover the

The St. George's Church charity school existed before free schooling and continued to be taught in the Old Dutch Church, Brunswick Street, after the school became part of the public system.

A classroom in Joseph Howe school on Creighton Street, which replaced Albro Street School, Albro being the earlier name of the same street.

societies to visit destitute members and dispense food, clothing, and fuel. By mid-century the need for a more systematic approach to relief began to take hold and the desire to differentiate among various categories of poverty also became a goal. Some church groups, such as the St. Matthew's District Visiting Society, responded with 'workfare' schemes which aimed to supply employment and domestic skills instead of unconditional relief. Also, a number of new, broader organizations and institutions appeared. For the relief of the "deserving poor," particularly women and their children, the St. Vincent-de-Paul Society was introduced in Roman Catholic parishes in 1853 and the Association for Improving the Condition of the Poor was established in 1867 by the Protestant citizenry. Institutions for children also came on the scene, such as the Protestant Orphans' Asylum and the Catholic (later St. Joseph's) Orphanage.

The middle decades of the nineteenth century saw a proliferation of churches in Halifax, many of them involving new varieties of

care of out-of-city patients and the doctors negotiated a managerial role for themselves, the City and Provincial Hospital (renamed Victoria General in 1887) opened in 1867, with help from Murdoch's estate. Shunned by the middle class who preferred home care or the private hospitals, which appeared from time to time, the facility catered largely to working class and destitute people, including hordes of visiting merchant seamen. In the meantime, establishment of the Halifax Visiting Dispensary in 1855 gave those who could not afford a doctor access to medical treatment and drugs. This facility received annual support from the city, as well as from the major churches, which held collections on Dispensary Sunday. Later the dispensary's building on Brunswick Street also housed the city's morgue.

Poverty, though widespread, was not something that attracted much government intervention. Outside the poorhouse, welfare remained a private sector activity, led by the churches. In most congregations, the wives and daughters of the more affluent members formed benevolent

Mount Hope Lunatic Asylum, later called the Nova Scotia Hospital.

Protestant experience. The Presbyterian secessionists, long active in eastern Nova Scotia, finally built a city church on Poplar Grove in 1843; the Free Church, resulting from the 1843 schism in the Church of Scotland, had two churches by 1850, on Gerrish (in Jackson's old Ebenezer Chapel) and Barrington streets. Congregationalism was briefly revived at Salem Chapel on Argyle Street between 1847 and 1854 and the Universalists opened a house of worship on Starr Street in 1843. Some older congregations replaced their churches with gothic-style buildings in brick and stone, including St. Matthew's Church of Scotland, rebuilt on Barrington Street after the Hollis Street fire of 1857, and Grafton Street Methodist Church (now St. David's Presbyterian), rebuilt after a fire in 1868. St. Mary's Roman Catholic Cathedral on Spring Garden Road was gradually decorated with a new granite facade. Even the humble wooden Zion Church,

The City and Provincial Hospital was renamed the Victoria General in 1887.

erected on Gottingen Street by the African Methodist Episcopalians, had gothic windows. Not everyone attended regular church services, something the more zealous Protestants set about to remedy. The interdenominational Halifax City Mission was established in 1852 and one of its missionaries produced *Halifax: "Its Sins and Sorrows"* in 1862 as an indictment of what good Christians deemed immorality and vice. Other initiatives followed. In 1868, the North End City Mission began a 100-year service to the poor people of the old north end who came to rely on the mission house on the corner of City (now Maynard) and Gerrish

Early ambulance, Victoria General Hospital.

streets. City missions spawned a number of specialized institutions, usually short-lived, such as the House of Refuge for "Fallen Women" in 1854, a sailors' home in 1862, and a "ragged" school which got absorbed into the city school system in 1865. For their part the Catholics delegated outreach after 1850 to the recently arrived Sisters of Charity.

businesses. A water supply, operated by gravity from the Chain Lakes along St. Margaret's Bay Road, was introduced in 1848 but two continuing problems soon emerged: excessive wastage and inadequate pressure for the north end. Mobility after dark was facilitated by the installation in 1849 of 80 gas lamps to illuminate the streets and the phasing out of old oil fixtures. By 1866 travellers had access to a horse-drawn street railway which ran from the south end of the city to the railway depot, established in the mid-1850s on the shoreline of the harbour narrows in Richmond. The new urban service provoked considerable opposition from Halifax's cabmen and operators of the multi-passenger vehicles known as omnibuses, who resorted to Luddite-like protests in a bid to protect their businesses from this more modern competitor with its protrusive iron rails. For those going farther afield, the Nova Scotian railway ran to Windsor, Truro, and

Modernization, Commemoration and Association

Creating the major services deemed necessary to improve the behaviour, literacy, health, and well-being of the citizenry consumed much of the energy and time of the city's leading administrators, professionals, and philanthropists. Yet these services comprised only a fraction of the new facilities and amenities promoted in this period. The desire of many to enhance the quality of everyday life in the city, to emulate what was in fashion elsewhere and to benefit from being part of something larger and more modern bore fruit in a number of ways.

A better standard of life depended on a cleaner, safer, and more accessible city. At the time of incorporation the city was drab, dirty, and smelly. Manifestations of improvement ranged from street name signs and house numbers (begun in 1843) to construction of water mains and sewer lines into a growing number of households and

Protestant Orphans' Home, North Park Street, May 1874.

This formal photographic portrait features the inauguration of the Crimean War Memorial in 1860 with the newly completed County Court House and Jail to the right, complete with a cupola which is no longer extant. Accompanying the dignitaries is a contingent of the Chebucto Greys, one of the volunteer militia units founded in 1859-60. One of the two militiamen, front left, is builder and mason George Lang who designed the monument and carved the lion.

Pictou by 1867. Scheduled steamer service to points outside of Nova Scotia connected Halifax to the wider world, as did the electric telegraph which came into local service in 1849 and transatlantic service in 1857.

Within the city, the Horticultural Gardens were developed in the late 1830s and early 1840s on a portion of the Common. Managed by the Horticultural Society, the gardens could be visited by those members of the public willing to pay a fee. Sport facilities, such as a skating rink and croquet lawn, formed part of the gardens complex. In 1867 the council began to transform an adjacent field on the north side into a public garden open to all. The two eventually combined to form today's Public Gardens. In St. Paul's Cemetery in 1860, Halifax raised its first war memorial to remember Captain

William Parker and Major Augustus Welsford, local heroes who died in the Crimean War.

This was an age of commemoration. Every year local ethnic societies of men turned out for marches, visits to Government House and banquets to mark their 'national day,' be it St. Patrick's for the Charitable Irish, St. George's for the St. George Society, St. Andrew's for the North British and Highland societies, Halifax's Natal Day for the Nova Scotia Philanthropic Society or Slave Emancipation Day for the African Society. In addition, royal events were recognized, often with public holidays. Competition between soldiers and civilians during the celebration of the Prince of Wales' marriage in 1863 precipitated a three-day riot, which demonstrated the inadequacies of Halifax's policing services the year before they were reformed.

The horse-car barn of the Halifax Street Railway Company was located in the north end (Richmond) at Barrington and Hanover Streets.

Three special occasions in this period were the 100th anniversary in 1849 of the founding of Halifax, the visit of the Prince of Wales in 1860, and Confederation with Canada in 1867. Although the settling of Halifax was celebrated every year on the ground that it fostered "a genuine patriotic spirit,"[3] political feuding threatened to interrupt the centenary proceedings in 1849. Fortunately, a co-operative spirit among the various ethnic voluntary societies prevailed such that the events of June 1849 proved successful. Royal visits provided an opportunity to show off the city's stylish society, aquatic scenery, military pageantry and picturesque Mi'kmaq warriors. In 1860, however, partisan bickering led to complaints that the prince's men, irrespective of class, colour or religion, belonged to fraternal, labour, sports, mutual benefit and self-improvement associations. They included lodges of Freemasons, Oddfellows, and Sons of Temperance, clubs of curlers, yachtsmen, and cricketers, and, after permissive legislation in 1864, trade unions of house joiners, shipwrights and caulkers, stone cutters and masons.

Since the major urban concern of this period appeared to be the moral, intellectual and physical well-being of young men, several organizations were aimed specifically at them. In the middle decades of the century the literary and debating societies tried to interest young men and the Halifax Young Men's Total Abstinence Society of 1847 included music in its programs to enhance its appeal.

The cast of the popular ice skating rink in the Exhibition Building is a composite one in this instance, showing skaters decked out for a masquerade.

entourage was being monopolized by the ruling Liberal Party. On the first Dominion (Canada) Day, anti-confederates dismissed the city's pro-confederate majority by hanging black crêpe on the statue of Britannia atop the new provincial building—soon to be the federal post office and customs house. The official street parade only drew about 600 people, "as many as have occasionally attended a decent funeral," suggested one disgruntled observer.[4]

Voluntary associations were central to such celebrations. Many

These groups were joined in 1853 by the Young Men's Christian Association, which also set its sights on respectable young men and tried to attract them with lectures. When the managers decided in 1857 that the young men were not heeding their advice to join, they took up the cause of early closing, which interested the clerks of the city. If employers could be persuaded to close their shops at 5 pm on Saturdays, then the YMCA could fill the clerks' evening hours with scriptural reading and edifying conversation.

Employer resistance led to establishment of the Young Men's Early Closing Association in 1867. The new organization continued to demand a shorter work day for white collar workers—office and shop clerks principally—to provide leisure time for elevating cultural and physical activities. It was more successful in providing opportunities for literary and athletic endeavour than in changing policies in the workplace.

Young men themselves were mainly interested in participating in sports teams, brass bands, and sponsored social events which included young women, along with playing soldier. The British "volunteer" militia movement swept through the province in the late 1850s and early 1860s. Several volunteer rifle companies were organized on the basis of ethnicity, religion and race. When they came together to form the Halifax Volunteer Battalion in 1860, the Victoria Rifles, a black

The first black Oddfellows Lodge, Wilberforce No.7336, Manchester Unity, is shown here in 1917.

The Marquis of Lorne, Canada's governor-general, receiving a delegation of Mi'kmaq in Province House during his visit in 1879.

company, was not included because of its poverty and the racism of the other units.

In 1863 ambitious young men who wished to enter the professions benefitted when Nova Scotia's two Presbyterian synods co-operated to reopen, on a lasting basis, Dalhousie College. The move engendered considerable opposition from other denominations which feared Dalhousie's expansionist ambitions, but S.L. Shannon, the lone Methodist serving as college governor, insisted that "Dalhousie was in reality a scheme to assist in the education of the middle class of Halifax."[5] Its motto *"ora et labora"* (pray and work) captured the ethos of the mid-Victorian city. Dalhousie students, a majority of whom continued to come from outside Halifax, were fortunate in the choice of the first cadre of professors, mostly distinguished scholars and good teachers, who, for a generation or more, contributed their intelligence, wit, and charm to the cultural life of the city, to say nothing of their prowess at quoits, the south end sport of choice. A medical faculty was established in 1868 in the wake of the opening of the city hospital. Although it briefly went its separate way as the Halifax Medical

College, this faculty reinforced the aspirations of Dalhousie to become a university.

People, Prejudices and Places

For a few years tension between Protestants and Roman Catholics characterized mid-nineteenth-century Halifax. Until 1851, Protestants were preoccupied with internal quarrels as Dissenters sought to dismantle privileges enjoyed by the Church of England. Latterly co-operation among evangelical Protestants, including some Anglicans like the reverends William Cogswell and Robert Fitzgerald Uniacke, spawned a number of inter-denominational Protestant organizations active in the realm of temperance, education and moral reform. Echoing developments abroad, Protestant militancy then slid into a paranoid crusade against what contemporaries defined as "papal aggression." Roman Catholics, who comprised 40 percent of Halifax's population in 1871, were chiefly Irish and their large numbers had been excluded from proportional influence in the city and the province during the period of immigrant adjustment and community formation. Taking their cue from the Irish nationalists, the city's Catholic leaders seized on the political reform movement in order to assert their right to a major share of power. Their claims fuelled nascent Catholic-Protestant antagonism within the city. This was encouraged by such incidents as Joseph Howe's apparently deceptive recruitment in the 1850s of Irish immigrants in the United States to fight in the Crimean War: the Irish Catholics thought they were coming to Nova Scotia for employment in railway construction.

Halifax Standards Baseball team in 1887.

HALIFAX
Young Men's Christian Association,
183 HOLLIS STREET,
OPPOSITE PROVINCE BUILDING.

Library & Reading Room,
Open every day (except Sunday) from 10 A. M. till 10 P. M.

PRAYER MEETINGS,
Every Thursday Evening, from 8 till 9 o'clock, and every Sabbath afternoon at half-past 4 o'clock, in the Mission Church, Barrack Street.

BIBLE CLASS,
Every Saturday Evening, from 8 till 9 o'clock.

Young Men are earnestly invited to attend, and those coming from a distance intending to take up their residence in the City, are requested to report themselves to the Secretary and leave their names and address

A. W. EATON,
SECRETARY.

J. B. MORROW,
PRESIDENT.

YMCA notice from Rogers' Photographic Advertising Album.

Nonetheless, unlike the turbulent social relations in many North American cities, the Irish Catholics in Halifax commanded enough respect from their Protestant neighbours to secure recognition for their culture as well as their citizenship. Conflict gave way to compromise as separate sets of institutions and a practice of political dualism emerged to characterize the public life of the city for generations to come.

While the ethno-denominational distribution of the population remained relatively constant, Halifax's population grew from 20,000 to 30,000 between 1851 and 1871, exclusive of the garrison. Most of

One of the Roman Catholic teams was the St. Patrick's baseball team shown here in 1906. Right: *Halifax Ramblers Bicycle Club in the Public Gardens ca. 1890.*

upheaval as soldiers and their families moved in and out of the garrison on rotations which ranged from several months to over five years.

The mid-century population of the city was still largely housed on the east side of Citadel Hill with some expansion spilling north along Brunswick and Gottingen and their cross streets as far as North Street, and in the south as far as Inglis Street. New houses appeared in Bauer's and Maynard's fields north of the Citadel and farther north west in Moren's and Bayers' fields, as well as in the more central Spring Gardens. On the fringes, people moved into the area north and west of the North West Arm where the peninsula met the mainland and along Lockman Street and Campbell Road (both now

the expansion derived from a high birth rate and rural to urban migration within Nova Scotia. Admittedly, infant mortality was high because of poor pre- and post-natal care, inadequate nutrition and frequent outbreaks of diseases, especially lethal for children, such as gastro-enteritis, scarlet and typhoid fever and diphtheria. Some deaths involved unwanted children, this being a period when infanticide was a common practice. At the same time, relatively few overseas immigrants came to Halifax or to the region as a whole. Instead they were drawn to the greater opportunities thought to exist in the Canadian colonies and the United States. Yet considerable turnover occurred in the city with people coming and going seasonally. As well, the military reinforced

part of Barrington Street), which skirted the narrows, as far as Africville on Bedford Basin. The rest of the peninsula consisted largely of grand estates, farms and commercial gardens like Thomas Leahy's Thornfield Nursery on Cunard Street and Herbert Harris's nursery on Upper Water Street just south of Richmond.

The People's Store on Gottingen Street, which had become a thriving commercial street by the 1870s. The dry goods/clothing store was first owned by James McPherson, then by McPherson and W.B. Freeman, before becoming Freeman's.

The Metropolitan Livery Stables were conveniently located opposite the Halifax Hotel on Hollis Street.

Business activity centred on the many private wharves along the harbourfront as well as on Water Street, Bedford Row, Hollis, Granville and Barrington streets. Small-scale commercial establishments competed on the "hill," soon to be known more commonly as the "upper streets"—Barrack (now Brunswick), Albemarle (now Market), Starr, Grafton, Poplar Grove and the steep cross streets of Sackville, Prince, George, Duke, Buckingham, and Jacob.

Among the many grand mansions and estates were the Bauld residences on the harbour adjacent to Point Pleasant Park and Oaklands on the North West Arm. The grounds of Oaklands, first owned as a summer home by William Cunard, second son of Samuel Cunard, were often thrown open to the public. It was, for instance,

the location in 1857 of the Sons of Temperance summer picnic. William Cunard also supported evangelical causes in Halifax. In 1858, for example, he joined forces with two of the Cogswells to buy a building for the Protestant Orphans' Asylum. In 1864 he gave a house for the rescue of prostitutes. On his departure for England in 1871 to become president of the Cunard Steamship Company, Cunard sold the estate to Philip C. Hill, then premier of the province, who had been mayor of Halifax in the first half of the 1860s. Hill, like Murdoch and Cunard before him, removed to England with his wealth in 1882.

Another estate, Jubilee, also near the North West Arm, was home to Isabella Binney Cogswell, a co-founder of the Protestant Orphans'

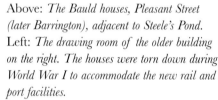

Above: *The Bauld houses, Pleasant Street (later Barrington), adjacent to Steele's Pond.* Left: *The drawing room of the older building on the right. The houses were torn down during World War I to accommodate the new rail and port facilities.*

Oaklands, North West Arm, ca.1870. This magnificent residence made of Philadelphia pressed brick with freestone trimmings and dressed granite foundation, boasted a conservatory, vinery, greenhouse, stables and barns, boating and bathing houses, and cottage. The property occupied 2000 feet on the waterfront and ran back from the eastern shore of the North West Arm about 3500 feet. The principal entrance to the estate, where the lodge still stands in 1999, was through iron gates on Robie Street. From here the main drive formed a curving avenue a half a mile in length, lined with oak, birch, pine, beech, maple, hawthorn, and poplar trees. The residence was situated 900 feet from the Arm on a beautiful terrace. The building was finished in black walnut, and birch. Although it escaped destruction during the construction of the railway cut, it had to be moved and was subsequently destroyed by an incendiary fire in 1928.

Asylum. Her activities expressed the way in which women were beginning to participate in public while maintaining their "proper sphere."[6] Daughter of Henry H. Cogswell, a financier, evangelical and "Halifax's leading philanthropist,"[7] Isabella used the wealth left her by her father on his death in 1854 to promote most Protestant charities during the last twenty years of her life. A wealthy single woman with time for good works, she adopted a hands-on approach to philanthropy and emphasized self-help for the poor. This was becoming the dominant middle-class approach to social welfare. Through her work on 'ladies' committees' and enthusiasm for women's organizations, Isabella Cogswell promoted the sisterhood of emergent female benevolence and set an important precedent for a later generation of Halifax women.

During the middle decades of the century, when Isabella Cogswell was active, there were better opportunities for many Haligonians hitherto marginalized because of religion, race, gender or class. While inequality continued to characterize urban life, all citizens could now secure a basic education and most men could vote and seek office. The sources of help for those needing short-term

The St. Paul's Church of England choir of 1865 included young men and women from such prominent families as Francklyn, Hill, Pryor, Tremaine and Uniacke. "The hymn tunes were pretty, the girls' voices were as fresh as their faces, the tenors and basses did wonderfully, but the harmony betrayed a diversity of opinion which led one to imagine that some of the men and maidens sang 'by ear.'" (R.V. Harris, The Church of Saint Paul in Halifax, Nova Scotia: 1749-1949, *245).*

Old Ladies' Home, Gottingen Street, more recently known as Victoria Hall. It was one of the many institutions supported by Isabella Cogswell, both in her lifetime and in her will.

assistance to overcome illness, hard times, or disabilities had expanded. The city was also becoming a more congenial place in which to live as municipal services and amenities increased. Literary and artistic talent found local outlets for both men and women. The many newspapers, for example, were supplemented by a number of short-lived periodicals conceived and edited by women. *The Mayflower* of 1851-52 was the creation of novelist Mary Eliza Herbert and *The Provincial, or Halifax Monthly Magazine* of 1852-53, was edited by historian Mary Jane Katzmann. If the cultural flowering of the mid-nineteenth century confirmed the ambition, talent and vision of Haligonians, it also demonstrated that competition was tough and financial resources inadequate for the success of more than a handful of aspirants. The city itself faced these same features as it adjusted to life as a Canadian urban centre torn between the new attractions of Confederation and the possibility of consolidating its traditional military identity as the "Gibraltar of British America."[8]

Chapter Five

INDUSTRIAL ASPIRANT
(1871-1901)

The chimney of Piercey's building supply firm on Robie Street once belonged to the cotton factory which opened in 1883 after local capital had been subscribed, existing factories elsewhere studied, a three-storey building with 148 windows constructed, and experienced Lancashire workers recruited. The Nova Scotia Cotton Manufacturing Company was important to three groups of people: the owners who hoped to realize a tidy return on their investment, the workers who sought steady, gainful employment, and the proud citizens of Halifax, and more especially their council, who wished the city to benefit from industrial development.

The owners, local men engaged in a variety of enterprises besides speculative industrial capitalism, included S.M. Brookfield, a building contractor and woodwork manufacturer who built the factory, Thomas Kenny, a wholesale dry goods and shipping merchant, the partners of Doull and Miller, a wholesale dry goods firm and clothing factory, J.P. Mott, a spice and soap manufacturer with establishments on both sides of the harbour, and Sandford Fleming, an occasional resident, renowned as an engineer and Canadian railway magnate. They each subscribed about $5000 to raise the capital needed for the factory. During the first few years they saw little return on their investment, and by the late 1880s they had to resort to debt financing in order to survive. Like other factories producing plain cotton, the Halifax establishment was acquired by Dominion Cotton Mills Company of Montreal (later Dominion Textiles) in 1891 at which time it was the seventh largest producer of cotton in Canada.

Cotton Factory, Robie Street.

In the year of the Montreal take-over, the cotton factory was Halifax's second largest industry with 317 employees, 146 of whom were women (131) and girls under 16 (15). Almost all the women were young and unmarried. Their factory labour was characterized by the classic features of large-scale mechanization of the Victorian period: strict discipline, long working days, low wages, wage discrimination against women, exploitation of children, and dangerous machinery. Workers had no means to protest against injustice except to quit and few in this period could take advantage of their strength in numbers to organize for better wages and working conditions.

For middle-class Haligonians, however, the factory personified progress. To encourage the company, City Council paid to have the water pipes laid for the factory and subsidized construction of a railway siding. Citizens demonstrated their interest by flocking to the building for a tour when it held an open house on Victoria Day, 1885. And yet the middle-class observers found the large factory unsettling. It upset the natural social order not only by employing women outside the domestic sphere but

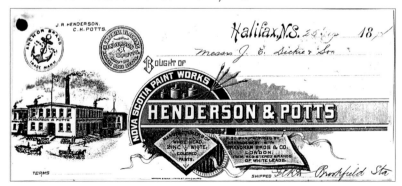

Samuel M. Brookfield.

also by throwing unrelated men and women together for a large portion of the day. Besides an interest in moral issues, observers expressed a concern for the health of the workers, particularly women and children subjected to long hours of toil in cramped and dangerous conditions. After pressure from middle-class women, a provincial factory act was passed in 1901 ostensibly to provide protection for female and juvenile workers.

The factory was one of the mixed blessings of Canada's industrial revolution. Sharing the profits and pain of industrialization became a major feature of Halifax life in the last decades of the nineteenth century. Another was the renewed determination to act as a major link between external markets and suppliers, on the one hand, and the interior of the new country, on the other. This ambition informed discussions about the needs of the port, the performance of the railway and the relationship with the federal government. But the city was also home to imperial forces and remained steeped in British traditions and cultural influences. Socially, times were changing: women had more opportunities; black citizens were resisting inequality; new ethnic groups were finding their niches within the city; and the working class was experimenting with organizational and political innovation. Urban reformers tackled alcohol abuse, cruelty both to animals and to people, and ubiquitous poverty. A combination of industrialization and lack of space forced people to live farther from the downtown and in these new locations they established the accustomed institutions of community life.

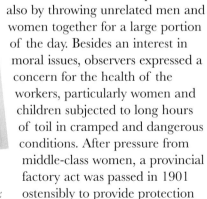

Fancy promotional poster for the Acadia Powder Company with offices in Halifax and works in Waverley, Halifax County.

Letterhead of Henderson and Potts, paint manufacturer, Kempt Road.

The lavishly draped interior of the People's Store on Gottingen Street.

Industrialization and Canadianization

After Confederation of the British North American provinces, which was a controversial change for Haligonians and other Nova Scotians, the federal government encouraged three major national policies. One policy, initiated in 1879, was tariff protection. It sought to encourage Canadian industry by making imported manufactured goods, especially from the United States, uncompetitively expensive. Of course industry was not new to Halifax in the 1880s. Small manufactories and artisanal enterprises of the mid-century, employing 22 percent of the city's labour force in 1861, first co-existed with and then gradually gave way to larger-scale mechanized establishments making everything from candy and boots to rope and steam engines. The new federal policy however created a more concerted, ambitious promotion of local industry. Halifax's entrepreneurs responded to protectionism by raising the capital to establish not only a cotton factory but also sugar refineries in Richmond (north Halifax) and Woodside (south of Dartmouth). The industrial strategy of producing high-demand consumer goods was pursued throughout Canada. Unfortunately, not enough domestic consumers existed to sustain so many competitive operations. The higher costs of production attendant upon a location like Halifax left the new industries open to takeover by external interests for purposes of consolidation or even termination. With Halifax's integration with central Canada after the completion of the Intercolonial Railway in 1876, first Montreal and then Toronto became ever more dominant within the Maritimes, reducing regional cities to a satellite status.

Halifax did not supplement the new consumer industries with the processing of local products to any great extent, whether Nova Scotian fish, forest products or coal and iron, as was occurring in other parts of the province. And when it came to attracting external investment, the city found its limited land base on the peninsula, even with the spread of industrialization to Dartmouth, as well as its water supply and tax revenue, insufficient to provide the necessary incentives. Nonetheless some enterprises thrived because they

Fader's meat market on Bedford Row in 1885.

Advertisement for Acme skates manufactured in its Dartmouth works by the Starr Manufacturing Company of Halifax.

Fish drying on flakes in Halifax, at the turn of the twentieth century.

skating was immensely popular and hockey attracted increasing attention. It also manufactured all sorts of iron goods from nails to bridges.

A second national initiative of significance to Halifax was railway policy entailing an interprovincial railway and the improvement of port facilities to link ocean traffic with rail transportation. Although the railway was only a qualified success since it facilitated interprovincial trade often to the disadvantage of the smaller producers in the Maritimes, federal funds improved railway access for both passengers and freight in Halifax. The handsome domed depot of the Intercolonial Railway at the foot of North Street opened in 1877. The Intercolonial's Deep Water Terminus, located on Upper Water Street immediately below the station, was built between 1877 and 1880. By the end of the century the dock complex, which stretched between Gerrish and Cornwallis streets, could handle twelve ocean steamers simultaneously. Among the many steamship lines

cornered the market on specialized products. For example, Starr Manufacturing, with a plant in Dartmouth and business offices in Halifax, made patented Acme ice skates at a time when recreational using the port of Halifax, the Furness Withy Company of Liverpool had the largest fleet engaged in shipping cargo. Pickford and Black, the only local firm that maintained a fleet of steamers, focused on the West Indies trade. The federal government also financed the construction of two successive railway bridges across the narrows to Dartmouth in the 1890s to service industries on the eastern side of the harbour. Unfortunately, both proved to be too poorly constructed to withstand raging storms and heavy traffic and had to be replaced with a longer line by land.

Another facility acquired by the modernizing port was waterside provision for shipbuilding and repairs. In 1889 the Halifax Graving Dock Company, under the presidency of S.M. Brookfield, opened its dry dock at the foot of

Pickford and Black Wharf where Historic Properties is now located.

Young Street. Built with city support, it was at the time the largest facility of its kind on the Atlantic seaboard. Halifax also needed modern storage facilities. A grain elevator, constructed of wood and located at the Upper Water Street end of Cornwallis Street in 1882, served until 1895 when, along with the freight and immigrant sheds of the Deep Water Terminus, it fell victim to fire. A replacement elevator and other facilities failed to help Halifax's bid to become Canada's dominant winter port. For central Canada the locational convenience and low cost of shipping through Portland, Maine, disadvantaged Maritime ports which had insufficient political clout to secure an all-Canadian trade route. Hard times of the 1880s and disappointed expectations produced political expressions of dissatisfaction with Confederation. Premier W.S. Fielding, a Haligonian and one of the many politicians who had honed his skills first as a city journalist, led a protest movement to repeal Confederation, which was largely economic in inspiration. Since Halifax had developed too many vested interests in the Canadian connection to sustain the agitation for repeal, Fielding, like Howe before him, decided to serve the local community through participation in federal politics. He went to Ottawa in 1896 as a member of cabinet of Prime Minister Wilfrid Laurier.

While Halifax businessmen were very concerned about the impact of rail communication on the city, they appear not to have worried about foreign-owned shipping in their port and other ports of the region. The failure to foster the creation of a subsidized Canadian merchant marine appears as a peculiar omission for a city with Halifax's traditions, and yet it was consistent with a past in which merchants remained more interested in the carriage of goods than in who carried them. It also reflected a shipping business in which low freight rates had considerably reduced profit margins by the late-nineteenth century.

Postcard of the Intercolonial Railway Station on North Street with the King Edward Hotel on the left.

The third aspect of the national policies which affected Halifax towards the end of the century was the encouragement of immigration. The measures taken to find settlers to farm, mine, build the cities, and labour on the public works in an expanding economy and a country acquiring new provinces reinforced Halifax's role as a national port. Although not many of the immigrants stayed in the region, the city had to be equipped to welcome newcomers, provide transportation to western destinations, treat the sick, deport the 'undesirables' and offer advice to people from many different lands, speaking many different languages. Until its replacement by Pier 21 in the late 1920s, Halifax's Pier 2 served as a major immigrant gateway to Canada.

The heightened activity in post-Confederation Halifax, especially in industry, required financing in an age when large-scale corporations were too costly to be underwritten by one or two individuals. For Haligonians and local companies in need of loans, the most significant financial institution was the Bank of Nova Scotia, the largest and most influential of the regional chartered banks, which

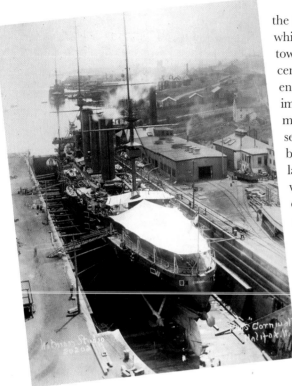

HMS Cornwall *in dry dock, looking south.*

also included the Halifax Banking Company, the Union Bank, the Merchants' Bank and the People's Bank. Under the general management of Thomas Fyshe between 1877 and 1897, the bank helped to facilitate the industrialization of the 1880s. It provided the working capital for the Nova Scotia Cotton Manufacturing Company, for example, and backed the Pictou County Nova Scotia Steel Company, in which Halifax businessmen prominently participated. Its loans to Halifax borrowers exceeded local deposits and so through the Bank of Nova Scotia the region as a whole contributed to Halifax's

Postcard of Halifax showing the view from the grain elevator, looking north across the railyards, naval dockyard and dry dock to the sugar refinery in the distance, its chimney belching smoke.

development. Unfortunately the depression of the mid-1880s left the bank with serious failures among its clients which encouraged Fyshe to look for safer investments outside the region.

When cotton became one of the major Maritime industries hit by the depression, the Halifax factory came under Fyshe's scrutiny as an auditor in 1888. He did not like what he saw and as a result the bank's support shrank and its influence over the factory's board became manipulative, climaxing in a takeover by Montreal interests.

During the 1890s, the bank became even less keen to make loans in the region and in 1900 the general manager moved to Toronto. Although the Bank of Nova Scotia remained committed to industrial development in Halifax, the new century saw more of its Halifax deposits leaving the region than being invested in the city.

Local enthusiasm for the opportunities and rewards of Confederation could not make up for the frequently disappointing impact of the national policies on the city. Even with the elevation of a number of Nova Scotian politicians to leading cabinet positions, the city's interests were often thwarted by economies of scale which combined with central Canadian banking policies to marginalize local enterprises. Additionally, inadequate transportation policies and the peripheral location of a small population were underlying problems.

At the same time, there were Canadian achievements to celebrate. Haligonians of the late-nineteenth century participated in such national developments as the formation of the Presbyterian Church in Canada in 1875, which affected seven congregations in the city. In

Assembly chamber of the Nova Scotia Legislature in 1879.

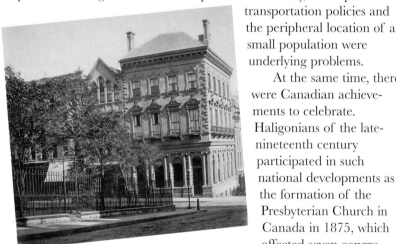
Union Bank, north-east corner Hollis and Prince.

1885 Halifax contributed a battalion to help defeat the North West Rebellion; and in 1888 a September Labour Day was inaugurated to recognize the contribution of the working class to nation building across the country.

Imperial Influences

For Haligonians, perhaps more than most other Canadians, British imperial influences remained paramount. By 1871 Halifax was one of only two British garrisons left in the country and the major one by far. The regiments posted to Halifax, along with the customary units of Royal Artillery and Royal Engineers, accounting for a military population of between 2000 and 4000 year round, and visiting crews of vessels in the North American and West Indies naval squadron, continued to influence people in all walks of life and to ensure good business for many local residents. For example, master baker William C. Moir used his profits as a military contractor to establish a large, vertically integrated factory producing bread, biscuit and confectionery, as well as milling flour, and making boxes. Another beneficiary of the military presence was the Oland family with its

William Robertson, Union Bank's turn-of-the-century president, whose ship chandlery store is now part of the Maritime Museum of the Atlantic.

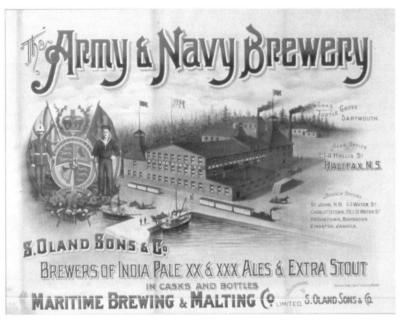

Advertising poster for Olands' aptly named Army & Navy Brewery.

A horse car passes the new City Hall and Grand Parade on Barrington Street in the early 1890s, a scene which reveals the many new electric power poles.

brewery on the Dartmouth side of the harbour and its wholesale and retail offices in Halifax. Both these long-lasting, military-fostered industries illustrate the crucial importance of market size for successful Halifax enterprises.

The public experience of the imperial forces centred on display (parades, drills, and regimental bands), disorder (from the mischievous to the criminal soldiers and sailors), and restricted access to vast stretches of property ranging from the Naval Yard in the north end and Fort George on Citadel Hill to the suburban and island forts, such as Fort Charlotte on George's Island and Fort Clarence south of Dartmouth. The military also had their own housing and social institutions, all exempt from city taxes. The increased financial needs of the city meant that the untaxed garrison was considered even more of a liability now than earlier. Not that the citizens were opposed to careers and reserve service in the armed forces. Local military culture

received a boost in 1899 when the Armouries, an imposing drill hall for the militia, opened on North Park Street. Many British soldiers and sailors settled in Halifax after they left the services and maintained their military identity through the Royal British Veterans' Society established in 1884. Haligonians also avidly followed imperial wars and campaigns and cherished any local heroes they created, such as Lieutenant William Grant Stairs who

Postcard of trooping the colours in 1903 in the grounds of Fort George (the Citadel). Note the signal flags on the right.

Parade on the Common by troops returned from South Africa, with the new Armouries in the background. The church to the right is Park Street Presbyterian.

Ceremony outside the Garrison Chapel, marking the death of Queen Victoria in 1901.

Anna Leonowens (Anna of Siam) in 1903.

accompanied H.M. Stanley on his exploits in central Africa in the 1880s. The Boer War established Halifax as an overseas troop station and attracted not only soldiers recruited locally but also several university-trained women to teach in South African concentration camps where Afrikaner families were interned.

Imperial interests focused more especially on Queen Victoria. 'Victoriamania' was best exemplified in Halifax by the jubilee celebrations of 1887 and 1897 marking the 50th and 60th anniversaries of Victoria's reign. Besides parades, feasting, commemorative songs and souvenirs, citizens also considered these suitable occasions to remember with permanent memorials. In 1887 one of these monuments was the Victoria School of Art and Design, the precursor of the Nova Scotia College of Art and Design, established with the help of Anna Leonowens who was later immortalized in Rodgers and Hammerstein's "The King and I." The public could enjoy the bandstand of 1887 and nymph fountain of 1897, both erected in the Public Gardens, which had become wholly city-owned in 1874.

British influences could be both direct and indirect. One of the latter was the organizational structure of the University of London which was adopted in 1876 with the establishment of the University

The Garrison Artillery Band grouped round their performance space, the bandstand in the Public Gardens, in 1902.

of Halifax. The idea was to maintain a common examining body for the various institutions of post-secondary education in Nova Scotia, a first step perhaps towards college amalgamation. The scheme failed in 1881 and with it the colleges lost their government support.

Undaunted and buoyed up by gifts from New York publisher George Munro, Dalhousie College added a law faculty in 1883. Many of the late Victorian graduates—lawyers, teachers, doctors, missionaries—left the city and the region to enjoy higher salaries or better opportunities in the United States, central or western Canada or overseas. More generally, the drain of youthful brains and brawn was not soon reversed though over the longer term it undoubtedly helped to promote the city's reputation externally as a place in which to study and vacation.

Halifax cast of Pirates of Penzance, *1885.*

A new imperial religious influence hit the city in 1885 when the Salvation Army "commenced bombarding the devil's Kingdom" on the upper streets.[1] The religious services of this offshoot of English Methodism had a military flavour with uniformed adherents, brass bands and chapels called citadels, all of which fit in very well in a garrison city. In the 1890s the Salvationists started their social work. It was well received and supported by the city's leading citizens and has been needed and available in various forms ever since. The first two projects, both in 1894, were a refuge for homeless men and a rescue home for "wayward" women. While the Salvationists' work with men in the "Salvation Harbour" led eventually to employment in the collection and repair of junk, and a thrift shop, the rescue home became a maternity home for unwed mothers, then for poor women,

and led to the establishment of a publicly-supported maternity hospital, the Grace, in 1922.

British cultural influences in this period ranged from Shakespeare to Gilbert and Sullivan. Beginning with noted actor E.A. Sothern at the Theatre Royal on Spring Garden Road in the 1850s, visiting dramatical, musical and variety troupes from overseas and the United States performed at various locations, particularly the Temperance Hall on Starr Street, later renamed the Lyceum, and then after 1877 at the Academy of Music on Barrington Street. These halls were also used by local performers and by lecturers, including the controversial Oscar Wilde in 1882 who impressed local audiences more with his outrageous clothing than with his sardonic wit.

Gender, Race, Ethnicity and Class

The last decades of the nineteenth century were eventful ones for the women of Halifax in a number of ways. First, women's organizations spread beyond their original bases in churches and children's institutions to address a variety of urban problems and opportunities which affected women. The Women's Christian Association (later YWCA), which began in 1874, focused in particular on the needs of young women, at first delinquent ones and later working women from

A teachers' meeting at Joseph Howe School. Guess which one is the principal.

when it became the Halifax Academy, governed by provincial legislation. Built on Brunswick Street by the board of school commissioners in 1879, the high school—formerly the Halifax Grammar School—began as a fee-paying facility for boys with provision for twenty scholarship places. Here and at St. Patrick's High School, opened in 1885, young women and men could also qualify for a teacher's licence. For the well-to-do, three private girls' schools were now available: Sacred Heart Convent School, Mount Saint Vincent Academy, and the Halifax Ladies' College. Closely allied with the Ladies' College was the Conservatory of Music which catered to the talents of both men and women. Post-secondary education was opened to women locally in 1881 when the first two women were admitted to Dalhousie College.

out of town, as well as on protesting vice and immorality in the upper streets. The Women's Christian Temperance Union, incorporated in 1881, not only gave women their own temperance voice but also rallied the members to address the needs of poor alcoholic women and to help working or unemployed women in distress or in need of a restroom and refreshment. It was also the first female suffrage organization in the city. The Local Council of Women of 1894 acted as a federation for mobilizing existing associations of women and took special interest in such concerns as factory conditions, female prisoners, immigrant reception, public health, child protection, and the promotion of domestic science. All of these local affiliates of national organizations were interested in women's rights—rights to education, employment, a safe environment, healthy children and public office.

This was indeed the period when opportunities for the younger generation of women opened up in educational institutions and in the professions. In 1885 girls were admitted to the public high school

Class photograph at Joseph Howe School. In the mid-nineteenth century Halifax's reputation was not enhanced by the old threat, common in New England, to send naughty children to Halifax as punishment for their misdeeds. This sentiment was an import from England where, in popular culture, law enforcement in Halifax, Yorkshire, acquired such a reputation for severity that to tell someone to "go to Halifax" implied a desire to subject that person to harsh treatment.

Sarah Howard's dry goods store on Hollis Street.

Native and black vendors in the market place.

While most women who entered the workforce with secondary or post-secondary educational qualifications became teachers, other opportunities also arose. Besides comprising 75 percent of the 208 full-time teachers—107 lay and 49 religious—in the public schools of Halifax in the 1880s, women began training for medicine in the city in 1888 and nursing in 1891. Not surprisingly the first professional women, such as Maria Angwin, Halifax's pioneer female physician, had been educated elsewhere before such opportunities sprang up in Nova Scotia. They also included women in religious orders. Various Roman Catholic and Anglican organizations gave women administrative training unavailable in any other contemporary context. The Sisters of Charity, for example, not only ran a motherhouse, several residential convents, and an academy, but also established and staffed St. Joseph's Orphanage, the Halifax Infirmary (1886) and the Home of the Guardian Angel (1886), a home for unwed mothers and infants.

For Halifax's black population the final decades of the century provided opportunities but also setbacks. The institutionalization of racially segregated schools in the 1870s was strongly resisted by individual members of the black middle class, and by the black population as a whole, through petitions and protest meetings in the early 1880s. Henry Russell sent his daughter Blanche to school in Boston until new regulations secured her the right to attend Brunswick Street Girls' School in 1884, despite a deluge of racist protest by white parents. In most aspects of social life, however, the black population remained separate from the mainstream. Separate black lodges existed in the local branches of such organizations as the Freemasons, Good Templars and Oddfellows. Employment practices

William Benjamin Thomas (1844-1937) epitomized the respectable black middle class. Son of the white Baptist preacher James and his black wife Hannah and related through his sisters to the leading Johnston and McKerrow families, William was the mainstay of the family's hat and fur business. He served his church as organist, deacon and lay preacher and was frequently master of Union No. 18, the black Freemasons lodge.

often disadvantaged blacks: for example, those employed on Intercolonial Railway trains and those applying for city jobs encountered discrimination. Black citizens experienced hostility in many of the city's restaurants, hotels and shops.

Most of the black population lived in the old north end, particularly in the area bounded by Brunswick, Cogswell, Robie and North streets. Here were located the two main black churches and the segregated school. This was a multi-racial neighbourhood where some black residents attained a degree of middle-class respectability

George Dixon (1870-1909), an international boxing champion, was born in Africville.

through savings in the bank and pianos in the parlour. Without a community hall as such, the residents depended on their churches to accommodate musical, charitable, educational and political events.

Although black and white citizens had lived in the city for generations and native people were frequent visitors by day, the addition of other cultures and the broadening of the population base beyond people of North American, West Indian or British birth, became noticeable in this period. The number of Jewish pedlars and shopkeepers increased so that by 1894 there were twenty families. Some came from England but most claimed German, Polish or Russian birthplaces. They formed the Baron de Hirsch Benevolent

Society which purchased a disused church on Starr Street for a synagogue to replace their temporary quarters in the Carpenters' Hall on Barrington Street. Jews numbered 120 by 1901.

Halifax also provided some opportunities for Chinese residents. Hand laundries operated by Chinese men began to appear in the 1890s and numbered a dozen by 1901 when census takers reported a mere 29 Chinese people in Halifax-Dartmouth. One laundry served as a community centre for religious worship. The tiny, vulnerable male population of. Chinese began to attract the attention of racist hooligans by 1899.

Regardless of ethnicity, class divisions became more obvious as people settled in the suburbs at a distance from their workplaces, and as poorly paid wage earners confronted larger employers under pressure from shareholders, creditors and competitors to make greater profits. Although by the end of the century the middle class was growing more homogeneous, with less rigid distinctions between the upper and lower ends, the working class continued to be divided by craft, workplace, and gender and thus lacked a cohesive class consciousness. Candidates for Halifax City Council did try to appeal to the working-class vote and men with artisanal jobs were elected as early as 1851. Most working men who became involved in politics seem, however, to have been motivated more by self-interest than by class solidarity.

The emergence of working-class leadership in the city centred on the Amalgamated Trades Union which was able to advance the interests of union men in the 1880s by fielding, albeit unsuccessfully, a labour-conscious painters' union president as aldermanic candidate in ward five. (Admittedly that same individual, Peter F. Martin, won election in 1898 and served as mayor during the World War I, but he had long since become an employer.) Only in a few

The first Jewish synagogue opened in a former Baptist church on Starr Street in 1894.

cases, such as a strike in 1889 of carpenters, did class-conscious tactics prevail. The results of that strike were a nine-hour day and 1.5 percent increase in hourly wages.

Social Development

Urban reformers of this period focused on cleaning up the city morally as well as physically. Moral crusades were sustained by religious interests, citizen concern for the reputation of the city and the desire of employers to promote productivity. Like-minded crusaders banded together in a range of organizations, such as the Law and Order League and the Evangelical Alliance, to promote a more sanitized city. The leadership provided by the clergy, men like George Grant of St. Matthew's Church of Scotland, and Thomas Connolly, Roman Catholic Archbishop of Halifax in the 1860s and 1870s, John Forrest, pastor of St. John's Presbyterian Church and later president of Dalhousie College between the 1860s and 1910s, and William Armitage, rector of St. Paul's Church from the 1890s to 1920s, was crucial. Through various levels of co-operation they

Union Badge of Local 83 of the United Brotherhood of Carpenters and Joiners of America which belonged to Benjamin Joseph Hollett who immigrated to Halifax from Newfoundland between 1902 and 1905.

The alternative to the tavern: coffee rooms run by the temperance societies.

did it have the only significant legal liquor trade in the province but it also was thought to have "more saloons than any other city in Canada for its size."[2] The campaign against taverns and licensed shops was prolonged because not everyone could agree on how dry Halifax should become and the revenues of the city had always included a significant amount from the sale of liquor licences. After public bars were abolished by the "pint law" of 1886, civil disobedience became so pervasive that they were restored in 1905. The city fathers included both purveyors and opponents of drink. Patrick O'Mullin, a Catholic brewery proprietor, who was mayor between 1887 and 1889, was blamed by temperance folk for failure of the 1886 legislation; Andrew Hubley, a Baptist grocer and realtor who first served as alderman between 1892 and 1911, became a convert to temperance and acted as the self-appointed temperance conscience of the

promoted a number of causes with support from leading laymen and women.

Temperance was the most popular but also the most contentious movement of the period. Besides encouraging individuals voluntarily to forsake alcoholic beverages, advocates wanted to reduce the number of licensed facilities in the city. Halifax maintained an unenviable reputation with respect to public drinking places. Not only

council. In the last years of the century, the temperance movement succeeded in reducing the number of licensed premises.

Concern about the effects of excessive drinking, which generated business for the hospital, poorhouse and prison, led to a number of new initiatives. An inebriate asylum for men was opened in Dartmouth for a few years and the various women's homes sought to reform drunkards. The domestic effects of alcohol consumption, especially among poor and working-class people, contributed to the conversion of the 1876 Society for the Prevention of Cruelty to Animals into the Society for the Prevention of Cruelty (SPC) in 1880, in order to enable it to intervene in cases of child neglect and wife harassment, many of which were associated with alcohol abuse. The SPC became one of the most important late-nineteenth-century community organizations because it laid the basis for the development of non-sectarian social work in the city through the promotion of protective legislation and case work. The long depression focused public attention also on poverty but ideas about what to do

Liquor for on-site consumption was available at two types of licensed facilities until probation in 1916, except for twenty years at the end of the century when the liquor licence legislation theoretically outlawed public bars. Shown here is the bar of the King Edward Hotel, the railway hotel, in the first decade of the twentieth century.

On the night of 7 November 1882 Halifax's poorhouse burned to the ground and thirty-one of its most feeble residents died. An inquest revealed that intended fireproofing features of the relatively new building had not been included and that management had been hopelessly inept in the crisis. Survivors were temporarily housed in the former provincial penitentiary on the North West Arm while a replacement building was erected on the same site on the South Common.

Other social ills of society which commanded attention included sabbath breaking, prostitution, and slum housing. The major response to the crowded, dilapidated and question-

about it did not advance, at least not in practice. Employment for men in the stone sheds, parsimonious relief for women without husbands and seasonal soup kitchens continued to dominate welfare in Halifax. Specialized institutions established in the second half of the century meant that certain elements in the population might end up in orphanages or industrial schools if children, hospitals or asylums if ill or disabled, homes for the aged if elderly, jail if incorrigible. The poorhouse, however, remained the major institution for the care of the aged and helpless poor.

able housing of the upper streets was to pull it down. Considerable attention was focused on Barrack Street, the street at the top of the notorious "hill" which seemed impervious to reform. Gradually its character was transformed. First it was declared out-of-bounds to the military, then its name was changed to allow it to become the southern extension of fashionable Brunswick Street. In due course some of its wooden tenements and dives were replaced with a series of brick buildings associated with the age of improvement: the Halifax Academy, the Halifax Visiting Dispensary, the central fire

The poorhouse or poor's asylum of 1869 on South Street after it burned down in 1882.

engine station, the Salvation Army Citadel, the Jost Mission house, Taylor's shoe factory. More was required than the renewal of one street. In the mid-1880s, Mayor James C. Mackintosh deplored the poor housing conditions and hinted at the need for rent control in the slums:

> *the dwellings of very many of the poor are really unfit for human habitation ... hundreds of hovels in courts, lanes and backyards, which are scarcely fit to house cattle, are rented by poor and hardworking people at rates proportionately higher than houses on some of our best streets.*[3]

The Suburbs

The population of Halifax slowly continued to grow between the censuses of 1871 and 1901, averaging about 3,500 a decade, with increases as well in the surrounding areas, such as Dartmouth and Bedford, where Halifax businessmen established mills and factories and citizens enjoyed occasional outings for picnics and sports. With a civilian population of almost 41,000 in 1901, Halifax had over eight times the population of Dartmouth and 40 times that of Bedford. The county as a whole—comprising the current Halifax Regional Municipality—numbered some 75,000. On the peninsula, the restricted capacity of the central core, especially as a result of the large amount of military property, and the check to private development of the Common west of the Citadel, pushed residential expansion to the north, west and south.

In the north end, Richmond included a working-class area adjacent to many of the new manufacturing, machine and transportation industries located on the harbourfront and close to the railway lines. One of the large landholdings in the north end, which was subdivided into streets and parks in the 1870s, was the Governor's farm between Richmond and Duffus Streets, part of which—the

Views from the Citadel about 1890 showing the Dispensary, corner of Brunswick and Prince, and the Halifax Academy, corner of Brunswick and Sackville, with three churches—(l-r) St. Matthew's Presbyterian, St. Mary's Roman Catholic and Grafton Street Methodist—in the background.

Grove—had been a public picnic ground. North of the farm and extending as far as the shoreline was an area long preserved as the glebe land of St. Paul's Church. The episcopalian provenance of the area was captured in some of the street names—Warden, Vestry, Rector, and Church. West of Richmond, Merklesfield—more farmland—was subdivided in 1891.

Residential expansion west and north-west of the Citadel broke up the private estate of the Cogswell family in the prime centre of the peninsula between Robie Street on the east, Oxford on the west, Jubilee on the south and Cunard and Chebucto on the north. Cognizant of his family's importance, Dr. Charles Cogswell, another of Halifax's rich exports to England, who had been an alderman in the late 1850s and was, on his death in 1892, the last surviving sibling of Isabella, gave to the city a small triangle of land on Windsor Street known as Cogswell Park.

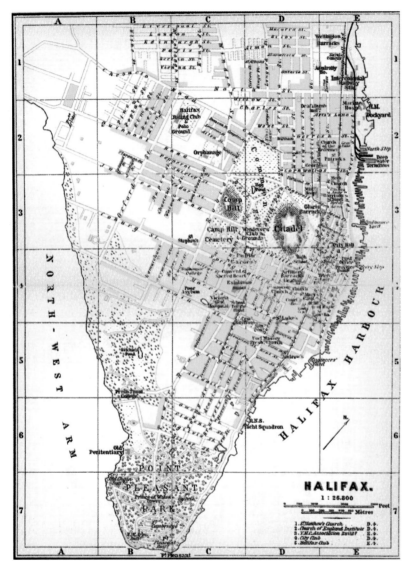

Map of Halifax from the 1894 Baedeker's Dominion of Canada guidebook for tourists. Note that Richmond is not included.

Kaye Street Methodist Church, Richmond.

In the 1870s Colonel Bennett H. Hornsby, a Confederate veteran of the Civil War, became Halifax's prime land speculator, laying out streets named after British, Irish, and European cities in Willow Park, located between Windsor and the future Connaught Avenue. He also planned streets on both sides of Almon Street between Windsor and Robie. Across Chebucto Road, the streets with names of trees were laid out about the same time. These areas did not fill up with houses and other facilities until later in the century. In the south end, development was mixed and included merchant villas and bourgeois townhouses on such streets as Tower Road, South Street, Victoria Road and Inglis Street, and working-class housing in the area of Greenbank at the south end of the harbour.

Important community facilities followed street planning and the initial house building: churches, schools, neighbourhood stores, public transport. The number of church buildings increased by almost 150 percent during the last thirty years of the century, an era when the population increased by 35 percent. In the working-class suburb of

Willow Park, corner of Windsor and Almon, ca. 1902, the home of W.B. Freeman, who owned the People's Store on Gottingen Street. The property had earlier belonged to John Thompson who began his career as a city alderman in 1871 and died in 1894 as prime minister of Canada. The Willow Park area was developed for housing about the time Thompson bought this house and some of the nearby lots in 1872.

all destined to be destroyed during the Great War. The Methodists and Baptists opened three new churches each in the west end and the old north end. Additionally, some of the older congregations decided to relocate closer to their members as the residential drift away from the downtown occurred. Thus St Andrew's Church of Scotland moved from Barrington to Tobin Street in 1871, Granville Street Baptist went to Spring Garden and Queen in 1887, en route to becoming First Baptist on Oxford Street, the Universalists' Church of the Redeemer moved to Brunswick from Starr Street in 1874, and in 1884 the Poplar Grove congregation built a new church on North Park Street. St. Patrick's Church remained where it was on Gottingen but secured a beautiful new building in the mid-1880s.

While neighbourhood facilities were obviously needed, residents often had to wait for them and in any case the location of their workplaces, businesses, and markets meant that public transportation was needed to convey them back and forth.

Richmond, for example, the Roman Catholics established St. Joseph's (Gottingen Street), the Anglicans, St. Mark's (Russell Street), the Methodists, Kaye Street, and the Presbyterians, Grove (Duffus Street),

Prime Minister Sir John Thompson's funeral cortège, Barrington Street, 3 January 1895.

After a ten-year hiatus the horse railway was restored to some of the city's streets in 1886, reflecting the reality of the new industrialism and residential expansion. Ten years later electric tram cars were introduced with routes to the western and northern suburbs.

The city maintained and expanded its parkland, including the newly acquired Point Pleasant Park, 75 hectares of woodland in the south end. The use of city revenues to enhance the park did not go unquestioned. In 1872 the city engineer's concern over the inadequacy of the sewerage system prompted him to suggest, "This is no time for laying out and adorning parks, pleasure grounds and lovers walks, when the very lives of our people are in the most imminent danger."[4] Most people could walk to the central recreational areas on the peninsula, especially the Common and the playing fields available on Quinpool Road in the period before the Catholic Church acquired that area for institutional development in the 1890s. Water sports were still largely confined to the harbour where all interested spectators could be accommodated on the wharves. Sports clubs became the vogue and most aspired to the acquisition of a club house for socializing after games.

Critical changes for the city centred on the Common and Grand Parade. The city's first exhibition building opened on the South Common in 1879 and another parcel of common land was leased to the Wanderers' Amateur Athletic Club in 1886. A grant of land on the western edge of the South Common went to Dalhousie College, where it constructed the Forrest Building in 1887. This migration finally cleared the north end of the Grand Parade for the construction of a new City Hall. Completed in 1890, the building housed the police station and court. It also accommodated the Citizens' Free Library, first established in 1866, a favourite project of Chief Justice Sir William Young, another of the city's benefactors, who had purchased the old Mechanics' Institute Library for the city. By 1900 the library had over 2500 borrowers.

Until it could build new schools, the city leased existing space such as churches and mission halls for classroom space. Some of the school facilities, both temporary and purpose-built, doubled as night schools, conducted by various benevolent organizations with city support. Such night-time opportunities were particularly valuable for young adolescents who worked during the day in the period before the

One of Sir William Young's legacies to the city in 1885 was a pair of gates for Point Pleasant Park. If he could see his gift today used instead as an entrance to the elitist avenue which bears his name, he would probably turn in his grave.

Labourers—black and white, men and boys—working on Cornwallis Street before World War I. On the left is a Chinese laundry at 64 Cornwallis operated successively during the first decade of the century by Shang Hong, Wing Chung, Quong Wing Chong and Hop Kee.

First Baptist Church, corner of Spring Garden and Queen.

council proclaimed day-time schooling compulsory in the 1890s. Without such legislation, less than 60 percent of children received regular schooling.

After the creation in 1872 of the board of city works, which was transformed into a department in 1894, and the appointment of E.H. Keating as city engineer, municipal services were addressed more

systematically. Improvements included additional brick sidewalks in the business area, expansion in the sewerage system, and the introduction of water meters and plumbing regulations in order to curb wastage. The first electric street lights were installed in 1886. On the darker side of the picture, "night soil" (human waste) and garbage—organic and inorganic—were dumped in pits on the Common at Camp Hill. In the mid-1870s, the night soil received separate accommodation, first on the Rockhead Prison grounds and, by the turn of the century, in hollows at the new provincial exhibition grounds on Windsor Street.

At the northernmost edge of the peninsula on Campbell Road, the African-Nova Scotian community of Africville struggled to provide a stable environment for the poorer and more agrarian members of the city's black community. But the railway tracks were in dangerous proximity which led to a number of fatal and near fatal accidents to local residents. When George Alexander was killed by the outbound Windsor and Annapolis train at the intersection of the rail line with Campbell Road in 1893, while trying to rescue his horse from the track, the coroners' jury, comprised of Africville residents, assigned no blame but recommended crossing gates.

The long trek or cart ride into city centre meant that Africville needed its own educational and religious facilities. Its Baptist church belonged to the African Baptist Association and its school—which was in fact suspended by the school board for several years in the 1870s and 1880s—provided rudimentary instruction. Towards the end of the century, the remote location also meant that the residents ran a gauntlet of racist abuse as they proceeded along Campbell Road and through Richmond into town. Moreover, their community was ridiculed by such white musical entertainments as the 'Cantata d'Africville' performed in 1894 by a group described as the 'Coonville Serenaders' in a program mounted by the St. Mary's Band.[5] But race relations were not uniformly bad. The residents of Richmond had purchased a horse for George Alexander. Replacing his former horse had been their way of thanking him for doing their errands in town. Ironically, the replaced horse was also killed by a train at the infamous railway crossing on Campbell Road.

Brown Bombers hockey team—an all-black team.

Cooper on the Halifax waterfront.

By the end of the nineteenth century, Halifax was physically a much larger city than it had been a few decades ago and no longer dominated by Citadel Hill. The Common now accommodated a wide range of public institutions as well as private facilities. The military was more accommodating as evidenced, for example, in the leasing of Point Pleasant Park to the City. As before, military pageantry remained a significant element in the life of the city. Municipal services were still fairly primitive and the roads unpaved. Not many citizens benefitted as yet from technological innovation, though electric lighting, flush toilets, and telephones had been installed in many institutions and in the wealthier residences. Although Halifax was still trying to become "Liverpool in America,"[6] the industrial development of the north end was the major new feature of the last quarter of the century. It was promoted by the Intercolonial Railway and the willingness of local citizens to work together in a range of business enterprises. The administration of the city was enhanced by the employment of a city engineer whose professionalism produced a running critique of waste, patronage, and inertia. His expert advice, along with that of other local and visiting professionals and reformers, created a more progressive urban agenda.

Chapter Six

PROGRESSIVE HALIFAX
(1901-1918)

During a period indelibly marked by military events—the return of the soldiers from South Africa, the termination of the imperial garrison, the establishment of the Canadian Navy, the slaughter of the Great War, the local carnage caused by the explosion of a munitions vessel in the harbour narrows—500 schoolchildren from Halifax and Dartmouth, some of them decked out as cadets and boy scouts, spent a sweltering noon hour on 14 August 1912 with the Duke of Connaught, Governor-General of Canada, in Fleming Park, on the western side of the North West Arm, inaugurating a monument to a non-military event which had occurred in 1758. The children sang the National Anthem and other "patriotic hymns." The introduction of representative government in Nova Scotia, the first step towards modern democracy in what would become Canada, was recognized by a memorial stone tower of 33 metres, designed by J.G. Dumaresq and Andrew Cobb, and constructed by S.M. Brookfield, near the shore of a 40-hectare tract of land, long known as the Dingle. Sir Sandford Fleming deeded the property in perpetuity to

Postcard of the Memorial Tower festively adorned for the opening ceremonies in 1912.

the lieutenant-governor in trust for use as a park for the citizens of Halifax after he realized that the alienation of the shoreline to private individuals had deprived the general public of access to the body of water they loved so well for its recreational charm. As for the children, they were accustomed to being trotted out to sing and perform on major occasions.

Improved facilities for recreation comprised only one of the features of city life before World War I. The early years of 'Canada's century' saw a number of initiatives launched in Halifax to attract new enterprises, reform the municipal government and clean up the city. Organized groups such as the Board of Trade and the Local Council of Women participated actively in 'progressive' movements such that pre-war Halifax revealed little of the stagnation and inertia that would overtake it after the war. The people enthusiastically endorsed the city's role in the Great War— after all, everyone knew that a wartime economy had always been good for Halifax. But in common with their contemporaries on the battlefields, Haligonians lost their innocence during the war in a way unparalleled anywhere else in Canada and with it much of the

Public occasions continued to be marked by a school children's demonstration, usually in the form of a choir. In 1897 children were trotted out to preside over the unveiling of the fountain in the Public Gardens, variously known as Jubilee, Nymph and Victoria. A new element was a cadet band; an old element was native people in ceremonial dress.

city and way of life they had known.

The Pre-War Economy

Although manufacturing remained the city's largest employer, Halifax did not emerge as a leading Canadian producer during the pre-war years, and, in fact, lost ground. But it was not from lack of trying because City Council devised incentives to attract new industry in order to counteract the city's locational disadvantage. One coup was the relocation of the Silliker Car Works from Amherst, achieved with help from the city fathers in 1906. The company was a woodworking firm specializing in rail cars and associated foundry work and provided employment for 250 men.

The other prospect, which did not in the end materialize before the war, was a steel shipbuilding facility on the harbour. This initiative generated a great flurry of activity in the opening years of the century. The problem with steel shipbuilding was that it was enormously complex and expensive and required technology and start-up capital of a sophistication and magnitude previously unknown in the city. Although a firm of British shipbuilders was interested in the project and Halifax City Council agreed to provide subsidies, support from the federal government in the form of a bounty and remission of duty on necessary imported materials was essential. In the end neither the company nor Ottawa officials would agree to the conditions that the other required. Not until after the destruction caused by the 1917 Explosion did the federal government commit itself to establishment of the Halifax Shipyards by Montreal-based interests.

What the province lacked in capital it tried to make up for in terms of technical expertise, by entering the field of industrial education. This interest was evidence of both a continuing commitment to an industrial economy for the city and faith in an industrial future for Nova Scotia. As early as the 1880s a lack of training in the applied sciences led to predictions that without informed technical knowledge Nova Scotians would remain proverbial 'hewers of wood and drawers of water.' Twenty years later pressure from the mining industry and the Board of Trade, allied with the post-secondary colleges, including Halifax's Dalhousie and St. Mary's, secured provincial government support for a

View of of construction of the new port facilities looking south in 1916. The gas works are on the right.

Young men and women taking an evening technical class in bookkeeping, 1911.

number of ventures. One was establishment of the Nova Scotia Technical College, which opened in 1909. Another program of the new provincial Department of Technical Education, under its first director, Frederic Sexton, featured night schools offering technical courses for male workers and, in the absence of support for job training for women, homemaking courses.

Most of the emphasis on economic development continued to stress Halifax's natural role as a port, particularly a winter port for Canada. In order to improve Halifax's ability to ship goods to and from central Canada, the Board of Trade sought better terminal facilities for storage and rail transportation, an expanded rail network and faster ocean steamers, measures which, it was thought, would give Halifax the edge over its rival, Saint John. The need to improve harbour facilities had long been recognized by the federal government and in 1912 a commitment to act was made by the new Conservative government. Although none of the components of the south-end Ocean Terminals was started before the war, the new railway track through the massive rocky terrain to the west and south of the peninsula was operational by 1917. Another initiative which came to fruition during the war was the establishment of an oil refinery. Imperial Oil had begun its Halifax operations in 1898. The city leased them a parcel of land on the northern fringes of the peninsula for oil storage tanks in 1910. In 1915 the company wanted to establish the refinery there, but fortunately for residents of Africville, the refinery located instead on the Dartmouth side of the harbour.

Above: Work on the railway cut in 1915. Construction of the ocean terminals and and the railway line drew foreign labourers to the city. On 26 March 1916 four Italians and three Russians lost their lives in a fire in a boarding facility at the work site, which was described as a shack. Their identity was unknown because no one had bothered to keep a list of their names. Right: *HMCS* Niobe

Another function of Halifax's status as a port was the maintenance of the armed forces as a major employer in the city. This was not substantially changed, though somewhat diminished, with the withdrawal of British troops in 1905-6, a policy occasioned by the closure of the naval yard and reduction to one vessel of the North American and West Indies naval squadron which the garrison had been designed to support. The British War Office also intended to demolish the garrison's clock on the eastern slope of the Citadel until the council persuaded the authorities to transfer Halifax's most famous landmark to the city "on account of its historical interest as well as its utility."[1] A replacement dockyard in 1906 and naval service in 1910 meant that Halifax became the principal Canadian naval base, equipped with one old British cruiser, HMCS *Niobe*.

With the removal of the imperial troops, Halifax was reborn immediately as an army town. It emerged as the centre of manpower and operations for the regular component of the Canadian army. The permanent force, which for the country as a whole was about half the size of the departing British forces in Halifax (that is, fewer than 1000 men) consisted of the Royal Canadian Regiment (infantry), the Royal Canadian Garrison Artillery, the Royal Canadian Engineers, the Canadian Permanent Army Service Corps and ordnance and medical corps. Its personnel was doubled in order to assume responsibility for the Halifax fortress, consisting of the garrison (citadel, barracks, workshops, training grounds) and the outlying system of fortifications. The augmentation favoured former British soldiers with the requisite experience and technical knowledge. The army in Halifax inherited from the British garrison state-of-the-art weaponry. Its operations between 1906 and 1914, including the establishment of good working relations with the new naval force and the part-time militia, helped prepare the city for its enhanced role during the war.

Two of the first naval recruits aboard Niobe *in dress uniform (above) and in their stoker's apparel (left).*

One block of the Wellington Barracks, built in the 1850s, with its new Canadian occupants in 1906.

Science building, Dalhousie University, photographed by Gauvin and Gentzel after World War I and the acquisition of a field gun.

Municipal Reform

While the Canadian army and navy were settling in, civic reform became another focus for united action in Halifax. It was promoted by a number of middle-class interest groups, such as progressive members of the Board of Trade, women's organizations, church leaders interested in social reform, and professionals with interests in health, architecture and planning. Many of these groups and individuals co-operated in 1906 in the formation of the Civic Improvement League which wanted to harmonize, humanize and beautify the city. In 1910 the League promoted such measures as the instruction of children in the evils of vandalism, prizes for attractive front gardens, and architect Andrew Cobb's plans for the redevelopment of George and Argyle Streets and the Market Wharf. The 1910-11 civic 'uplift' campaign had all the hallmarks of a religious revival. Haligonians boasted about the new stone structures then taking shape, such as Cobb's science building on the recently acquired Studley campus of Dalhousie University and the Anglican All Saints' Cathedral on Tower Road.

City Council continued to improve the city's services and amenities while grappling with intractable problems. Street paving was undertaken in earnest but in some cases created more difficulties than it resolved, at least during the last years of horse-drawn transportation. In acknowledging the slippery effect of paving on the steep east-west streets beneath the Citadel, city engineer F.W.W. Doane obliquely criticized the founders of Halifax for laying out the town on a formal grid pattern.

It does not seem to have occurred to the City designer that it is harder to raise a team and load one foot than to move it three feet on the level, and that consequently less power is expended in going one mile around a hill than one-

third of a mile up it. In fact, after a sleet storm, many of our hills are practically impassable for loaded teams .... Across the Atlantic they are much more particular to-day in these matters than they must have been when the man who planned Halifax came out. Strenuous efforts are made not to exceed a four per cent grade. The power required to haul a load on a four per cent grade is 3 times as great as on a level street yet some of our grades are more than four times four.[2]

Another perennial problem was the water service which continued to involve excessive waste. The estimated daily water usage in 1908 was a phenomenal 1323 litres for every man, woman, and child. In 1913 the construction of a water tower on Shaffroth's Hill at the north end of Robie Street equalized the pressure for consumers in that part of town. An outbreak of typhoid fever that same year underscored the need to protect the reserved supply lakes against pollution.

In the old town, after decades of complaints about the inadequate market facilities near the waterfront, a new building was opened in 1916, on Market Street.

In the midst of the reformist zeal of citizen groups and the persistent problems encountered by the civic administrators, many came to see Halifax's municipal government as being out of date. Encumbered with the parochialism of ward politics, a vast aldermanic committee system and endless, counter-productive Council meetings, City Hall seemed unable to perform as an agent of good government. As a result vital matters such as taxation reform, increased industrialization, and the provision of municipal services were being hampered. A perceived solution was at hand in the form of 'progressive' structures of urban government which promoted "efficiency, planning and expertise."[3] Two models of reform were open to consideration. One involved a

Electric street car No.11, Barrington at Roome in Richmond, 1897.

'board of control,' a directly elected executive arm of the council. The other was government by commission, a far less democratic approach which saw the council replaced by a ruling committee of experts. In a plebiscite in 1911, Halifax ratepayers opted to establish a board of control, together with a council reduced from 18 to 12 members. While the controllers and councillors were elected every two years, the mayor, who chaired both board and council, was still elected annually. Civic power primarily resided in the board since council could reject its decisions only by a two-thirds vote.

Government by paid controllers lasted only from 1913 to 1919 and proved disappointing. The first board (1913-15), filled with doubters and traditionalists, could not cope with its first major challenge, a violent strike by employees of the Halifax Electric Tramway Company. Caught between a group of streetcar workers who commanded considerable public support and a company which brought in strike breakers and wanted the mayor to call out the militia, the board sided with the workers but failed to play a role in settling the dispute. The second board, elected in 1915, got caught up in the crises of wartime, particularly the onset of shortages and runaway inflation. It failed to take over the city's electric power grid, which became American-controlled by 1919, and to gain public approval for changes in municipal taxation. The third and final board, elected in 1917, drew criticism because of its opting for an unprecedentedly high million-dollar budget. As well, the board found itself effectively shut out of the redevelopment of the north end, after the 1917 Explosion, by the federally appointed Halifax Relief Commission. Finally Mayor Arthur C. Hawkins, elected in the final board's second year, proved so controversial that the aldermen resigned, forcing the board to run the city alone for the ensuing year. In 1919 another plebiscite resulted in the abolition of the board and the city returned to the tradition of government by mayor and aldermen.

Another much older reform measure which required widespread support in order to succeed was prohibition. Although the number of licensed premises steadily fell after 1911, an emergency was needed to encourage the city to let itself be disciplined by the Nova Scotia Temperance Act of 1910. That emergency came with the war as prohibitionists demanded that young recruits be protected from the temptation of the bar-room. Accordingly on 1 July 1916 the legal sale of alcohol ended in Halifax except through prescriptions issued by medical practitioners. Illicit manufacture, sale and consumption of booze flourished, however, especially on the fringes of the city, a development which helped to create an unsavoury reputation for dance halls in Africville and roadhouses on the St. Margaret's Bay Road.

Organized Womanhood

Organized women in Halifax represented some of the most stalwart prohibitionists. On this matter and many others, they served as effective lobbyists and astute politicians in the early years of the century. While their interests usually built on the more modest pioneering efforts of the previous generation and were often pursued in conjunction with other groups, their leadership became ever-more prominent in the community. A cadre of educated, experienced, and relatively affluent women emerged to play a role in reforming Halifax. The women whose names occurred most frequently were Edith Archibald, Eliza Ritchie, Agnes Dennis and May Sexton. Ritchie and Sexton were university graduates with attainments unusual in women of their day: Ritchie had earned a PhD from Cornell University while Sexton had studied at the Massachusetts Institute of Technology. Both Ritchie and Dennis came from Halifax. Archibald, the daughter of a diplomat, was Nova Scotian but had been raised mainly in New York. Sexton, from New Brunswick, was married to the first director of the Department of Technical Education and principal of the new Technical College. Archibald's husband served as president of the Bank of Nova Scotia and

Dennis's husband was not only proprietor of the Halifax Herald but also a senator. Ritchie remained single but received the support of her prominent Halifax family.

Although these female leaders and their associates pursued their aims both as individuals and as members of specialist organizations, they also relied on the Local Council of Women (LCW) to coordinate and publicize their efforts. The LCW threw its weight behind the establishment in 1910 of a day nursery for the care of pre-school children of working mothers at the Methodists' Jost Mission on Brunswick Street. May Sexton was the chief organizer of that project. The Children's Hospital, opened in 1910, the same year it held its first 'kermesse' or fair, had a group of 24 trustees, half of whom were women, including Edith Archibald. The hospital was a popular project and attracted the support of smaller, less conspicuous groups as well. For example, the newly formed social club of the wives of non-commissioned officers of the Royal Canadian Regiment endowed a bed in the hospital.

Another child-centred interest involved the establishment of playgrounds to keep unsupervised children occupied and out of harm's way. In 1910 LCW members Agnes Dennis, Eliza Ritchie, Marshall Saunders, author of children's animal stories, and May Sexton attended the end-of-summer closing ceremony at the Wanderers' Grounds of the city's three supervised playgrounds located at St. Mary's (city centre), Joseph Howe (old north end), and Bloomfield (Richmond) schools.[4] As chair of the Halifax Playgrounds Commission, Sexton made a speech. Activist women were also concerned about neglected and abused children and supported the establishment of the Children's Aid Society, the functions of which remained, until 1920, part of the work of the Society for the Prevention of Cruelty.

Women's concern for children and young women was not just environmental. Like the wider society of the day, they also turned their attention to health problems, including the care of what were described as feeble-minded children. The Nova Scotia League for the Protection of the Feeble-minded was formed in 1908 with Agnes Dennis as vice-president and became part of a widespread eugenics movement. A home for girls aged 9-19 years, diagnosed as being mentally challenged, was opened by the affiliated Imperial Order of the Daughters of the Empire (IODE) in 1918 when its home for unclaimed children of the 1917 Explosion was no longer needed. Located on the grounds of the Halifax Industrial School, between the western end of Quinpool and Chebucto roads, it was supervised by Eliza Brison, the city's first female psychiatrist. The first five residents were in fact Explosion victims. Its premises were those earmarked earlier for the Home for Coloured Children, a project which does not seem to have held much interest for the Halifax feminists. Black Haligonians who led the campaign for this facility found an alternative location on the Preston Road, east of Dartmouth, where the home opened in 1921.

Another area of interest to Halifax's middle-class women related to young working women living on their own, a new phenomenon in the twentieth-century city. For such women the LCW established a girls' club, promoted the boarding facilities of the YWCA, opened a welcome hostel in 1909 for newcomers (usually looking for work as servants), urged the study of domestic science, and advocated sports and entertainment, especially for factory girls. Factory workers however were not particularly enamoured of the council's attention. The author of a paper entitled "The Factory Girl of Halifax" observed: "Any attempt at welfare work has to reckon with a very strong prejudice against being regarded as objects of charity; there is a certain strong pride among these girls and they resent the inference that their social condition requires betterment."[5]

The sick and helpless also commanded the attention of the LCW. They supported public health campaigns like that run by the Anti-Tuberculosis League; they agitated successfully for the establishment and later re-establishment of the Victorian Order of Nurses; and they promoted a more positive image for some of the welfare institutions, securing, for example, the cosmetic renaming of the poorhouse as the City Home. Matters of health and welfare were also dear to the hearts of the city's Roman Catholic women, organized since the mid-nineteenth century in parish societies of the Children of Mary. Vitally important work was also undertaken by the Halifax's Catholic religious

Local Council of Women House, Young Avenue, gift of George Wright, as it looks in 1999.

Maids serving tea in the garden of A.A. West's house on Brunswick Street in the early 1890s.

orders, especially the Sisters of Charity and the Sisters of the Good Shepherd. Sister Agnes Gertrude, superior of the Halifax Infirmary, encouraged the hospital's female Aid Society to establish a free ward and send the hospital's nurses out to the homes of the poor infirm.

Despite opposition from the male Catholic hierarchy and other traditionalists, the LCW promoted civil rights for mature women, namely the right to vote and hold public office. Unmarried and widowed women in Halifax had secured the civic franchise in 1887. Other women had already gained parallel rights within some of the Protestant churches. For example, progressive men in the diocesan synod of the Church of England voted in 1910 to change references to men in the description of church officers to persons, thereby providing for the possibility that women might assume lay leadership roles in the church. Eliza Ritchie, a member of a prominent Church of England family, was a frequent spokesperson for comprehensive female suffrage. At the conference of the National Council of Women held in Halifax in 1910 she expressed her willingness "to stake everything she owned" in favour of female suffrage. It "would make political life purer, would lesson graft and give women a better opportunity in individual life."[6] Although Halifax feminists were instrumental in securing the introduction of a suffrage bill in 1917, a cautious male legislature defeated it and the Explosion later that year effectively interrupted further suffrage activism. Almost unremarked, provincial legislation giving women the franchise and right to run for public office passed in 1918.

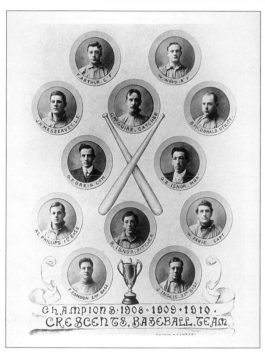

The Halifax Crescents' Baseball Team managed by businessman Gordon B. Isnor, 1910.

In 1912 the Local Council of Women benefited from the loss of the supposedly unsinkable *Titanic* when the will of George Wright, a victim of that disaster and a former Halifax businessman, left the council his mansion on Young Avenue. They were well placed to launch into war work in 1914 when they turned their house over to the Red Cross which co-ordinated the various female wartime volunteer activities with much the same leadership as the LCW.

Leisure

Activities for filling the increasing amount of leisure time that the citizens began to enjoy with shorter working days drew participants and spectators. The early twentieth century became something of a 'golden age' for athletic and musical organizations. The former ranged from baseball teams through college varsity teams to associations such as the St. Mary's Amateur Athletics and Aquatic Club (open to members of that Catholic parish's Total Abstinence

Shop window of Gauvin and Gentzel, photographers, on the south side of Spring Garden Road between Queen and Birmingham. Outside is an organ grinder and his family, a type of street busker common in Halifax during the summers since at least the 1840s.

An early executive committee of North West Arm Rowing Club in their striped blazers.

Society) and 'country' clubs like the Waegwoltic, organized in 1908, and open to both men and women of appropriate social standing and religion. The careful ordering of Halifax society into Catholic and Protestant, black and white, semite and non-semite, to say nothing of class and gender, was usually reflected in sports clubs.

Musical clubs too had special identities. The college co-eds had

Businessmen's gym class at the YMCA during the war.

activities, as they were also of the public holidays like Natal Day and Labour Day.

For spectators or audiences a variety of amusements and entertainments was available. Besides visiting theatrical troupes and musical ensembles, circuses and black-face minstrels (as well as black minstrels) attracted large crowds. Occasionally the city enjoyed the performances of a great celebrity. Nellie Melba, the famous Australian diva, began her Canadian tour of 1910 in Halifax. She arrived in her own private rail car, claiming that "she had heard so much about this being a musical city."[7] Melba drew a capacity crowd to the Academy of Music where she performed a program which one reviewer did not find particularly challenging, perhaps even a little condescendingly popular.

Motion pictures came to Halifax in the first decade of the century. Silent films, accompanied by live music, attracted a mass audience because they were cheap and novel. But they were not without controversy with respect to morals and sensibilities. As a result, censorship legislation was passed in 1915. Public opinion also played a

their glee club. The talented black musicians had their bands for providing entertainment for their own community and for hire. The Ladies' Musical Club, formed in 1905 with Edith Archibald as president, was a performance group for women with its own orchestra and chorus. It also ran a lecture series for members. One of the early presidents was Kate Mackintosh, a public school teacher with 46 years' service by the time of her retirement in 1916. She was a well-known local composer and champion of other female composers.

For public holidays and a summer treat for children, institutional picnics remained popular. Sunday school picnics, for example, were held on most of the public grounds in the city and environs such as Francklyn Park in the south end, McNab's island in the harbour mouth, Cow Bay on the eastern shore beyond Eastern Passage. Wealthy families also continued to lend their estates for picnics in the pre-war period. Competitive races were usually a part of the day's

Circus on the Common about 1900. A high wire act is in progress.

Program for Orpheus Club presentation of Mendelssohn's "Elijah," 1894.

part. When the racist film about the American Civil War and Reconstruction, *The Birth of a Nation*, was slated to open in 1915, the leaders of the black churches succeeded in delaying its showing in the city for a year.

Other spectator events included band concerts. The Public Gardens was partially maintained by the admission fee to the summer concerts which were exceedingly popular until the early years of the century when they began to feel the competition of other attractions. The well-to-do established the Gorsebrook golf course in the south end in 1900. Spectator sports had a large following. Halifax had its own professional baseball league by 1911. The game was well enough established by the war to provide both an activity for troops awaiting transport overseas and a means of raising money for the patriotic fund and local charities.

The Great War

The overwhelmingly patriotic response to the outbreak of war in 1914 was hardly surprising in Canada's major military city.

Enlistments, speeches, support services, and mobilization of resources occurred in an orderly but enthusiastic fashion. The appeal to help the children of Belgium resulted in large-scale collections as Haligonians expressed horror over the alleged barbarity of the Germans. Peacetime concerns were put on hold; in the short term everyone pulled together.

The deluge of troops strained the resources of the city. Except for the embarkation of the First Contingent from Quebec, Halifax was the only Canadian troop port and oversaw the departure of 284,455 personnel during the war. Many Commonwealth and American soldiers also departed from Halifax. Local enlistment of young men emptied the college classrooms and depleted the workforce in the factories, offices and services of the city. For example, one-third of the male students registered at Dalhousie University in 1914-15 enlisted. In the wake of the horrendous battlefield casualties, Halifax also

An evocative portrayal of Barrington Street nightlife about 1917, including the Green Lantern Restaurant, the Orpheus Theatre, early motor cars, wet cobblestone streets, and tram lines.

Halifax Harbour in Time of War *by Arthur Lismer who was principal of the Victoria School of Art and Design from 1916 until 1919.*

Mrs Maude Foley, tram car conductor in her winter uniform.

became a major convalescent centre, with a new hospital being built at Camp Hill for returned soldiers.

In wartime Halifax, women found it was possible to do things they had hitherto been denied. These opportunities included hospital work for female physicians, access to educational programs such as law and dentistry, more senior positions in the teaching profession, and employment in jobs usually reserved for men such as streetcar conductors and delivery van drivers. The variety of volunteer work increased each year and many young women served as VADs (Voluntary Aid Detachment).

Although Halifax was Canada's most easterly port of major size and the centre for troopship convoys, it was not until September 1917, after the menace of German U-boats was felt and the United States entered the war, that Halifax became a convoy port for merchant shipping. In the last year of the war the naval vessels stationed in Halifax were engaged mostly in the protection of coastal shipping.

Despite the deaths overseas of the rich and the poor, the war was not a social equalizer. African Nova Scotians were not welcomed into the ranks and in 1916 a separate battalion was established with white officers, reminiscent of the black volunteer company of 1860. Nonetheless, the 2nd Construction Battalion was heartily endorsed by the local black leadership. Late in the war Canadian and American members of the Jewish Legion were sent to Halifax before

The first policewomen were appointed during the war, including May Virtue with credentials as a nurse, Salvationist, and social worker.

transferring to their camps at Windsor. Several members were stationed at York Redoubt, which guarded the harbour approach, and the battalion was demobilized in Halifax.

The arrival of telegrams with news of the deaths of the city's young men in France continued relentlessly. Some died on the battlefield, others in hospital of their wounds or, at the end of the war, of the Spanish influenza, an epidemic which also hit Halifax in the fall of 1918. Servicemen also died in the Explosion of 6 December 1917, which intially must have seemed to be part of an enemy attack but was caused by a collision in the narrows between the inbound *Mont Blanc*, a French munitions ship, and the outbound *Imo*, a Norwegian vessel chartered for Belgian relief. The *Mont Blanc* represented, in the words of Archibald MacMechan, the

German officers, prisoners of war, incarcerated in the Citadel during World War I.

contemporary historian of the Explosion, "a floating bomb charged with more than two thousand tons of high explosives, attacking the City of Halifax."[8]

Although both vessels had pilots aboard, they were in each other's paths because of a combination of heavy traffic in the channel, misunderstanding of the whistle blasts, and, possibly, distortion caused by the sun's glare on the water. After they collided at 8:50 am, the benzol stowed on the deck of the *Mont Blanc* caught fire and the resulting pillar of smoke drew the people of the north end to the shore, the streets and their windows. There was ample time for a warning but the crew of the munitions ship chose to concentrate entirely on saving themselves and did not even run up the red explosives warning flag. At 9:05 am, the *Mont Blanc*, now an inferno, exploded and the vessel was blown to smithereens. An air blast, laden with razor-sharp fragments, swept across the north end of Halifax and the opposite Dartmouth shore, destroying the lives or the sight of many hundreds of onlookers. The shock wave flattened buildings within a 130-hectare area, blew out windows across the rest of the city and created a tidal wave which flooded the harbourfront.

While the effects of the Explosion could have been worse, especially if the land-based magazines and south-end gas works had been ignited, they were devastating in their impact on the population, geography and industry of the city. An official total of 1,963 deaths occurred in Halifax, Dartmouth and the harbour, 9,000 people were injured, 6,000 lost their homes completely. Almost all residents and sojourners were touched by the disaster, either as relatives or friends of those killed or maimed, householders with damage to their houses or helpers in the aftermath. Although the city was well-placed in some respects for disaster relief in terms of trained military personnel who could be deployed for the rescue effort, the Explosion, which destroyed most of the north end on a clear, calm day, was immediately followed by innumerable fires in buildings where lighted stoves had been overturned. The next day a blizzard hampered rescue efforts and the following day bitter cold froze many of the trapped who had not already been burned to death in the fires.

The losses were devastating: whole families went to their deaths, not necessarily together but by virtue of the functions of their everyday lives—the father at work, the mother in her kitchen, the children in their classrooms or on the way to school. Most of the north-end industries on which the pre-war industrial capacity of the city was based were laid waste—the massive sugar refinery on the

The Imo *beached on the Dartmouth shore. The cargo of the* Mont Blanc *consisted of 2,366.475 tons wet and dry picric acid, 250 tons TNT, 62.062 tons gun cotton, 246.022 tons benzol.*

water's edge collapsed, the Hillis foundry was shattered, the cotton factory burned in the aftermath, the dry dock was badly damaged, and the roof of the Intercolonial Railway station on North Street fell onto the tracks. All of the social institutions on which the community of Richmond depended—the schools and the churches—were little better than shells if they remained standing at all. The area looked like the killing fields of France—a devastated war zone marked by blackened tree stumps, smouldering fires and piles of rubble. The city had unwittingly been called upon to make a supreme wartime sacrifice.

In the aftermath, life could hardly return to normal. The scale of relief was enormous. As black rain descended on the people and places of Richmond on that fateful morning, people outside the north end walked or drove to the site as best they could in difficult circumstances to aid in the rescue work and help the injured. At 11 am the first out-of-city doctor fortuitously arrived by a train which could proceed no farther than Africville on the outer edge of the destroyed north end. He was grateful for the supply of morphine he carried. All available public buildings and many private ones were soon turned into hospitals, operating rooms and dressing stations,

some 57 in total. Additional medical personnel were recruited first from the province, then from farther afield. Many of the homeless were housed in military huts on the Common and when they were filled, tents were added to increase the amount of emergency shelter. Former Mayor Robert T. McIlreith used the experience he had gained as supervisor of the *Titanic* identifications to give advice on how to deal with bodies in the morgue he established in the basement of Chebucto School. By the time local people were ready to drop from exhaustion, an international relief effort was under way, led by the despatch of medical aid from Massachusetts, which began to arrive on 9 December.

One of the survivors of the Explosion was fourteen-year-old Barbara Orr, who lived on the corner of Albert and Kenny Streets. She left her house with a brother and sister to watch the spectacular fire on board the *Mont Blanc* and was near the shore of the harbour when the Explosion occurred. The blast carried her to the top of Fort Needham. Blackened by the fallout and injured in the leg, she

Bodies of the unidentified dead.

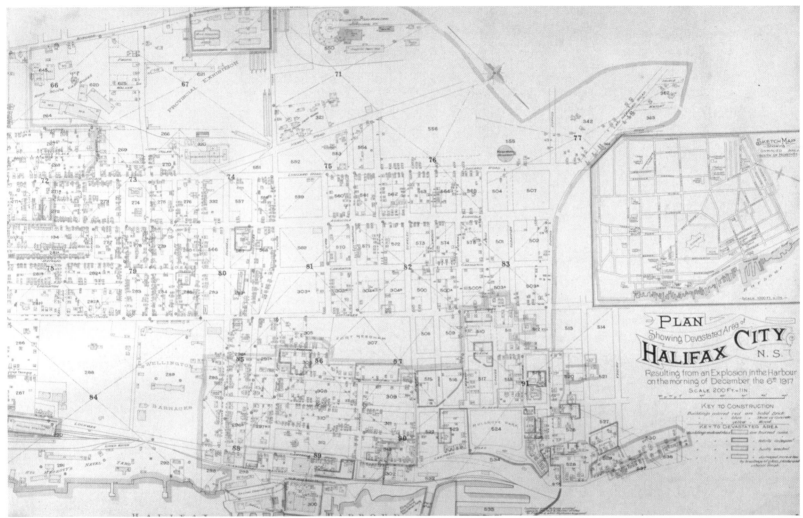

Map of the devastated area of Halifax.

eventually ended up in the new Camp Hill Hospital though not before she had seen the remnants of her family house in flames. The Explosion killed the brother and sister, who had gone with her to watch the drama in the narrows, along with her three other siblings and her mother in their home, and her father at work. The homeless orphan moved in with close relatives. As a memorial to her family,

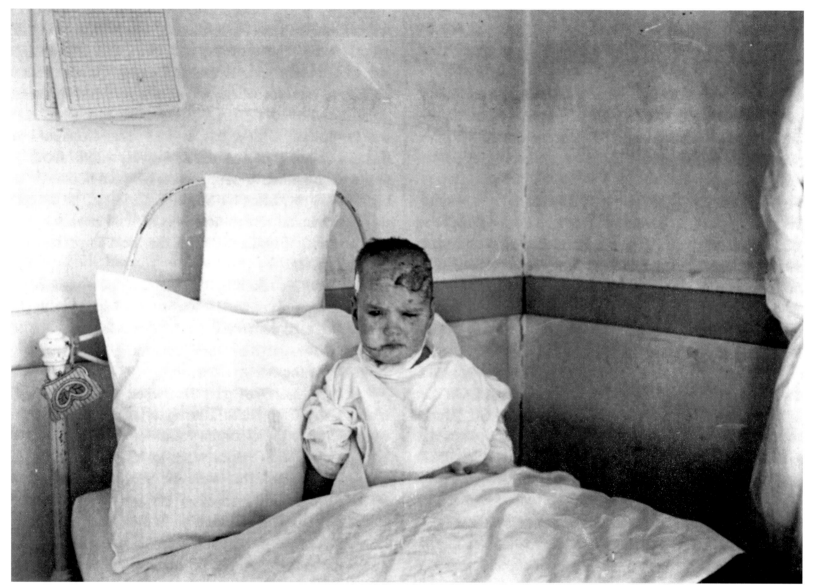

Injured child.

Looking south along the railway track after the Explosion.

Barbara Orr donated a carillon of bells in 1920 to the United Memorial Church, which was itself a memorial to the members of the Methodist and Presbyterian churches killed in the Explosion. Many years later, in 1985, the carillon was removed with her concurrence to the new Halifax Explosion Memorial Bell Tower on the top of Fort Needham Park overlooking the area that was once Richmond.

The Explosion and the end of the War had devastating effects on the shape and character of the city. The obliteration of Richmond led to a rebuilding program which provided new housing in the north end but little employment once the reconstruction had been completed. The destruction of many major industries on the peninsula helped to reinforce the long-term trend toward locating plants and factories on the fringes of the city but, in the short term, it meant privation for many. Returned soldiers and sailors joined the local unemployed in the hard times of peacetime, a destiny familiar to Halifax but no less severe for all that. Such problems as shell shock for veterans and bereavement for Explosion survivors complicated the city's adjustment to the post-war era.

Chapter Seven

WRESTLING WITH ADVERSITY
(1918-1945)

This period of the history of Halifax is set between two very different kinds of explosions. In 1917 it was the explosion of the *Imo* and the *Mont Blanc*. In 1945 Halifax experienced an explosion of pent-up anger and frustration when the announcement of victory in Europe triggered two days of rioting, vandalism, and looting. The years between were difficult ones. Haligonians had to contend with two dreary decades of depression. Severe unemployment and widespread poverty plagued the city. While labour unions tried to protect their members, and reformers reorganized private charity and lobbied governments to provide for the needs of the poor, many people simply gave up and left the city to find work in the United States. In an era when thousands of immigrants flowed through the city to other parts of Canada, the population of Halifax continued to hover around 60,000. In the 1920s, dissent coalesced in the Maritime Rights movement which took regional grievances to Ottawa, where it met with limited success. By the time war broke out in Europe in the fall of 1939, hard times had taken their toll. Although war once again brought a brief boom to Halifax, the city would be sorely tested in meeting the special demands placed on it during the six-year conflict.

Thousands of Canadian veterans of World War II returned to Canada through Pier 21 in 1945, hoping for a brighter future.

Adjusting to Peace

In Halifax, as in much of the rest of Canada, the coming of peace marked an abrupt end to the wartime boom and signalled the beginning of a period of social unrest. Although the economy of the city was buoyed briefly by the rebuilding program which came in the wake of the 1917 explosion, by the end of 1919 the city was experiencing a postwar recession. In addition, tensions ran high in the city, with racism was very close to the surface. In February 1919 soldiers and civilians turned their anger against Chinese Haligonians, causing severe damage to six restaurants and their owners and staff, who then struggled for years to obtain compensation for their losses. For the city's tiny Chinese community in Halifax, which numbered fewer than 200 at the end of the war, the losses were very significant. Outbursts of racism and xenophobia were frequent in Halifax in the inter-war years; attacks against African Nova Scotians and Chinese

Unveiling the Memorial Cenotaph in the Grand Parade to honour those who served in World War I. Sir Robert Borden, Col. J. Ralston, Lieutenant-Governor J.C. Tory, and Hon. E.N. Rhodes, Premier of Nova Scotia, were among the dignitaries who attended.

citizens occurred almost every year, however, police and city officials showed little interest in addressing the problem.

In the rebuilding of the area devastated by the 1917 Explosion, progressive reformers manifested their optimism in the grand plans drawn up for revitalizing the north end. In late January 1918, the Halifax Relief Commission (HRC) was established to investigate losses, damages, and injuries and award compensation to victims. It was also given a mandate to redevelop the 130 hectares worst hit by the explosion, an area bounded by Barrington, Russell, Robie, and Leeds streets. British-born town-planning pioneer Thomas Adams proposed a dramatic new design for the area, with broad thoroughfares for cars, Tudor-style townhouses for workers, and large green spaces. Controversy briefly swirled around the proposal as north-end residents protested their lack of a voice in the process of rebuilding. But the ten-block Hydrostone district—named for the locally produced cement blocks used in the construction of the houses—proceeded, becoming the HRC's lasting monument in Halifax, and the country's first experiment in public housing. Designed by Montreal architect George Ross, the 324 terraced homes were modelled on the garden suburbs in England. The design of the houses, as well as the plan for the whole area, reflected the belief of many progressive reformers that providing workers with 'ideal surroundings' would not only improve public health, but also transform and uplift their personal lives.

During the 1920s the Hydrostone district emerged as a distinctive working-class neighbourhood. Most of the residents had lost their housing in the disaster, but they were joined by many newcomers. Several of the tenants of HRC housing belonged to old railway families, and many, too, supported

Harry Thompson stands proudly in his Kane Place garden in the Hydrostone district after receiving first prize in the Halifax Relief Commission Garden Contest in 1923.

The Girls Manual Training Class at the School for the Blind on Morris Street in 1921 demonstrates the commitment of progressive educators in this period to learning by doing.

the new Labour Party. No other polling district in Halifax was so consistent in its support of Labour candidates in federal and provincial elections during the early 1920s.

Because of its concentration of industrial workers, the Hydrostone district and surrounding streets were especially hard hit by the recession and the deindustrialization of the city's economy. In 1926 the *Halifax Citizen*, a Labour paper, published a poem signed 'Old Timer' that expressed the bitterness of area residents. It began:

> *I remember in Halifax, not long ago,*
> *When our boys leaving school had a chance;*
> *They could learn a trade,*
> *And in time, lead a maid*
> *To a home, not a joy ride or dance*
> *When the old shops at Richmond were going full swing,*

> *With the cotton mill, dry dock and Moirs,*
> *The Acadian refinery, the dockyard and Gunn's*
> *We had then lots of work for our boys.*[1]

Two Decades of Depression

As the Old Timer's lament suggests, economic conditions in Halifax in the inter-war years were bleak and Haligonians did not share the prosperity of the 1920s enjoyed in western and central Canada. After the wartime boom, the city's economy slumped precipitously for several reasons. Canada's peacetime navy was greatly reduced, and the Naval College, which had begun classes in 1911, was moved from Halifax in 1918, further reducing the size of the naval establishment. The once vital military establishment was barely visible in the inter-war years. Moreover, between 1920 and 1930 the city lost nearly half its manufacturing jobs. Many of the factories destroyed in the 1917 Explosion were never rebuilt. Others survived only to be closed. The new Halifax Shipyards began laying off workers right after the war and by 1922 its workforce had shrunk to only 100 workers from a high of nearly 2,000 in 1918. A wave of business mergers during the 1920s further concentrated manufacturing in central Canada, and new freight rates and changes in tariffs made it even more difficult for Halifax industries to compete in the Canadian market. A crisis in the region's resource industries proved equally devastating for the city's economy. Coal markets lost during the war were never regained; Europeans offered stiff competition for Maritime fish products; British Columbia's lumber

The arrival of the Sparks Circus, shown parading along Barrington Street in 1925.

For members of the South End Tennis Club the depression seemed to make very little difference.

Haligonians adopted a wide range of strategies to cope with economic hard times. The generosity of friends and family was always vital and usually the first line of defence. But as the bad years ground on, personal charity often proved inadequate. In the 1920s hundreds of people despaired and left the city in search of work. Most of them went to the United States until the American government prohibited further immigration in the early 1930s. Labour unions, churches, and charitable organizations all played important roles in seeking to ease distress. Halifax charities, like their counterparts across the continent, banded together to coordinate services. Along with the labour movement, they lobbied governments to take action to help the casualties of what had become a prolonged economic crisis.

The collapse of the city's economy took the local labour movement by surprise. When World War I ended, the movement in Halifax was large, powerful and committed to political reform. In January 1920 the *Citizen* editorialized,

The new day will be ushering in a new era, in which the working class must be prepared with leaders and policies that will direct and build a new nation conceived in brotherhood and devoted to the cause of humanity.[2]

saturated the North American market. The general decline in the regional economy soon had an impact on all Halifax businesses. Once the rebuilding was finished, the construction industry went into a steep decline. Similarly, wholesale and retail operations entered an era of relative inactivity.

Although business conditions slightly revived in the late 1920s, the depression of the 1930s brought a return to hard times. Some claim that the depression did not hurt Maritimers as much as other Canadians but the poverty and hardship faced by Haligonians challenge that myth. The cumulative effects of another decade of depression took their toll. Low tax revenues for the Province and the City made it virtually impossible for Haligonians to benefit from cost-shared social programs, such as old age pensions offered by the federal government. Maritimers, worse off than most of the country before the depression began, continued to be significantly disadvantaged for the next quarter-century.

But militancy faltered in 1920 during a bitter three-month strike by a coalition of unions against Halifax Shipyards. The strike was a last gasp of Canada's postwar labour revolt—best known for the Winnipeg General Strike in 1919. Workers in Halifax, along with their counterparts in the

Churches and other organizations sponsored athletic teams, such as the Halifax Cardinals, who were intermediate League Champions in 1930, 1931, and 1936.

rest of the country, had taken the idealistic rhetoric spawned by the Great War to heart. When the war ended they anticipated a prosperous peace based on a commitment to social justice. Instead, they had to contend with spiralling inflation, a severe recession and repressive employers backed by anti-trade union governments.

Following the defeat of the shipyards strike, the labour movement in Halifax shrank in numbers and lost its cohesion. A small group of Halifax activists joined the communist movement. In 1921-22 the radicals were also prominent in leading the Halifax Unemployed Association which held large protest demonstrations. More conservative labour leaders emerged, however, and supported a less radical rival organization of the unemployed, the United Workmen of Nova Scotia. By the mid-1920s the dominant conservative wing of the labour movement had abandoned labour politics to participate in the Maritime Rights campaign for regional economic rehabilitation, a movement led by middle-class professionals and businessmen concerned with the adverse effects of federal transportation and tariff policy.

The depressed economic conditions and divisions within the labour movement made it difficult to advance—or even defend—the position of workers in the city during the 1920s. For example, job security was the main priority for the Halifax Building Trades Council in 1927 when it began issuing cards to members in an effort to reduce competition from non-union workers. This action proved useful during the brief construction boom in the city in the late 1920s, but offered little protection during the nationwide depression of the 1930s.

The early 1930s brought the craft unions to their lowest level in the century. Mass unemployment meant that workers were scrambling for any available jobs and even the most skilled lost out to competitors willing to work for lower wages. The association of construction companies imposed wage cuts in 1932 and 1933. In 1933 the

While most Mi'kmaq people lived outside the city, many such as Jeremiah Bartlett Alexis, also known as Jerry Lonecloud, were regular visitors. Clara Dennis, who frequently wrote about Alexis in her newspaper columns, photographed him in her garden.

provincial government passed legislation to protect Nova Scotia workers from competition from those coming from outside the province, but the most dramatic change in the situation came in 1936 with the passage of the Industrial Standards Act which brought binding arbitration to the building trades in the Halifax area.

Private charities were at the forefront of efforts to help Haligonians weather the depression. Charitable organizations met the prolonged economic crisis by coordinating their efforts to increase efficiency and pressing all levels of government for action. In 1925 the Community Chest was established to mount one annual appeal for funds. In 1930 many charities joined the new Halifax Council of Social Agencies (later the Halifax Welfare Council) to coordinate their efforts. A plethora of private charities, churches and religious organizations remained vital in helping the poor survive. The Jost Mission, for example, continued to provide inexpensive child care for working mothers, and the Halifax Association for Improving the Condition of the Poor maintained its long-standing breakfast depots for children. Personal generosity was also important. During the worst years of the depression, Evelyn Theakston, the daughter and granddaughter of missionaries at the North End City Mission, lived with her family in a tiny flat above the Mission house at the corner of Maynard and Gerrish Streets, a short walk from her teaching job at Bloomfield School. She later wrote to a friend, "teaching at Bloomfield School ... in the days of the Depression I helped many a pupil with shoes from my own small salary and [provided] school supplies for entire classes until the war brought prosperity."[3] Her generosity is underscored by the fact that teachers had to take a "voluntary" pay cut during the 1930s.

Through the 1930s, the Halifax Council of Social Agencies, under the leadership of Anglican minister and sociologist Samuel Prince and American-trained social worker Gwendolyn Shand, actively lobbied governments to improve welfare services and address the continuing housing crisis in the city. Prince, staked his claim to leadership of the welfare reform movement on the publication of his PhD thesis, *Catastrophe and Social Change: Based Upon a Sociological Study of the Halifax Disaster*, about the social impact of the 1917 Explosion. In

1924 Prince was appointed Professor of Sociology at King's College and Dalhousie University, and became very active as a social reformer. He transformed the Anglican Diocesan Council into an effective lobby group for improved social legislation and social services. He was president of the Nova Scotia Society for Mental Hygiene for 20 years, and president of the Halifax Council of Social Agencies from 1934 to 1945. He held directorships in most of the city's charitable organizations and was instrumental in the establishment of the Maritime School of Social Work in 1941. In 1932 Prince conducted a study of city housing which revealed Halifax was

infested with a high percentage, per house population, of tumble-down shacks where whole families eat, sleep, bathe and live in a single room, where cellars reek with filth and vermin... unfit for human habitation, and typical of the worst slum conditions to be heard of anywhere.[4]

Newly married country singer Hank Snow and his wife Minnie experienced these appalling housing conditions first hand. In 1935 the couple was expecting a baby and moved into a bigger apartment in downtown Halifax. The place was filthy, and Minnie and Hank's mother immediately started to clean it up, but,

as soon as the stove was hooked up and fire started, something bad happened. The heat hit the kitchen, and cockroaches started coming out of every crack in the woodwork and from everyplace else! Those roaches were an inch long and as fat as wooden pencils. You could see them on the ceiling even. They would drop off the ceiling and hit the floor with a thump.[5]

The next day they moved again, into two cold shabby rooms entered through a rickety outside stairway, but without bugs.

In the 1920s and 1930s the major responsibility of providing for the poor fell to the municipal government. Under the terms of the city charter, the local government was explicitly forbidden to provide what was known as "outdoor relief"—income maintenace payments to support those who continued to live in their own homes. Instead.

From 1932 to 1936 unemployed single men were housed at the Halifax Citadel and spent their days working on restoration work as part of the system of federal government's system of relief camps operated by the Department of Defence.

the City continued to provide what had long been known as "indoor relief," through the incarceration of the most destitute in the City Home (the old poorhouse) at the corner of South and Robie streets. During the 1930s the city did provide "outdoor relief" for some at the shockingly low rate of $3.77 per month. Belatedly the provincial and federal governments made token gestures to help out. In 1930, Nova Scotia introduced mothers' allowances which gave widows with two or more dependent children a monthly pittance. And in 1933 Angus L. Macdonald, the newly elected premier of Nova Scotia, introduced old age pensions after the federal government agreed to pay 75 percent of the cost. Even then the pension benefits of $14.49 a month paid to Nova Scotians were well below the national average of $18.24.

In November 1932 the Halifax Citadel became one of the hated Department of National Defence relief camps for single unemployed men. It was a very last resort. Although facilities were provided for 300 men at the Citadel, there were rarely more than 200 at the camp. The admission process was humiliating and conditions in the camp proved grim. Inmates received the standard relief camp twenty-cents

a day, military rations, and a room shared with a dozen or more others. Initially the facility had only 14 toilets. All inmates' efforts to protest conditions were quickly suppressed.

The major work of the relief camp was the restoration of the old fortifications as a heritage project. In 1934 Nova Scotia archivist D.C. Harvey, a member of the national Historic Sites and Monuments Board, reported satisfaction with their progress, but when the project was cancelled in 1936 much remained to be done and Citadel's future looked uncertain.

Many Haligonians, especially skilled workers, gave up on Halifax during the 1920s and moved to the United States or other parts of Canada, where work was available. Those who stayed behind, many of them women and children abandoned temporarily or permanently by the men in their families, relied on friends and neighbours for help. On the outer fringes of the peninsula families kept hens, pigs and even cows to supplement their food supply. As they had for decades, peddlers sold fish and seasonal vegetables and fruit through residential neighbourhoods undercutting local grocers and providing cheap produce. Many older Haligonians still have warm memories of the help they received from friends and neighbours, but conditions were grim and many of the strategies people resorted to

Prize-winning high school athlete Josephine Labba. Because she competed in shorts, she was not allowed to take the stage on her graduation from St. Patrick's High School.

Women were very active in team sports in the interwar years. Members of 1925 YWCA Be Square Volleyball team included R. Muir, J. Bond, E. Hartlen, K. Wagner, A. Pitcher, and D. Ray.

Modernization in the Midst of Depression

One of the bright spots in the Halifax economy in the late 1920s was the resumption of work on the Ocean Terminals which had been interrupted by the war. In 1926 the Royal Commission on Maritime Claims recommended that federal funds be provided for port development. In 1928 the Halifax Port Commission was established to oversee completion of the new terminals with financial help from the federal government. Further federal funds were spent on port facilities after the National Harbours Board took over the management of the port in 1936. Seasonal work on the docks provided the income that kept many families afloat during the depression.

damaged their health and future prospects. Children, for example, often had to cut short their education and work for pitifully low wages. Young people stayed at home to help their families and delayed marrying and having children of their own because they lacked the money to set up their own households. Mothers had to leave young children at home alone while they went out to earn a living. The poorest survived by crowding into the wretched slums with inadequate plumbing, little heat and too little food.

In 1928 the federal Department of Immigration opened a new facility at Pier 21 in the south end of Halifax's waterfront. During the 1920s immigration was heavy and in the last years of the decade an average of 130,000 people a year passed through Halifax. Pier 21 housed a complex of buildings that contained Immigration Services, Customs, Health and Welfare, Agriculture, the Red Cross, a waiting room, a restaurant, and a canteen for purchasing supplies for the long train trip to other parts of Canada. New arrivals were processed through the appropriate government departments, but many were also met and cared for by Haligonians, who served as volunteers for religious and social organizations. Between 1930 and 1939 immigration slowed

Many Haligonians, such as these members of the Nova Scotia Baptist Federation, served as volunteers at Pier 21 to welcome new immigrants.

to a trickle. Thousands of earlier immigrants were returning home— some voluntarily, having abandoned the hope of finding a better life in Canada. Others were deported, many through Pier 21 where they had earlier entered Canada full of hope for a better life.

The longest serving and best known volunteer at Pier 21 was

The Lady Boats provided some glamour for the drab Halifax waterfront during the late 1920s and 1930s, and Canadian Steamships actively promoted its passenger service to the Caribbean.

Sadie (Mrs. Morris) Fineberg who spent more than four decades helping newcomers, first as the representative of the Jewish Immigrant Aid Society, and after 1948 as the official representative of the City of Halifax. She was well qualified for the job—she spoke seven languages, seemed to have unflagging energy and unlimited compassion. When immigrants arrived without money or food, Sadie Fineberg sent for boxes of provisions from her husband's food service business. Her contribution to easing many people through their arrival in Canada earned her the respect and affection of hundreds of families, and reminds us that although few of the new immigrants settled in Halifax, Pier 21 had a significant impact on the life of the city and its residents

The new immigration facilities at Pier 21 were just one of the changes on the Halifax waterfront during the 1920s. Two years after Canada and Jamaica renegotiated a trade agreement to provide regular passenger and mail service between the Atlantic port of Halifax and Saint John, Montreal and the West Indies, the "Lady Boats" began to visit the port. In 1927 the federal government provided Canadian National Steamships $10 million to assist with the building of specially designed new vessels. The beautiful new white ships were named for the wives of British naval admirals. Throughout the depression they carried passengers, sugar and bananas as well as

Workers packing barrels of salt fish at A.M. Smith and Company in 1942.

the mail between Halifax and Saint John, New Brunswick and the Caribbean and Bermuda. Even in the depths of the depression passengers signed up for special excursion rates for southern cruises. During World War II the Lady Boats were armed and painted in the drab colours of war as part of the merchant fleet that kept Canada and its allies at war. Only two survived the war, the *Lady Rodney* and the *Lady Nelson*. In the early 1950s Canadian National Steamships abandoned its West Indies' service, and the last two vessels were sold to Egypt.

Other new vessels appeared on the waterfront as mechanized fishing trawlers

Maritime National Fish also produced Sea-Seald *Cod Liver Oil with elegant art deco labels.*

The traditional Grand Banks schooner fishery and the salt fish industry remained important elements of waterfront life in Halifax until the end of World War II. Cod was brought ashore and dried on waterfront wharves and rooftops.

began to replace traditional schooners. The fishing industry in Halifax modernized to meet the growing market for fresh and frozen fish. Changing conditions in the industry created conflict among both those who went to sea and those who worked on land. By the late 1930s fishers and plant employees followed the lead of their New England counterparts and began to organize unions. They faced keen resistance from fish merchants and processors, combined with little sympathy from the provincial government but enjoyed strong popular support. In December 1937 Captain Angus Walters, the captain of the famous Bluenose, proclaimed a "tie-up" of vessels to support demands for a quarter of a cent per pound increase in the price paid for haddock. Most of the schooners stayed tied up for several weeks, and the fishers found new allies. A Fish Handlers' and Fish Cutters' Union then taking shape within the two large Halifax fish processing plants publicly supported the Fishermen's Federation. When the National Fish Company retaliated by firing 60 union members, the

In 1928, the new Lord Nelson Hotel, situated opposite the Public Gardens at the corner of South Park Street and Spring Garden Road, opened with considerable fanfare and provided a boost to the local economy.

workers went on strike demanding union recognition and the reinstatement of their members. In January 1938 fish buyers agreed to price increases, but refused to recognize the Fishermen's Federation. Settlement of the Fish Handlers strike required the direct intervention of Premier Angus L. Macdonald, who promised a certification vote under the new (1937) Trade Union Act.

During the 1920s and 1930s tourism emerged as one solution to the city's economic woes. Halifax was promoted to Americans and other Canadians as a beautiful historic seaport city, and the municipal government issued a steady stream of tourist propaganda to encourage visitors. Local tourism promoters applauded the opening of two large modern hotels in the 1920s— the Lord Nelson on South Park Street and the Nova Scotian Hotel at the new train station. When the seven-storey Lord Nelson opened in the fall of 1928, it was hailed for its modern conveniences, beautiful design and fine location, across from the Public Gardens. The hotel opened in October with a "brilliant ball" attended by 500 people; hundreds more stood outside with their noses pressed to the glass. Elizabeth S. Nutt, principal of

This colour postcard presented a somewhat idealized view of the Nova Scotian Hotel and the adjacent new train station, built to replace the North Street Station destroyed in the 1917 Explosion.

the Nova Scotia College of Art, put an aesthetic stamp of approval on the new building, praising its "modern equipment and rich fittings." In addition to lavish decoration, the hotel offered phone service in every room and had its own orchestra. Radio station CHNS moved its studios into the hotel, and plate-glass windows and were provided to allow guests to watch the work of the radio station. The construction of the hotel gave a major boost to the local economy. For example, L.E. Shaw provided the brick and Cape Breton's Dosco provided the steel for the hotel.

Despite the economic malaise of the inter-war years, modern mass popular culture and new mass consumer products were welcomed in Halifax. Radios brought American popular music into many households and the rooftops of the city held a forest of radio aerials to catch the signals. Going to the movies was a favourite entertainment for young and old. Shopping changed with the arrival of new national department store chains. For many Haligonians trips to Simpson's and Eaton's were confined to window shopping, but there were those whose standard of living was very little affected by the depression. Limousines continued to drop off students at the Halifax Ladies College on Barrington Street, and car dealers advertised the latest models for those few who could afford them.

In 1930 the end of prohibition brought back a limited form of legal drinking. Halifax had never been completely "dry" in the intervening years, of course. The legendary Nova Scotia rum runners kept local bootleggers well stocked. But the change in the law meant that alcohol could be legally purchased in government-run liquor stores. Commercial establishments, however, continued to be denied the opportunity to serve liquor to their customers. Private clubs could get special licenses to serve alcohol to their members, and many of these continued to thrive years after the arrival of commercial competitors.

These new signs of modernity had a special impact on the lives of women in Halifax. Although domestic work continued to be the most important employment for women throughout the period, new jobs were opening up, especially for young un-married women, in stores, laundries, restaurants, and as telephone operators. Many women also found work in offices, and their youth and stylishness attracted admirers on downtown streets. The fashions of the new mass consumerism

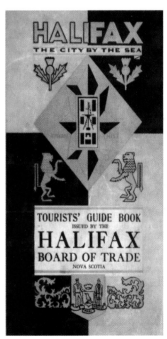

In the 1920s and 1930s the city of Halifax produced advertising material to attract tourists to the city.

had wide appeal, especially for the young, and masked the older, starker class differences in clothing.

Some Haligonians, many of them artists, poets and musicians, responded to the changes in the city with a nostaligic lament for what they regarded as Nova Scotia's "golden age" of wooden ships and iron men. In the 1920s a group of poets calling themselves the "Song Fishermen" organized lectures and recitals in Halifax and produced poetry broadsheets illustrated by local artists. Led by Andrew Merkel, who ran the Canadian Press office in Halifax, they turned to traditional ballads, old sea shanties and Gaelic literature to evoke a sense of Nova Scotia's glorious past. Folklorist Helen Creighton also began her career of collect-

Black women contributed actively to community activities. This photograph shows the executive committee of the Ladies Auxillary of the African United Baptist Association for 1919-20.

Regular tram service opened up suburban shopping at the new Simpson's Department store in the west end.

ing songs and stories in the inter-war years, and her work has continued to enjoy a wide audience ever since. The ideals represented in the folklore found visual form in the romantic photographs of McAskill.

As the fishery modernized, nostalgia extended to the celebration of the traditional skills of the heyday of the schooner fishery on the Grand Banks of Newfoundland. An

international racing competition was held in Halifax Harbour, organized by W.H. Dennis, publisher of the Halifax *Herald*. The North Atlantic Fishermen's Trophy was open only to *bona fide* fishing schooners. In 1921 and 1922 the Trophy went to a Lunenburg-built schooner, the *Bluenose*—immortalized by the schooner on the Canadian dime. Haligonians filled the streets leading to the harbour to watch the races, and the Herald hung models of the contenders from wires high above the street to keep spectators in the upper street abreast of the race. The races were suspended in 1923, and resumed again from 1931 to 1938.

Built in Lunenburg, the famed fishing schooner Bluenose drew large crowds to international races held in Halifax harbour in the 1920s.

World War II

During World War II, Halifax became a "conscripted city." No place in Canada turned as much of its land and resources over to the war effort as Halifax. Every aspect of life in the city and the surrounding area was dramatically affected by being the home of Canada's main

The recruitment of large numbers of young women into clerical work during the 1920s also opened up new opportunities for women such as Theresa Murphy who offered training in the new skills needed by stenographers and bookkeepers.

naval port, a ship-repair centre, and the port of embarkation for more than 150 troop convoys. The navy commandeered hotels, fairgrounds, Victorian-era army barracks, and the campus of King's College which had moved to Halifax from Windsor in the 1920s. Army huts sprouted like mushrooms on the Halifax airport on Chebucto Road.

Municipal officials hoped in vain that the federal government would recognize the special strains the war placed on Halifax and provide extra money to help with the crisis. Only 51 of the city's 114 miles of streets were paved. The city had no traffic lights to cope with the increased traffic. The decrepit water system had trouble coping with the bottomless demand for fresh water for ships. Patriotic groups, churches, and war charities set up hostels and recreation huts, but there were never enough. Repeatedly the city asked for help with housing and improvements to over-strained municipal services such as public transportation. After two decades of depression Halifax was barely able to cope with the doubling of the population from the influx of military and civilian personnel. The housing crisis, already the cause of concern before the war, became desperate by the early 1940s. And despite the appeal of the new forms of mass popular culture, few new restaurants or commercial leisure activities had actually been established.

Between the two wars Halifax had been the east-coast headquarters of the tiny Royal Canadian Navy. Early in 1939, seeing war on the close horizon, Britain's Royal Navy moved its North America and West Indies Squadron from Bermuda to Halifax. After Canada declared war on 10 September 1939, Halifax became a

In the summer of 1939, shortly before the outbreak of World War II, King George VI and his popular wife Queen Elizabeth visited Halifax.

strategic centre for both the British and Canadian navies. From 1941 to 1943 it was part of the U.S. controlled naval operations on the Atlantic seaboard. In mid-1943 the Royal Canadian Navy assumed responsibility for the pro-tection and control of shipping in the northwest Atlantic. By then its peacetime complement of 1800 had increased to more than 75,000 men and women. The navy's appetite for facilities proved insatiable. Buildings all over Halifax were put into service; new buildings, many of them designed to be temporary, were built and the demand spilled off the peninsula into the surrounding suburbs.

The role of Halifax as a ship-repair centre was one area where the city's strategic role overlapped with economic interests. Halifax's location made it an obvious choice for ship-repair facilities. Although C.D. Howe, Canada's Minister of Munitions and Supply had spent his formative years in Halifax, his wartime policies "were detrimental not only to Maritime industries

Early in the war a submarine net was stretched across the mouth of Halifax Harbour to keep out enemy U-boats, but stories abounded of German submarine crews picked up with ticket stubs from the Capitol Theatre in their pockets.

People of all ages and all walks of life were encouraged to contribute to the war effort, and Haligonians such as this group of Girl Guides conducting a paper salvage drive, responded to the call to action.

but also to Canada's war effort."[6] In 1940 the British government complained to Howe about his insistence on developing ship-building and ship-repair facilities along the upper reaches of the St. Lawrence and the Great Lakes, which remained ice-bound for part of the year, instead of in Halifax. When Howe turned a deaf ear, Britain turned to the United States for repair services. The Americans were equally critical of Howe's reluctance to develop a ship-repair industry in Halifax, arguing that Canada's naval efficiency was undercut by this failure to develop east coast repair facilities. Although Halifax Shipyards were very busy on both sides of Halifax Harbour in the fall of 1940, as soon as the ice moved out of the St. Lawrence River in the spring of 1941, Halifax workers were laid off as the repair industry was shifted inland. By the time Howe changed his position it was almost too late. Labour shortages meant that skilled workers were not available. Even if the necessary workers had been attracted to the city, the acute housing shortages would have left them virtually homeless.

Convoys of merchants ships and their naval escorts formed in Bedford Basin to prepare for the dangerous trip across the North Atlantic.

Overall, the short-term economic impact of the war on Halifax was enormous, featuring bustle but minimal long-term development. Demand for goods and services outstripped the capacity of local businesses to deliver them, especially in the face of government rationing. Demand for labour also outstripped the supply because large numbers of skilled workers had left the city early in the war to find jobs in central Canada or had joined the armed services.

Unionized workers capitalized on the labour shortages. By 1943, despite appeals to workers' patriotism, a number of strikes erupted for union recognition and higher wages. Prime Minister Mackenzie King, anxious to hold the political support of workers, introduced federal legislation which greatly improved trade union rights. A month-long strike by 3000 Halifax Shipyards workers for the check-off of union dues in 1944 was one of the largest wartime strikes. It ended when the Regional War Labour Board ruled in favour of the union.

During the war, military and civilian workers and their families flooded in, looking for food, housing, and entertainment. Convoys of up to 150 merchant ships and their naval escorts left the city every

Children evacuated from Britain during the war arrived at Pier 21 in Halifax.

to fill the gap by establishing canteens and hostels where servicemen and women could find food and entertainment. It was their concerts which provided the stage to launch the international career of Halifax contralto Portia White. White, daughter of a Baptist minister, the first black graduate of Acadia University, taught school to pay for her training at the Halifax Conservatory of Music, and began performing in churches and at Sunday evening concerts organized by her father, at the Casino Theatre on Gottingen Street. On April 19, 1940, Portia White sang "A City called Heaven" during the first radio concert broadcast from the new YMCA Hostel for service personnel. A week later, in true Hollywood fashion, when a featured soloist fell ill, White replaced her—the first step towards stardom. By the end of the year she was appearing regularly at the weekly concerts for servicemen in the Knights of Columbus Hut on Barrington Street. Edith Read, a Toronto teacher with a reputation for talent spotting, heard White sing and invited her to perform in Toronto. This performance launched her career as an international star which included sold-out concerts at prestigious venues such as the New York City Town Hall.

The biggest problem facing Halifax during World War II was the housing shortage. Until 1944 half the naval personnel in Halifax lived outside barracks, competing with civilians for accommodation,

eight days. Thousands of soldiers and newly trained pilots awaited embarkation. German prisoners-of-war passed through the city on their way to internment camps inland. Newfoundlanders flocked to Halifax to join the Royal Navy and the merchant marine, or to work on the docks. American servicemen arrived in 1940, a year before the United States entered the war. Dispossessed sailors and refugees came to town, along with British schoolchildren evacuated under the threat of invasion. Later on, war brides began to arrive, often with young children. Prostitutes, bootleggers, and drug-dealers came to cash in on demand for their services.

Haligonians did their best to cope with the influx in the face of government indifference. Newcomers and long-time residents alike faced long waits for service at the city's few restaurants, and movie line-ups were a regular part of wartime life. A number of voluntary organizations, such as the YMCA and the Knights of Columbus tried

transportation, food and other commodities made scarce by wartime shortages and rationing, although price controls curbed inflation. The federal government built 1000 small pre-fab bungalows in the Halifax area, but only a handful were allotted to service families. Public transit

Long lineups for movies were part of the wartime experience of naval personnel and civilians alike.

was another problem. There were too few "Birneys," as the local electric trams were known, to meet the demand, and finding more during the war was nearly impossible.

The Canadian government was no more responsive to social needs than it had been on the issue of ship-repair facilities. The

Halifax had very few restaurants to serve the bulging population of the city, but the Green Lantern, pictured here, was usually a very busy place.

federal government persisted in turning a blind eye to difficulties associated with using Halifax and surrounding area as the primary Canadian operational, training, administrative, supply and repair base for naval forces and merchant shipping. Despite the unique and vital role that Halifax played, Ottawa continued to claim that all Canadian cities were equally affected by the war and Halifax received no special consideration.

In 1943 Halifax City Council began to prepare for the transition to peace by establishing a Civic Planning Commission. The

commission was chaired by Ira P. Macnab, a well-known engineer and a member of the Nova Scotia Public Utilities Board. Although the commission did not complete its work until 1946, many Haligonians threw themselves into the process. Briefs were presented by labour organizations and community groups, such as the Halifax Council of Social Agencies. In 1944, for example, the Halifax Club of Business and Professional Women created a civic planning committee to prepare a brief urging the city to adopt a program of slum clearance, construction of low-income housing, especially for young women, improved public transit and city sanitation and the expansion of recreation services. The Business and Professional Women's agenda reflected many of the concerns of other groups and of the commission itself.

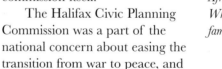

African Nova Scotian contralto Portia White began her ascent to international fame in Halifax during World War II.

The Halifax Civic Planning Commission was a part of the national concern about easing the transition from war to peace, and preventing the social and economic dislocations that had followed World War I. During the war the federal government put in place a set of programs and policies that served as the foundation for the welfare state in Canada as it formed in the 1950s and 1960s. However, there was to be no easy transition to peace in Halifax.

The pressure on the city erupted on VE Day, 8 May 1945. Haligonians and historians have been debating who was to blame ever since. No one could have doubted the potential for trouble. Naval personnel had made no secret of their resentment of the high rents and lack of services in wartime Halifax, and there had been persistent rumours that they would take their revenge when the war ended. In 1944 Mayor John E. Lloyd met with military officials to plan for the

Civilians participated in looting local stores.

Rear Admiral L.W. Murray was criticized for his failure to control naval personnel.

coordination of military and civilian forces to prevent disorder when the war was finally over, but no plans were put in place.

The riots began at 10:30 pm on Monday, 7 May, when naval passengers on a tramcar bound for downtown threw the driver out and, with the help of hundreds more sailors walking along Barrington Street, set the vehicle on fire. Ten city police, thirty unarmed military police, and a contingent from the Halifax Fire Department were unable to control the crowd. While the southbound sailors pushed the tramcar along Barrington Street, a second incident erupted downtown, where sailors and civilians were taking over the Sackville Street liquor store. The next target was the well-stocked Hollis Street liquor store, followed by the new Buckingham Street store. Well lubricated by the liquor store raids, the rioters spent the night and much of the next day—when their ranks were augmented by an additional 10,000 naval personnel and large numbers of thrill-seeking civilians—smashing windows and looting downtown businesses. A successful raid on Olands Brewery kept the liquor flowing. The rioters caused damages worth $5,000,000 before they were finally stopped.

The rioting ended Tuesday night. Rear-Admiral Leonard Warren Murray, Commander-in-Chief North West Atlantic, the senior naval officer in Halifax, was finally persuaded a crisis existed late Tuesday afternoon. He rounded up a convoy of nine trucks of Shore Patrol-men and a loudspeaker, and drove through the downtown streets an-nouncing that all leave was cancelled as of 6:15 pm and ordering all naval personnel to return to their ships and their bases. The trucks picked up drunks; hundreds more walked back to the north end. A heavy rain that night provided further inducement for the sodden celebrants to give up the party. The next day the Army sent 1000 soldiers from Debert, Nova Scotia, to Halifax to patrol the streets. Two days later, on 10 May, a Royal Commission of Inves-tigation, led by Supreme Court Justice Roy Lindsay Kellock, was appointed to investigate the causes of the riots. As the commission began the work of

The unofficial VE Day celebrations and riot included this attack on the Liquor Commission Warehouse on Hollis Street.

interviewing witnesses and collecting information, Haligonians saw the name of their city blackened in the nation's press. Newspapers across the country placed the blame for the riots on the greed, ineptitude, and lack of generosity of Haligonians toward the military. Kellock, however, placed the blame squarely on the naval command in Halifax, and especially on Admiral Murray. He was critical of the navy's lack of planning and inadequacy of the Naval Shore Patrol, responsible for policing navel personnel in the city. Further, he defended the city's restaurants, establishing that they had continued to operate during the riots, serving over 10,000 customers on 8 May, and paid tribute to the volunteers who had worked hard to provide for the entertainment and well-being of service personnel. Although Kellock established the legal culpability of the Naval Command, popular debates over who was to blame continued for many years.

The final explosion of World War II was a minor replay of the 1917 Explosion. On 18 July 1945 the Halifax Magazine on the Dartmouth side of Bedford Basin was the site of a series of fires and explosions lasting for 24 hours. Halifax residents who lived north of Quinpool Road were ordered to leave their homes, but thousands

An explosion of at the munitions depot on the Dartmouth side of the Bedford Basin 18-19 July 1945 provided spectacular fireworks but little damage. Although all city residents north of Quinpool Road were evacuated from their homes, many refused to leave, and some enjoyed the sight from the hillside overlooking the Basin.

The end of the war brought another group of new Canadians to Pier 21, the wives and children of Canadian military personnel who had married women from Britain, Europe, and Newfoundland. The warbrides in this photograph arrived aboard the Mauretania.

immediate and concrete ways than those living in other Canadian cities. In 1945, as in 1918, Halifax would have to rebuild. Following two decades of depression the city was very poorly equipped to provide for the demands the war put on the city and it paid a high price for its contribution to the war effort. Despite years of lobbying the federal govern-ment for an acknowledgement of the unique situation in their city, Haligonians received little recognition for the sacrifices they had made and the national reputation of the city was tarnished by the VE Day riots and the complaints of service personnel who returned to their homes after the war telling stories of the hardships they experienced at the hands of rapacious landlords and shopkeepers. As a port and naval station, war had exacted a heavy toll on the city. The consequences of the explosions of both 1917 and 1945 were severe and long lasting and not compensated by the brief wartime booms.

The role of Halifax was unique in Canada during the wars. Haligonians not only enlisted in very high numbers to serve their country in the military and the merchant marine, but also lived in the major North Atlantic centre of operations for naval and

refused. Instead they lined the northern slopes of the city to watch the spectacular fireworks.

The role of Halifax during both world wars was unique in Canada. While all Canadians made sacrifices to support the war effort, the role of Halifax as the major North Atlantic centre of operations for naval and merchant shipping meant that Haligonians, both long-time residents and newcomers, lived with the war in more

merchant shipping. Civilians, side-by-side with military and merchant marine personnel, contributed and sacrificed to support the war effort and shared many of the same frustrations. In 1917 the special role of Halifax created the conditions that led to the explosion of the *Imo* and the *Mont Blanc*. In 1945 war once again created the conditions that led to the destructive VE Day riots.

Chapter Eight

URBAN RENEWAL
(1946-1980)

In the summer of 1949 Haligonians celebrated 200 years of European settlement with much fanfare and a program that included concerts, parades, and fireworks. A Bicentenary Operetta—"a bright and attractive musical based on the Founding of Halifax"—was performed. Many events drew Haligonians to the waterfront. The British and American navies visited, and a parade of decorated boats lit up the harbour. There was a Bicentenary Art Display, "200 Years of Halifax in Pictures." The Halifax Press Club and the Nova Scotia Branch of the Canadian Women's Press Club sponsored a special beauty pageant. According to Mayor Gordon S. Kinley, "The 200th birthday party of beautiful old lady Halifax needed to recognize modern beauty," and "girls" from the American seaboard were invited to compete with Maritimers. Those who wanted the glamour of American popular culture could watch the "Congress of Hollywood Auto Daredevils," attend a Wild West Rodeo or go to the circus.

Although Haligonians pulled out all the stops to celebrate the bi-centennial in 1949, the city was still drab and war-weary, the scars of a lengthy depression and the six taxing years of World War II were still visible. For the decade following the war the pace of change was very slow in Halifax, but in June 1946 the council adopted a master

The juxtaposition of the horse-drawn cart photographed against a billboard advertising cars symbolizes the persistence of older ways in the midst of a modern postwar city.

Even the post office got into the act of celebrating Halifax's 200th birthday, with a special stamp and an official first day cover.

plan for postwar reconstruction, and a rebuilding process began. By the 1960s the pace had quickened, and Haligonians witnessed and participated in changes in every aspect of the life of the city. Urban renewal and suburbanisation changed the look of the city and the way Haligonians lived in it. Residents joined the war against poverty, participated in a vital and lively citizens' movement, and prospered as a result of massive amounts of federal funding designed to ease regional disparity and expand the defence, medical, educational and research establishments in the city.

The Post-War Economy

Canadian Prime Minister Mackenzie King was determined to achieve a smooth transition to peace. He desperately wanted to avoid a return to depression or a repeat of Canada's 1919 labour revolt. During the war the federal Liberals commissioned a series of studies and reports designed to ensure a prosperous peace for all Canadians (and fend off the challenge of growing support for the CCF). By the end of the war

labour unions had been given new legal rights, and veterans' benefits were adopted to assist the return to civilian life. Social programs such as Unemployment Insurance and Family Allowances were introduced. The federal government also announced a number of large public works projects to provide employment for Canadians. These programs and projects offered little to Halifax in the short run. Some, such as construction of the St. Lawrence Seaway, were greeted with justifiable concern in the city because it would draw shipping directly to Montreal and away from Halifax.

The Maritimes did not share in the postwar prosperity enjoyed in much of the rest of the country. Neither the region nor the city shared in the benefits of increased investment and employment in the resource, manufacturing and service sectors. The continuing decline of manufacturing in Halifax was a legacy of C.D. Howe's wartime policies of encouraging the development of a strong, industrial economy centralized in Quebec and Ontario through federal

Cartoonist Robert Chambers provided a daily dose of satire for generations of Haligonian newspaper readers.

Harness racing on the Halifax Commons was a regular occurance during the 1940s and 1950s until the opening of Sackville Downs Raceway.

government investment. By the end of the war, central Canada had considerably strengthened its manufacturing base in a number of key areas, including rubber, chemicals, and electrical appliances, all of which experienced strong demand during the years following the war. Halifax had received almost no federal investment to encourage or stimulate manufacturing, and local manufacturers found it difficult to compete. In the summer of 1945 Haligonians, worn out from the stresses and strains of six years of war, were still clearing up the debris from the VE Day Riots. With the abrupt ending to the economic boom of war, Halifax was left with few benefits. It was not until the late 1950s that the impact of new federal spending brought prosperity to the city.

The boom had aggravated many of the city's pre-war problems and little money had been spent on the city's infrastructure. The housing crisis remained acute, exacerbated by the flood of returning veterans. For many years Haligonians, unable to find affordable housing, lived in temporary wartime barracks dotted all over the city. The crumbling nineteenth-century waterworks were badly in need of repair—half the water being pumped through the city's water supply system was leaking into the ground. Getting on and off the peninsula remained difficult. Long lines of cars waited for the ferry to Dartmouth, and the growing volume of commuter traffic was slowed by bottlenecks at the end of the North West Arm and the entrance to the Bedford Highway.

Postwar inflation combined with the removal of price controls and rationing added to the problems. In early January 1948 citizens interviewed by the Halifax *Mail* complained about the high cost of living, especially food prices. Mrs. John Hayes complained,

It's wicked the way prices have been going up and up. I actually don't know how some people on really small incomes manage to live at all. Personally, I notice the difficulty of buying when I go shopping for meats and butter. It's time we had some helpful controls back again.[1]

A coalition of housewives and workers protested rising prices and called for a federal investigation. The Halifax Housewives and Consumers Association held a public meeting to address the problem, and on 15 January 1948 over a hundred members took the issue to Halifax City Council and planned a house-to-house petition campaign for the re-imposition of 1946 price ceilings on food. Employees at the Halifax Shipyards formally protested rising food prices and members of the Halifax Trades and Labour Council signed the housewives' petitions and took their campaign to the radio airwaves. Lloyd Shaw, provincial secretary of the Cooperative Commonwealth Federation (CCF)—the forerunner of the NDP—expressed his party's concern about high prices. Wartime price controls were not reinstated and the cost of living continued to rise, causing hardship for many families.

Nor did Prime Minister Mackenzie King's policies ensure peace on the labour front. In April 1949 the Halifax waterfront was the scene of one of the most violent confrontations in the domestic politics of the Cold War in Canada. In 1948 Canadian shipping companies, with the collusion of the Canadian government, invited the U.S.-based Seafarer's International Union (SIU) and its gangster-leader Hal Banks to come into Canada to break the Canadian Seamen's Union (CSU), which was accused of being Communist led. The political hysteria which accompanied the allegations made by Igor Gouzenko, an employee at the Soviet embassy in Ottawa, that there was a Russian a spy ring operating in Canada was further inflamed when CSU leader Pat Sullivan admitted he was a communist.

During World War II Canada had developed the fourth largest merchant marine in the world and through the CSU merchant seamen had improved wages and working conditions. In March 1949 the CSU struck the Lady Boats. In the cold early morning hours of 6 April a dozen or so strikers were walking the picket line in front of the *Lady Rodney* when a freight train rolled onto the dock. Two hundred armed SIU-recruited replacement workers got off the train and boarded the ship. Two hundred helmeted and armed CNR police prevented the handful of legal CSU picketers from interfering. Once aboard, the replacement workers taunted the CSU picketers and opened fire on them from the deck. Eight men were injured, one seriously. As soon as the barrage let up the CSU picketers gathered up their wounded members and took them for medical treatment.

The next morning the Halifax labour movement reacted with shock and outrage. Tugboat seamen walked off the job. Four thousand marched on City Hall demanding action. J.K. Bell, head of the Marine Workers Union denounced the "goons," and the Halifax District Labour Council issued a statement that the "shooting of seamen engaged in a legal strike by imported gangsters is one of the most disgraceful things that has ever happened in the history of Halifax." The CSU finally conceded defeat in October, although Banks' reign of intimidation and corruption in Canada's merchant marine continued until the early 1960s when the Canadian TLC demanded a government inquiry. When the Norris Commission reported in 1963 it confirmed what the Halifax strikers had known all

In 1949 Haligonians bid a sad farewell to the old tram cars known as "Birneys."

On the tram car:

GOOD-BYE, MY FRIENDS, GOOD-BYE.

GOOD-BYE MY FRIENDS, THIS IS THE END; I'VE TRAVELLED MILES AND MILES
AND WATCHED YOUR FACES THROUGH THE YEARS, SHOW ANGER TEARS AND SMILES;
ALTHOUGH YOU'VE CRITICIZED MY LOOKS AND SAID I WAS TOO SLOW,
I GOT YOU THERE AND BROUGHT YOU BACK, THROUGH RAIN AND SLEET AND SNOW

health care. Over the next decade military and social spending had an enormous impact on Halifax, home to several universities and a large hospital complex, as well as the east coast headquarters of Canada's navy. Expansion of the government services at the provincial and municipal levels in the 1950s and 1960s also created new jobs for Haligonians and their suburban neighbours. Finally, during the 1950s, Maritime provincial premiers were successful in persuading Prime Minister John Diefenbaker to introduce a series of regional development programs which also helped revitalize the Halifax economy.

In January 1960, Mayor John Lloyd sponsored a "Halifax 1980 Conference" and appointed a Citizens' Planning Committee to take stock and make plans for the next two decades. The committee hired Dalhousie University economist Alasdair M. Sinclair to study the local economy and suggest future trends. His report confirmed the importance of the defence services industry, and identified it as the fastest growing employer of labour in Halifax since 1921. The armed forces provided year-round employment, and military spending was largely recession-

along: Banks was an "outlaw, hoodlum, rogue and villain."[2] Following the release of the report Banks returned to the United States and eluded extra-dition to Canada to face trial.

Despite the bumpy transition to peace by the 1950s there were signs of hope for the local economy. The federal government increased military expenditures as the Cold War heated up, and adopted new funding programs for post-secondary education and proof. Trade was also important. Halifax functioned as the distribution centre for much of Nova Scotia, and both retail and mail-order businesses were major employers. Sinclair also identified education and health as "basic industries" in metropolitan Halifax. During the 1959-1960 school term over 4000 students were enrolled in the nine post-secondary education institutions in the Halifax area. The manufacturing sector, however, continued its decline. In the early 1960s Burnside Industrial Park was established in Dartmouth, and many of its first tenants were Halifax manufacturing and distribution companies who found land on the peninsula too expensive to allow for expansion. However, most of the businesses in the new industrial park were not manufacturers, but wholesale distributors, providing Halifax and the region with goods manu-factured outside the region.

Government spending has always been vital to the well-being of Halifax. The city's role as the major Atlantic coast station meant that the Navy continued to be an important employer—even more important after the reforms of the 1960s which substantially increased military salaries. However, in the decades following World War II there was dramatic expansion of the civilian role of government, especially administration, education and health care. The Massey Commission in the 1950s recommended federal assistance to post-secondary education, which, in combination with the much larger numbers of students attending universities as the baby boom generation began to finish highschool in the early 1960s, resulted in major expansion at all the city's universities. And Halifax had a large number of universities and colleges, including Dalhousie, Saint Mary's, Mount Saint Vincent, the Nova Scotia College of Art and Design and the Nova Scotia Technical College. The introduction of government funded hospital insurance in 1958 and medicare in 1969 greatly expanded the city's medical establishment, and augmented government payrolls in the city. The Nova Scotia government also expanded its services in the 1950s and 1960s. The baby boom caused a boom in school construction and created an insatiable demand for teachers, who were able to bargain effectively for higher wages.

Halifax joined the postwar boom a little later than most of Canada, and when it did its prosperity was based in very large

measure on both new and old forms of government services. Halifax continued its important role as Canada's major east coast naval base and expanded its role as a regional centre for post-secondary education, scientific and medical research, and health care. Although there were a number of private companies which benefitted from the expansion in the emerging knowledge-based economy in the city, the new pillars of the Halifax economy were to a large degree sustained by government spending. By 1975, in the face of rapid inflation and economic stagnation, the federal government began to curtail the social and military spending so vital to Halifax, and the provincial and municipal governments had little choice but to follow suit because their own revenues were so dependent on federal funds. Ottawa's decision to tighten the purse strings presented a challenge to the city in the late 1970s, and for a while it looked as if the city's prosperity might falter. Haligonians would once again be challenged to find new economic strategies in the coming decade.

Modernizing Halifax

The social and political geography of Halifax underwent substantial changes in the years following World War II. Like people in the rest of the country, Haligonians joined the exodus to the suburbs. In 1969 the old city of Halifax annexed the mainland western suburbs of Jollimore, Purcell's Cove, Spryfield, Armdale, Kline Heights, Fairview, Rockingham and Kearney Lake. These areas experienced significant residential and commercial growth in the postwar period, and suburban residents wanted city services such as sewerage, water, and public transit. The amalgamation increased the population of the city by 35,000 to 123,000, making Halifax the thirteenth largest city in Canada, and outstripping once again the population of its traditional rival, Saint John, New Brunswick. The land mass of the city increased by 300 percent, from 4,500 acres to 13,500. The *Chronicle Herald* pointed out that Dartmouth was actually larger in land mass than Halifax, although it had only about half the population. However, its growth had, in fact, been the most remarkable in the metropolitan area. Stimulated by the building of two harbour bridges and the

Official motorcade inaugurating the Angus L. Macdonald Bridge in 1955.

insatiable post-war demand for suburban housing, Dartmouth had grown from a small town of about 10,000 during the war to a city of 60,000 people. Other suburban areas also flourished and grew after the war. In the 1950s the Nova Scotia government stimulated residential development in Sackville through its co-operative housing program. In the 1960s, Clayton Park, a huge middle-class residential development, began to fill the land between Fairview and Rockingham. Federal programs designed to assist home ownership provided the impetus for suburban townhouse developments in areas such as Cowie Hill in Armdale and Cole Harbour, in the early 1970s, and a municipal public housing project in Spryfield further stimulated the move to the suburbs. The contrast between the old city and the new suburban development was more marked in Halifax than in many other Canadian cities because other than some building in the west end, there was very little home construction in the inter-war years. The architectural legacy of two decades of depression was the virtual absence of neighbourhoods built in the 1920s and 1930s.

Among the most visible signs of change in Halifax were the changes in urban transportation. In 1949 the old tramcars were retired from duty and replaced by bright yellow electric trolley coaches. These provided service until 1970 when the Halifax Transit System was formed and a fleet of diesel buses took over public transit. In 1955 the long awaited Halifax–Dartmouth bridge, named for Nova Scotia's long-serving premier Angus L. Macdonald, opened to considerable fanfare. The same year

Leroy Zwicker, Halifax Looking North, 1959. Oil on canvas. Dalhousie University Art Gallery. Leroy Zwicker and his wife Marguerite Porter Zwicker were central figures in the Halifax visual arts community. Both had distinguished careers as painters, but they also owned and operated the oldest and best known art store and commercial gallery in Halifax—Zwicker's Gallery on Doyle Street.

construction began on a new civilian airport at Kelly Lake, almost 50 kilometres outside the city on the road to Truro. The old airport on Chebucto Road had been closed and the naval airport at Shearwater, on the Dartmouth side of the harbour, served as the civilian airport until 1960, when the Halifax International Airport opened. It has served the city ever since and within a few years of opening could be reached by Bi-centennial Drive, which allowed commuters to bypass the sprawling suburban development in Sackville, Bedford and Rockingham.

The port also underwent major changes in the period, especially with the building of the first container port in the late 1960s. The Port of Halifax fell on hard times after the war as convoys disappeared and shipping lines increasingly used the port of Montreal. Canada's sea-going merchant marine was effectively disbanded in the late 1940s, and traffic through the port slowed. Despite the opening of the St. Lawrence Seaway in 1956, and more aggressive ice-breaking efforts in the Seaway a decade later the situation gradually improved. The amount of cargo entering and leaving Halifax increased slowly and steadily from the early 1950s until the mid-1970s. In 1952 the Halifax Port Commission was established to promote the port and encourage the development of improved facilities. The increase in shipping had little impact on waterfront employment, however, and work on the waterfront supported a smaller proportion of the Halifax workforce than it had in earlier decades.

The Port Commission, headed by lawyer J.W.E. Mingo,

recognized that the port would have to make significant changes in order to continue to compete successfully with other Atlantic ports. It faced the challenge in typical postwar fashion, by hiring an expert. In 1965, New York consultant John Kneiling recommended the construction of a container terminal. The introduction of standard sized shipping containers that could be transferred from ships to trains and trucks with a minimum of handling was being adopted by many shipping lines in the 1960s. Port officials quickly embraced Kneiling's recommendation, and in 1969 the Port of Halifax opened the

Halifax's new public library at the corner of Spring Garden Road and Grafton Street was a memorial to those who had died in World War II.

first purpose-built common user container terminal in Canada. The new facility, just south of the older Ocean Terminals, was operated by Halterm, a consortium of the Canadian National Railways, Clarke Transport of Montreal, and the Halifax and Nova Scotia governments.

The introduction of containerization changed the look and feel of the Halifax waterfront:

> *The finger piers and complex docks in the heart of the city, worked by gangs of men and highly visible to passers-by, were replaced by brightly lit large open spaces on the periphery of the old downtown area, served by container cranes, conveyor belts or pipelines.3*

It also changed the rhythm of work on the waterfront. Containerization reduced the stevedoring workforce, but the work changed from a seasonal and casual occupation to a year-round highly paid job.

The media, both old and new, also underwent change in this period. On 1 January 1949 the first editions of newly merged city newspapers hit the streets of Halifax. The morning edition was called the *Chronicle Herald*, and provided more provincial news. In the afternoon the *Mail Star* appeared. These two newspapers, really two editions of the same paper produced by the Halifax Herald Limited, dominated the newspaper market throughout the period. However, from 1969 until 1977 the dailies faced competition from the lively weekly the *4th Estate*. In December 1954 television broadcasting began in Halifax, from the new CBC television studios on Bell Road. No longer would Haligonians be faced with the frustrating evening task of trying to tune into snowy American channels. A few years later CJCH radio also expanded into television production and broadcasting, and Halifax become a two-channel town.

In the summer of 1957 the opening of the Bayers Road Shopping Centre inaugurated the era of the suburban mall. While Simpson's had pioneered suburban shopping when it built its Halifax store in Armdale in the 1920s, its success was due in large part to the trams which brought shoppers to its door. The Bayers Road Shopping Centre was designed for cars. When the Halifax Shopping Centre opened in the Bayers Road area in the early 1960s, the suburban west end became the major retail shopping district. By the mid-1960s there were no longer any major department stores in downtown Halifax.

For many Halifax children in the 1950s and 1960s, Christmas included a visit to Nova Light and Power's Fantasy Land, shown here in 1959. Each year the basement of the Capitol Building on Barrington Street was cleared of merchandise and became Fantasy Land, designed by Carl Edwards, long-time company display artist.

Barrington Street entered a long slow decline; Gottingen Street lost business more quickly under the combined impact of suburban shopping and urban renewal.

Wartime residents in Halifax had complained bitterly about the dearth of restaurants and bars in the city, something largely related to highly restrictive liquor laws. In 1946, and again in 1948, the citizens of Halifax voted two to one in favour of allowing the sale of beer and wine by the glass—to men. Women had to wait until the 1960s for the same right. At ten o'clock on the morning of 27 September, 1948, the Sea-Horse Tavern, the first to pass the stringent inspection of liquor license inspectors, opened for business. Within 20 minutes the Sea-Horse had served over fifty thirsty customers, and later in the day would-be drinkers lined up for beer. In 1961 liquor laws were further liberalized to permit restaurants to apply for lounge licenses, which permitted not only beer and wine, but also spirits, to be served. The Carousel Restaurant on Barrington Street, for example, opened the Peppermint Lounge and attracted customers with live performances by local musicians. In 1964 the law permitted establishment of ladies beverage rooms where men and women could sit and drink. By the 1970s restaurants and bars had multiplied rapidly in the city, providing a boost to the local economy and the music industry. Despite liberalized liquor laws, private clubs, the post-prohibition sites of public drinking, such as Graham and Bill Downey's Arrows Club, which billed itself as the "soul centre of the Maritimes," continued to be popular.

The Politics of Urban Renewal

The Sea Horse Tavern was the first to open for business when tavern licences were re-introduced in Halifax in 1948.

Urban development dominated City Council's agenda from the late 1940s into the mid-1970s. Council followed up its 1946 master plan for postwar redevelopment with an official town plan in 1950. These committed the city to implement slum clearance, construct public housing, complete the Westmount subdivision on the site of the former Halifax airport on Chebucto Road, improve city streets and build a bridge across the harbour to Dartmouth. In 1957 Halifax City Council hired Toronto town-planner Gordon Stephenson to develop a comprehensive plan for urban renewal.

Lack of adequate housing was a perennial theme at council meetings throughout the twentieth-century. After 1945 the council regarded the provision of more, better and cheaper housing as a great panacea. It would provide construction jobs, bring in attractive funding from provincial and federal governments, and beautify the city. In the late 1940s, while the housing shortage remained acute, the

A map of the city of Halifax from the Stephenson Report which proposed sweeping redevelopment of the city's older neighbourhoods.

limited supply of public housing was shrinking thanks to the sale of wartime pre-fabs and the houses owned by the Halifax Relief Commission in the Hydrostone district. At the same time, the city acquired some of the temporary military barracks to use as emergency shelters. These quickly became permanent homes for families caught in the housing crunch. In the early 1950s the city developed a new public housing project in the suburban northwest end of the city, just north of Bayers Road.

Suburban development was less controversial than "slum clearance" in older residential neighbourhoods. In January 1954 property owners and community groups complained about plans for the northend neighbourhood bounded by Charles, Gerrish, Gottingen and Agricola Streets. The Rev. W.P. Oliver, representing the Nova Scotia Association for the Advancement of Coloured People, opposed the rezoning and proposed slum clearance in the area because of the negative affect it would have on black homeowners and tenants. Oliver feared that black homeowners who allowed their properties to be cleared would not obtain adequate alternative housing. He pointed out that black families were not welcome in the city's new Bayers Road public

housing development. In a short speech that in many ways set the political tone for the later destruction of Africville, Oliver said,

We cannot conscientiously support anything that suggests segregation, which is alien to our way of life in a democratic country. Segregation serves only to create ghettos resulting in segregated schools and other unfavourable situations that will handicap a wholesome development in the city as a whole.[4]

In 1957 Gordon Stephenson, Professor of Town and Regional Planning at the University of Toronto, drew up a plan that was to have far-reaching consequences for Halifax. Although he pointed out that Halifax "is one of the oldest cities in Canada, also one of the most beautiful," Stephenson recommended that a large tract of land

Aileen Meagher, Brunswick and Buckingham 1951. *Despite the enthusiasm for redevelopment in the old core of the city, artists such as Aileen Meagher and John Cook preserved images of the old city in their work.*

now occupied by Scotia Square be completely cleared and redeveloped. He also recommended removal of the community of Africville. Spurred on by the availability of substantial federal funding under the revised terms of the National Housing Act, City Council acted quickly on Stephenson's recommendations.

In October 1958 plans were unveiled for Mulgrave Park, a large public housing development at the north end of Barrington Street. All the units would have electric stoves and fridges and shared laundry facilities would be provided. Streets in the development would reflect the city's seaport heritage—they were named for famous ships such as the Jarvis Bay, the Niobe, and the Aquitania. The total estimated cost of the project was $4.3 million and the federal government would pay 75 percent, with the remaining 25 percent to be shared equally by the Province and the City. Although the new project was greeted with general enthusiasm by members of the council, some members expressed an anxiety

This 1961 photograph, taken from Hurd Street looking northeast along Star St.

that recalled the parsimonious and paternal attitudes toward those in need that had characterized the 1920s and 1930s. Alderman Abbie Lane, who had long advocated action on the housing crisis, was worried about whether the tenants would take good care of their new electric appliances. Alderman Dennis Connolly was concerned that the development would quickly become another slum—a fear repeated frequently at City Council and which arose from time to time in the local press.

The Novelli family—Frances and Clara and their eight children were the first residents of Mulgrave Park. They moved in with considerable fanfare just before Christmas 1960. Representatives from the Halifax Housing Authority wished the Novellis "good health and

good living" in this "big wonderful Mulgrave Park," and Mr. and Mrs. Novelli were reportedly very pleased with their home. The Novellis probably already knew most of their new neighbours. Priority was given to people whose homes had been destroyed by the slum clearances in the Maitland and Jacob Street areas. Once these people had been provided with housing, those living in the city's emergency shelters were permitted to apply, and after their needs were taken care of, others who met the income qualification (a maximum annual income of $3,900) were eligible to apply.

The destruction of Africville is justifiably one of the most written about chapters in the history of the city. A tragedy for the people who lived in the community and their descendants, Africville has become a

The north end suburb of Africville was destroyed by the urban planners of the 1950s and 1960s.

The residents of Africville took pride in their community, and resentment about the relocation continues to shape race relations in the city.

compelling example of the dangers of urban redevelopment. It has also become an important rallying point for Haligonians of African descent as they continue the struggle to eliminate racism in the city. No incident so clearly illuminates the social and political currents eddying through Halifax at this time. Rather than offering clearly recognizable heroes and villains, the story of Africville presents an uneasy coalition of Halifax boosters seeking industrial development and people of good will and social conscience, both black and white, strongly imbued with the integrationist ambitions of the mid-twentieth-century black civil rights movement.

Throughout Africville's long history, the City of Halifax refused to deliver basic municipal services to the community. The absence of city water was a particular hardship for residents who lacked safe drinking water and the water pressure essential to combat fire. While the Public Service Commission was putting in new water mains along Dutch Village Road on the western edge of town, the much older suburb of Africville continued to rely on inadequate wells. In December 1947, six Africville homes were destroyed by fire. Lack of water supply was identified as the cause of the extensive damage, and early in the new year City Council commissioned a report on the possibility of providing water to the community. Instead, in 1954 the City Manager recommended that the resident population of 300 people be moved. In 1962 City Council agreed, and began what was euphemistically called the "relocation" of Africville.

Once again the City Council hired an expert, this time Toronto social worker Albert Rose, to develop a plan. Rose recommended that people who had a deed to their properties should receive market value, which was not a fair or defensible approach under the circumstances because the council's failure to provide adequate services to the community, especially water, had resulted in a deterioration of property values in the area. Other residents would receive a minimum of $500, depending on their family size. The displaced people would be moved to public housing, but Rose recommended that the residents should be dispersed in order to promote racial integration in Halifax. The term "relocation" is not a description of what happened to Africville. Residents were not relocated together to a new location, but rather were dispersed. Rose also argued that all should receive guidance about employment and help in adjusting to their new surroundings, although follow-up studies suggest this did not happen.

The process did not lack for critics. In April 1965, city welfare director H.B. Jones drew the anger of Council when he pointed out that if the city had provided water and sewer to Africville the relocation would be unnecessary. In June the CBC presented a program critical of the move, and in October 1967 *Maclean's* magazine followed suit. But the most severe criticism came from black human rights organi-zations in support of Aaron Carvery, the last

A large tract of land in the heart of the city's downtown was cleared to make room for Scotia Square.

resident to reach a settlement with the city. Carvery believed his property to be worth $35,000. In 1966 the City offered him $30,000, which he refused to accept. In the fall of 1969, Council decided to offer him just $14,387.76 for his property, and to expropriate it if he refused. In December, Carvery was invited to City Hall and shown a suitcase containing $14,000 in cash as an inducement to settle. The plan backfired when Carvery went to the Nova Scotia Association for the Advancement of Coloured People and the Black United Front with the story. Both organizations were outraged, and demanded an investigation. City Solicitor Murphy and Social Planner Harold Crowell, who had both attended the meeting, apologized, but the tide of public opinion had obviously turned on the issue of the relocation of Africville.

Unfortunately it was too late to save the community. Resentment about the destruction of Africville continued to surface in Halifax, and the community has been remembered in music, literature, and politics ever since.

Urban renewal struck in the heart of the city as well as on the periphery. In the 1960s the area just to the north of City Hall was demolished. Poplar Grove, and Buckingham, Jacob, Hurd and Starr streets disappeared entirely, along with houses, stores, restaurants and the Clayton's Clothing Factory. An old residential and business district was replaced by the sprawling, modern Scotia Square complex. The project included apartment and office towers, the Trade Mart, a hotel, and a shopping mall, and covered several blocks immediately to the north of City Hall and the Grand Parade.

Among the buildings razed for Scotia Square was the "new" city market. In 1917 the Halifax Farmers' Market, known for years as the Green Market, moved into brand new quarters on Market Street. The building was renovated in the early 1950s when the Police Department moved in upstairs. But the market building did not survive the passion for urban redevelopment. Saturday, 31 May 1969 was the last day area farmers brought their produce to the old location: the building was razed for the third phase of Scotia Square. The market moved first to temporary quarters in the Industrial Building at the Halifax Forum, a few years later to a temporary location in the Devonshire Rink at the foot of Fort Needham. In the 1980s the Farmers' Market found new quarters in the former Keith's Brewery on Water Street.

Every summer Halifax children held neighbourhood fundraisers in support of Camp Rainbow Haven.

Political Reaction

In 1970 Mayor Allan O'Brien told the dozen international experts assembled for Encounter on Urban Environment,

In spite of the notes of doubt or cynicism which you may find among municipal politicians, we do welcome the experts. We are used to hiring them. We sometimes think by the bushel.[5]

In the years following World War II "bushels" of experts told Haligonians what was wrong with their city and how to fix it. Experts on urban renewal, regional economic development, social work and human rights offered their criticisms and their cures, and for a long time—perhaps too long—Haligonians listened. But by 1970, as the tone of Mayor O'Brien's comment suggests, Haligonians were becoming more sceptical of the advice of the experts and were banding together to demand a louder voice in urban planning and government policy. Their voices changed the face of the city.

Urban renewal provided concrete evidence of more elusive social changes in Halifax. In some respects economic and social change went hand in hand. The expansion of government services increased the number and importance of health, education and research professionals. Urban renewal and suburban expansion created new opportunities for developers, architects, and construction companies. Lawyers proliferated and flourished amidst the changes. Contrary to popular mythology, membership in the financial elite was not confined to the old Halifax merchantocracy. The board of directors of Halifax Developments Limited, the consortium formed to build Scotia Square included members of old merchant and industrial families and lawyers along with newcomers to the Halifax business community such as Roy Jodrey of Hantsport and Frank Sobey of Stellarton.

A steady trickle of immigrants from other parts of the world, particularly from countries bordering on the Mediterranean, and migrants from other parts of Nova Scotia and from the rest of Canada, also contributed to the changes in the city. Many newcomers reported difficulty in feeling accepted in the city, but recent arrivals and long-time Haligonians often found ways to work together to change the face of the city and its personality.

As the population of the city became more diverse, there were also changes in the peculiar institutional accommodation between Protestants and Catholics. In the nineteenth century Haligonians had created an unusual—perhaps a unique—system of parallel institutions. For example, Halifax had one board of school commissioners which, since 1866, had maintained separate schools for Protestants and Catholics. In the 1940s and 1950s new high schools were constructed for protestant and catholic students, replacing buildings opened in the 1870s. Queen Elizabeth opened for protestant students in 1942, and St. Patrick's, the catholic high school opened in 1952. They were both within a stone's throw of the central Willow Tree intersection.

In 1954 Montreal-born Joseph Gerald Berry, moved from Peterborough, Ontario, to become the archbishop of the Halifax archdiocese. In a letter to a friend he commented on what he regarded as the comfortable relationship between Catholics and Protestants in Halifax. He noted for example, that both Richard A. Donahoe, mayor of Halifax and Angus L. Macdonald, the premier of Nova Scotia, were Catholics, and claimed that social relationships between Protestants and Catholics were more amicable in Halifax than was the case in Montreal, and that Catholics enjoyed considerable political power and prestige in the city.

In 1966 the local press lamented the end of what it claimed was a century-long tradition of alternating protestant and catholic mayors in Halifax when catholic Mayor Charles Vaughan decided to run for a third term of office against the protestant candidate Allan O'Brien. The myth of a "gentlemen's agreement" of a rotating mayoralty has been remarkably durable. It was, in fact, a short tradition in Halifax, dating back only to 1946, a short twenty years before its demise in the Vaughan-O'Brien election. In the years between 1918 and 1966 there were three examples of protestant and catholic mayors succeeding one another in Halifax. During World War II, Halifax had had two protestant mayors in succession. John E. Lloyd served from 1943 to 1945, and Allan M. Butler, 1945-46. The symbolic importance of an electoral race between a protestant and a catholic mayoralty candidate in 1966 must have been seen as significant by Haligonians as they participated in changes in the social structure of their city. In the 1970s, as a result of the amalgamation of the western mainland suburbs—where there was no tradition of separate denominational schools—the system of protestant and catholic education gradually withered away.

The changes reflected a combination of the increasing secularization of civic life and a new commitment to human rights. In the first half of the twentieth century many social clubs in Halifax discriminated in the selection of members on the basis of race, religion and ethnicity. In 1962 Oakfield Golf and Country Club was established on a different basis: its constitution forbade such discrimination. In 1964 in the wake of embarrassing publicity, the Waegwoltic Club finally eliminated its policy of not admitting Jews. In 1978 the newspaper *Barometer* reported that when it came to joining clubs in Halifax "blueblood's no longer needed but lots of the long green [cash] is."

The sensitivity to cultural diversity was manifested at the amalgamation of the old city of Halifax with its mainland western suburbs. On 1 January 1969 these areas were annexed to the city, and the event was marked by a special midnight ceremony of civic officials in front of City Hall. The event, chaired by Deputy Mayor Nick Meagher, symbolized new attempts at inclusiveness in Halifax. Dr. Max Wallach, rabbi of Shaar Shalom Synagogue gave the invocation, Anglican Bishop W.W. Davis and Father Richard Murphy of St. Mary's Basilica offered prayers, and the Rev. Wrenford Bryant, pastor of Cornwallis Street United Baptist Church blessed the city's flag.

In February 1970 Haligonians took a long and critical look at where they had come in recent decades. Encounter on Urban Environment was a week-long planning exercise organized by Nova Scotia Voluntary Planning and the Nova Scotia government. A dozen male experts from a variety of fields were invited to meet with representatives from industry, government, the arts community, as well as with education and voluntary organizations. They conducted nightly televised public meetings. It was an ambitious project, and in some respects, it was the last gasp of the era of outside experts.

The Encounter team, nicknamed the Twelve Apostles, found fault with all levels of government, with economic development strategies, and with the education system. They discussed racism, poverty, and inadequate housing. They pointed out that incomes in Halifax were less than two-thirds of the national average. They charged

Haligonians generally, and the media particularly, with racism and a complacent acceptance of the status quo. The city's 1200 citizen groups, they argued, had "indignation without strategy."

Haligonians followed the process with growing interest. Each evening the public meetings attracted larger audiences; ratings for the televised proceedings shot up. Many brought their grievances. The labour movement complained about the treatment of labour issues in the media and education system. The destruction of Africville resurfaced vividly when Hattie Carvery told the story of the destruction of a once vibrant community and spoke of the indignity of being moved out in garbage trucks and put "right down in the slums." Gus Wedderburn, president of the Nova Scotia Association for the Advancement of Coloured People (NSAACP), and a member of the Encounter planning committee claimed that "[t]he blacks who manage to make progress in Nova Scotia were the blacks with black masks and white souls."

Amateur sport continued to attract players and fans in the postwar years. In 1957 the Halifax Royals Midget baseball team were provincial and Maritime champions.

The Encounter team showed much less interest in women's issues than in racism. In part this lack of attention reflected the times, but women's issues were on the national and the local political agenda in the late 1960s. Members of the Encounter team were dismissive of women and their concerns. Sociologist Scott Greer, for example, referred mockingly to a "powder puff assault by the Women's Liberation Movement" at one of the sessions. And suggestions that well-known urban theorist and activist Jane Jacobs would have made an excellent contribution to the Encounter process were greeted with ridicule. When Muriel Duckworth of the Voice of Women asked why no women had been appointed to the team, the experts responded patronizingly, some claiming that the process was too arduous for women, others suggesting that it would have been impossible to find suitably qualified women.

The Twelve Apostles obviously misjudged the vigour of the revived women's movement in Halifax in the early 1970s. *The 4th Estate*, in addition to carrying on a detailed commentary on the city's war on poverty and the struggle of the black community for civil rights, provided extensive coverage of the activities and issues of the city's burgeoning feminist organizations. Women in Halifax organized to fight for better wages, access to male-dominated occupations and credit, and improved social assistance rates. They pressed for more extensive medical services, including abortion and birth control. Until the mid-1970s a number of Halifax physicians refused to prescribe the birth control pill to unmarried women, despite the public outcry against rising numbers of unmarried mothers. The Women's Bureau, formed in 1971, received funding to document women's economic, political, and legal disadvantage, and encouraged the labour movement to take a more active role in unionizing women workers in Halifax. Women's centres, film festivals and new organizations proliferated.

The lack of adequate and affordable daycare services in Halifax was a persistent problem throughout the 1970s. Although Nova Scotia passed daycare legislation in the 1960s, by the mid-1970s only nine daycare centres were operating in the city, some of them just on a part-time basis. Parents faced high costs; daycare workers were paid low wages. And although the city's churches initially supported improved child care, by the early 1970s at least three churches had evicted centres from their premises. The women's movement lobbied hard to improve the services and increase provincial funding for daycare.

The report of the Nova Scotia Task Force on the Status of Women, appointed in 1975 to advise the province on the implications of the report of the federal Royal Commission on the Status of

Women, which had reported in 1970, confirmed women's grievances and recommended redress. Among its recommendations was the establishment of a Nova Scotia Advisory Council on the Status of Women, which opened its Halifax offices in 1980, to provide women with a conduit to provincial bureaucrats and politicians.

Encounter also heard the voices of those involved in the war on poverty in Halifax. In the late 1960s Haligonians, like many others in North America, rediscovered the poverty in their midst. Voluntary organizations and government agencies worked to develop new forms of social welfare and community development, especially in the city's old north end. At the Neighbourhood Centre, for example, community workers investigated the causes and the impact of poverty and worked to find new solutions such as a north end employment centre and a medical clinic. Welfare recipients organized to fight for more adequate social programs and a larger voice in the administration of programs.

Encounter served as a catalyst to bring those concerned with poverty, women's issues and urban planning together in a new coalition of citizens' groups much like those developing in other North American cities in the late 1960s and early 1970s. It brought together groups such as the Heritage Trust, the Downtown Business Association and the Business and Professional Women's Club of Halifax and the Nova Scotia Association for the Advancement of Coloured People, with the newer organizations such as the Africville Action Committee, the Voice of Women, welfare rights groups, single parent family organizations, and public housing tenants associations which had

For over a hundred years several orders of religious women, wearing their distinctive black and white habits, provided social services in Halifax and formed an important element in the streetscapes of the city.

mobilized as part of the social and political ferment of the 1960s.

A new coalition, Movement for Citizen Voice and Action (MOVE), quickly became a force to be reckoned with, demanding much greater public input into the urban planning process. In late 1970 a number of community groups began meeting to discuss their dissatisfaction with the process of the newly created Metropolitan Area Planning Committee (MAPC). By mid-May the coalition had incorporated as MOVE and was beginning the difficult job of juggling the responsibilities of lobbying all levels of government for social change with providing services and training programs for its member organizations.

MOVE's greatest political successes were the in the area of urban planning. These efforts were hard won and generated considerable controversy and sometimes bitter attacks on the coalition. MOVE was sharply critical of the Halifax archdiocese for the sale of its Quinpool Road property to developer Ralph Medjuck, and equally critical of Medjuck's plans for high-density housing the site. However, after years of negotiation a much lower density development was accepted. MOVE's most visible legacy is the Cogswell Street interchange, the elaborate intersection which leads into the narrow, cramped one-way street of the old downtown waterfront district. The Cogswell interchange was designed to connect to Harbour Drive, an expressway planned for the waterfront. Plans for Harbour Drive were scrapped in large part due to the outcry from citizens orchestrated by MOVE and its member organizations, especially Heritage Trust.

The successful campaign to block the construction of the

expressway was part of the broader struggle waged by heritage activists to preserve historic buildings on the waterfront. Although concern about the preservation of these buildings dates back at least to the 1950s, it was not until the 1960s that a concerted move to save the area took shape. Heritage Trust hired Peter John Stokes, a restoration architect, to survey the buildings and prepare a brief for City Council, and enlisted the support of Alderman Allan O'Brien, who remained a steadfast ally. The first success in the campaign was the decision of the city works committee to delay the demolition of any of the waterfront building until the committee had met to discuss it. The city works superintendent ignored this decision, however, and despite Halifax historian and heritage activist Lou Collins' heroic efforts to stay the bulldozers, some buildings were lost. To increase public awareness of the problem, Collins led newspaper reporters on a tour of the buildings. Heritage Trust president Gilbert Hutton appeared on radio and television. Heritage Trust established a "committee of concern," and recruited architect Allan Duffus. In 1966, when Allan O'Brien became mayor, he revived the civic advisory committee on the preservation of historic buildings and chose Lou Collins to chair it.

In the spring of 1967, Harbour Drive, the waterfront expressway was at the top of the council's agenda. City planners and engineers promoted the project, while aldermen were divided on the issue. Many deferred to city staff, but a handful, including Mayor O'Brien and Aldermen Hedley Ivany and Bob Matheson, were more sympathetic to the idea of preserving historic buildings. Despite the best efforts of Heritage Trust it was touch and go, and once again the historic waterfront buildings were slated for destruction. On 19 June 1969 City Council voted to demolish waterfront buildings, but by 1971 it had reversed its stand and was calling for proposals for a redevelopment which would preserve many of the buildings. Two major tenants, the Nova Scotia College of Art and Design, and Parks Canada were secured, and the successful redevelopment of the waterfront was underway.

After 1976 the redevelopment of the Halifax waterfront was controlled and coordinated by the Waterfront Development Corporation (WDC), a provincial crown corporation jointly funded by the provincial government and the federal Department of Regional Economic Expansion (DREE). The mandate of the WDC was to revitalize and restore the downtown harbourfronts of Halifax and Dartmouth in preparation for private development. It spent millions of dollars, especially until the DREE funds dried up in 1982, acquiring property, and improving ferry services, sewerage, power and water utilities. Controversy regularly swirled around WDC, especially in its first years of operation. For several years plans to demolish the Fisherman's Market, a waterfront shop where fresh seafood was brought straight from the dock to customers, attracted a vehement public outcry. In 1981, the destruction of the Irving Arch, built in 1878, and the last of the arched buildings so characteristic of the Halifax waterfront a century ago, occurred over the strong objections of the council and the Ecology Action Centre, and was at the centre of another storm.

By 1980 the full force of the citizens' movement in Halifax was spent, but for a critical time it had mounted an effective campaign against the experts and bureaucrats who had seen the bulldozer as the most effective way to improve the city. Although the next decade would bring severe social and economic challenges some of the best solutions would be found in the preservation and revitalization of the city's historic waterfront, a legacy of the citizens' movement—not of the "bushels" of experts who had come to Halifax in the postwar years.

Chapter Nine

THE NEW OLD CITY
(1980-1999)

The pace of change in Halifax was as rapid in the 1980s and 1990s as in any of the preceding periods in the city's history. Politically, the biggest change in the period was the creation of the new Halifax Regional Municipality in 1996 by the Liberal government of Premier John Savage. The new municipal unit was opposed by many who feared the erosion of municipal services, especially the network of social programs for those in need. The economic life of the city continued to follow trends established in early in the post-World War II years. As manufacturing continued its slow, steady decline, new efforts were made to develop an economy based on tourism, high-tech industries, and offshore gas and oil, and the cultural life of the city entered a new period of vigour and productivity. Art, music, literature, film, and theatre flourished as never before, stimulated by the work of artists and cultural producers themselves, government policies, and some elusive ingredients that provided Halifax with a reputation as "hot" or "cool" depending on one's perspective. Haligonians seemed to enjoy their city more. In the warmer months festivals and special events drew huge crowds to the waterfront and the downtown streets. All year bars, restaurants, theatres, and concert halls drew large appreciative crowds, and the night life regularly continued into the early hours of the next morning.

The new old city is captured in this photograph of Historic Properties in the foreground against the highrises that now make up the city's skyline.

signing of the Free Trade Agreement with the United States in 1988 was an important indicator of the new direction. Employment dropped in all government sectors, including defence, education, and health care. With reductions in public sector employment, local service industries were also affected. By the late 1980s, as Canadians began to talk about the demands of the new global economy, 'downsizing' became a fact of life in the private sector as well.

Manufacturing and the fishery, both important in Halifax in the late-nineteenth and early twentieth centuries, offered little hope of a secure economic future for the city. After the initial burst of industrial investment, manufacturing in Halifax went into a long, slow decline and throughout the twentieth century employment in manufacturing represented an increasingly small proportion of the workforce. Many manufacturers left the peninsula for suburban locations, especially the sprawling Burnside Industrial Park in Dartmouth. In 1998 Volvo closed its Dartmouth car assembly operations after 35 years, resulting in the layoffs of over two hundred workers. At the same time, Irving Shipbuilding Inc announced that the prospects for the 600 workers

Left: Halifax is still a "navy town", and the Naval Yard, located just below Barrington Street, photographed here in the 1980s, remained a highly visible feature of the life of the city. Above: In 1967 the old Ferry Terminal was still an important landmark on the Halifax waterfront, but it was soon to be replaced as part of the renewal of the area.

Restructuring the Economy

Achieving sustained economic prosperity has been a challenge for Haligonians since the city was founded in 1749. Halifax has always depended, to a greater or lesser extent, on government spending for its well-being. Wartime economic booms have been a recurrent theme, and from 1950 to the early 1970s military and social government expenditures played a vital role in city's economy. As the postwar boom gradually petered out, the federal government replaced the goals of social security, regional development, and full employment with policies designed to increase global economic competitiveness through decreased government spending and decreased deficits. The

During the 1980s Haligonians hoped that an offshore oil boom would provide the long-term prosperity that so long eluded the city.

The schooner Bluenose II *berthed at Historic Properties.*

employed by the shipyard were "bleak." The fishery also fell on hard times with the collapse of groundfish stocks, and the fishing industry ceased to be a presence on the Halifax waterfront.

However, the economy of Halifax remained very strong. In 1992 Halifax tied for fourth place with Edmonton in average household income, and the overall unemployment rate remained relatively low. The success of the Halifax economy stood in stark contrast to that of much of the rest of the province, where poverty, unemployment, and rural decline resulted from the collapse of fish stocks, and the continued erosion of Cape Breton's industrial economy. Investment, jobs, and population continued to be more and more centralized in the greater Halifax area.

Despite cutbacks in defence spending, Halifax remained a navy town. In 1985 the Canadian navy returned to its distinctive "navy" blue uniforms, after nearly 20 years of wearing the drabber colours of the unified Canadian armed services, restoring greater visibility of naval personnel in the city. The important role Halifax played in preparations for Canada's participation in the the Gulf War in 1991 provided a vivid reminder that the city is still Canada's east coast naval station. The naval dockyard, which covers a large section of the Halifax waterfront north of Historic Properties was visible evidence to commuters who crossed the Angus L. Macdonald Bridge.

In the early 1980s, the prospect of offshore oil and gas caused considerable optimism among the Halifax business community. For several years the huge drilling rigs moored in Halifax harbour fostered hopes that the future would lie in the offshore. By the late 1980s the rigs were gone and so was the dream. In the late 1990s offshore gas became a modest reality with the Sable Gas project. Downtown office vacancy rates were low and real estate prices were increasing.

Business leaders in Halifax also actively promoted the development of high-tech industries in the city such as information technology and telecommunications, bio-technology, pharmaceuticals and transportation. These new industries continued to build on the health, education, and transportation infrastructure created as a result of federal and provincial government spending of earlier times. One of the great benefits of spending was the development of a highly educated workforce. In the late 1990s the number of post-secondary graduates in Halifax area exceeded the national average by 50 percent. The city's five universities continued to attract students from all over Nova Scotia, Canada, and the world, and provided not only trained workers but also excellent research facilities in a number of areas including marine biology and bio-technology. The program of hospital building in the 1990s, in addition to creating jobs for highly trained workers, also increased the role of Halifax hospitals in regional health care. Education and health care remained vital to the well-being of Haligonians and the local economy.

As in the past, the Port of Halifax continued to play a role in the city's economy. During the 1980s conditions in the international shipping industry were especially favourable to Halifax. The use of larger vessels, load-centre ports and the practice of following the great circle route all increased the competitiveness of the port. Conditions in the 1990s were less favourable to Halifax, but the city was served by two container facilities and an autoport and continued to handle bulk cargoes such as forest products and nickel oxide from Cuba for mines in Alberta, and break bulk cargoes such as crude and refined oil, gypsum and a small amount of grain for local consumption. "Roll on-roll off" cargoes including cars, and heavy equipment for the military and the construction industry also passed through the port. In 1998 a new, more autonomous agency, the Halifax Port Corporation, was created to replace the National Harbours Board. Employment in the port remained fairly constant during the 1980s and 1990s at about 2400 jobs, with an additional

The Halterm Container Terminal located at the south end of the Halifax waterfront.

5000 spinoff jobs. The port also continued to generate revenues from side wharfage, harbour dues from visiting ships, and pilotage fees.

Amidst what appeared to be a new wave of prosperity in the city, poverty remained a problem for many. The social activism of the 1960s and 1970s carried over into the 1980s when serious efforts were made to address the city's perennial housing problem, and the initiatives in the provision of affordable housing reflected the activism of groups such as Mothers United for Metro Shelter, and the establishment of Halifax Non-Profit Housing. The Canada Mortgage and Housing Corporation provided funding for housing co-operatives and for the Neighbourhood Improvement Program which provided funds for individual low-income home-owners and neighbourhoods to upgrade. However, the heyday of the large public housing development was over, and while the city maintained its developments in Spryfield, Bayers Westwood, Mulgrave Park, and Uniacke Square, no new public housing was constructed.

Hope Cottage on Brunswick Street continued to provide the essential service of feeding the needy throughout the 1980s and 1990s.

Hope Cottage, on Brunswick Street, served its one-millionth meal to the hungry in the fall of 1998. Neighbourhood churches expanded breakfast and meal programs, and coordinated their services to try to fill the gaps left by the erosion of income support programs. There were few vestiges of Halifax's war on poverty in the 1990s and fewer social reform activists pressing for change.

By the mid-1980s the impetus for reform was waning. Cuts to government welfare services, and moving the post-mentally ill out of custodial institutions increased the numbers of homeless people living on city streets and in emergency shelters. Changes in the local administration of social services, and the elimination of the federal Canada Assistance Act in 1996 reduced the resources available to help those in need. Voluntary charitable organi-zations tried to fill the gap, but as in previous eras, the voluntary approach was inadequate. The Metro Food Bank, begun in the early 1980s as a temporary measure, became an essential agency for many people.

The Halifax Regional Municipality

In 1996 the cities of Halifax and Dartmouth, the town of Bedford, and the rest of Halifax County were amalgamated by the provincial liberal governemnt of John Savage to form the Halifax Regional Muni-cipality (HRM). The establishment of the HRM on 1 April 1996 was greeted with no more enthusiasm than had been Confederation in 1867. While the concept of the Halifax metropolitan area was obviously not a new one, the distinctive communities which had developed around Halifax harbour and Bedford Basin resisted giving up their individual sense of identity and their political autonomy.

The social geography of the HRM reflected a long history of suburban development; the fact that the old city of Halifax was built on a small peninsula limited development possibilities. Since the eighteenth century a number of separate cities, towns and villages had grown up around the shores of the harbour and gradually spread inland along lakes and rivers. By the middle of the nineteenth century a number of industries had moved to Dartmouth to take advantage of sources of water power, and once regular ferry service was established, residential development increased. Fishing villages grew up on both sides of the outer harbour. Farmers worked the fertile soils along the Sackville River which empties into the head of Bedford Basin. The villages of Windsor Junction, Bedford, and Rockingham were served by commuter trains in the 1920s and 1930s. After World War II virtually all the suburban development occurred off the peninsula. Dartmouth's population growth outstripped that of Halifax for decades. The population of the Halifax Regional Municipality increased substantially in the last decades of the twentieth century, and the distribution of the population reflected suburban development. Between 1976 and 1996 the old city of Halifax actually lost ground, dropping from 117,882 to

Mounted policeman at the Quarry Pond in Point Pleasant Park.

113,910, while the population of the region as a whole increased from 278,531 in 1976 to 342,966 in 1996. Bedford and the Cole Harbour area east of Dartmouth have seen the most rapid population growth, but new residential development quickened in both the eastern and western ends of the region. Manufacturers and distributors began to move to the suburbs in the early 1960s and the trend continued in the 1980s and 1990s, as Burnside expanded and new industrial developments such as Bayers Lake on the western mainland side of Halifax were opened. By the 1990s the industrial parks had also become important retail shopping districts with the rise of factory outlets and "big box retail."

Despite their shared social and economic interests, residents of the diverse communities showed no interest in political amalgamation. The municipalities in the region had participated in a number of joint planning and services initiatives, such as the Metropolitan Area Planning Committee, the Regional Transit Authority, and the Pockwock Water Supply. In 1969 Halifax took a first step toward amalgamation in annexing adjacent areas to the west of the peninsula, and during the 1980s added the Lakeside and Bayers Lake industrial parks. But the impetus for the creation of the Halifax Regional Municipality came from the government of Nova Scotia. As

The visit of the Tall Ships in 1984 was one of the first events to bring large crowds to the waterfront.

The visit of the Pope to Halifax in 1984 drew huge crowds to the Halifax Commons. Bottom: *The Pope with Archbishop James Hayes who created a special ministry to the Italian community in Halifax.*

cultural, as well as the geographic, distance between downtown Halifax and small rural communities on the periphery of the HRM gradually lessened over the twentieth century, but it remained great. Forging appropriate electoral and administrative structures to respond to the needs of such a diverse population was both difficult and expensive. Residents experimented with new institutional forms with mixed results. The new 23-member elected council of the HRM was plagued by financial problems. Start-up costs were very high as new administrative systems were put in place to coordinate services in what were previously four different municipal governments. The HRM also faced a "garbage" crisis resulting from the closure of the solid waste facility in Sackville and attempts to reduce solid waste through the introduction of more recycling including a new composting system have been costly. A long-proposed and much-needed harbour clean-up was placed on hold. In 1998 the HRM was involved in an expensive round of labour

metropolitan area residents vigorously resisted amalgamation, the provincial government tried to sweeten the deal by offering a "service exchange." It agreed to assume the cost of social services in the new municipality, while the new municipality would pay for roads and policing in previously rural areas of Halifax County. However, the transfer of social assistance from municipal to provincial responsibility was not welcomed by social services professionals or by those who relied on their services because the change resulted in less money for social support programs. The creation of the HRM also resulted in steadily increasing traffic flows which raised concerns about the consequences to the environments, and pleas for improved public transit in the municipality.

The new HRM was not only a very large geographic area, but also characterized by significant economic and social diversity. The

negotiations with virtually all city workers set off by the end of the unpopular wage-freeze legislation imposed by the provincial government.

Cultural Renaissance

In the 1980s and 1990s many visitors to Halifax, especially those who had known the city in the bleak, drab years of World War II, were surprised by the new streetscapes, and cultural dynamism and diversity they found. The redeveloped historic waterfront attracted thousands

to outdoor festivals. The visit of the Tall Ships in the early 1980s, when thousands of people were drawn to waterfront to enjoy the spectacle, was a significant turning point. For several years a huge Halloween costume party, known as Mardi Gras, drew celebrants to the city core. The International Buskers Festival brought enthusiastic crowds. The Word on the Street, an annual one-day event on Spring Garden Road, attracted participants to hear authors read from their work and browse stalls set up by publishers and booksellers.

The revitalization of "downtown" spread from the waterfront to the streets at the base of the Citadel. Argyle Street, for example, became home to popular bars, restaurants, and coffee shops. The Spring Garden Road area witnessed an explosion in upscale retail development. Barrington Street, the former heart of the retail business in Halifax, showed fewer signs of recovery despite the promotional efforts of downtown boosters. Gottingen Street, the northern extension of the downtown area, suffered acutely from the blight of urban renewal and the impact of the rise of suburban shopping. Stimulated by community development, it became an area of service agencies and businesses serving the Mi'kmaq and African Nova Scotian communities. In the late 1980s the alternative art community trickled into the area, bringing galleries and cafés. Throughout the 1980s and 1990s downtown merchants faced stiff competition from developments off the peninsula.

In the late 1970s the arts in Halifax began a virtual renaissance. While Haligonians have long enjoyed and supported local musicians, in the 1980s and 1990s the music industry grew and diversified, fuelled by a combination of talent and self-promotion through events such as the annual East Coast Music Awards. Each year the Scotia Festival of Music and the Atlantic Jazz Festival brought a wide variety of artists to Halifax, and provided workshops and master classes for musicians. Regional talent was encouraged by television and CBC radio, and was supported by a plethora of recording studios. For a number of years Wormwood's Dog and Monkey Repertory Cinema operated as an alternative movie theatre, but unfortunately closed its doors in 1998. The Atlantic Film Festival, established in 1980, drew moviegoers and industry personnel, while live theatre was also part of

the cultural renaissance. In addition to older institutions such as Neptune Theatre and the Theatre Arts Guild, new companies such as the Eastern Front Theatre, Shakespeare-by-the-Sea, and an annual fringe festival brought new plays and players to the city.

One striking example of the success of the cultural activity in Halifax was Salter Street Films, established on a street named for Malachi Salter, the eighteenth-century merchant. Begun on a shoestring by brothers Michael and Paul Donovan, by the late 1990s Salter Street was involved in a wide range of film and television productions, including the award-winning and highly rated comedy series "This Hour has 22 Minutes," the family drama series "Emily of New Moon," and the science fiction series "LEXX." It also operated Electropolis, a large sound stage on the waterfront. The success of Salter Street Films both stimulated and reflected the growth of the cultural industries in Halifax and contributed to the revitalization of the city's downtown.

Long dominated by a large Anglo-Celtic majority, Halifax experienced a steady trickle of newcomers from more diverse national and ethnic backgrounds in the 1980s and 1990s. Despite a tragic legacy of persistent racism, Haligonians began to show more willingness to celebrate cultural diversity. The small Chinese community in the city, harassed by racist hooligans earlier in the twentieth century, was commemorated by a special exhibit at the Nova Scotia Museum in 1997. St. Mary's University established an Irish Studies Program which would have been unthinkable in the nineteenth century. The small Greek, Italian and Lebanese communities established strong institutions in the city, and invited their fellow citizens to enjoy their cultural traditions in well-attended events such as the annual Greekfest.

One of the new groups of immigrants that had an impact on the life of the city was a group of Tibetan Buddhists, many of whom moved to Halifax from the United States under the leadership of Chogyam Trungpa, Rinpoche. In 1978 Trungpa decided to move the world headquarters of his Tibetan Buddhist organization, Vajradhatu International, from Boulder, Colorado to Nova Scotia. Trungpa believed Nova Scotia mixed basic amenities with traditional values

The New Old City (1980-1999)

Each summer the International Buskers Festival attracted large crowds to the revitalized waterfront area.

and pace. In 1986 Trungpa himself moved to Halifax; where he died in 1987. More than 500 adults came to Halifax, and about 420 stayed. By the late 1990s the community was no longer comprised only of U.S. immigrants. Many Canadians joined the community, along with a small number of European immigrants, although the overwhelming majority were educated, white, middle class and born and raised in the United States. "Sangha" members are psychiatrists, crafts-people, teachers, film-makers, entrepreneurs, media and health professionals.

The economic, political and social changes Halifax underwent in the 1980s and 1990s reflected the challenging blending of old and new. The new industries, whether tourism or high tech, arose out of the city's long tradition as a seaport and as a regional service centre. The new political institutions of the Halifax Regional Municipality were a concrete manifestation of long-standing social and economic relationships in the area drawn together by Halifax Harbour. The new cultural and multi-cultural vitality represented changes set in motion decades earlier, rooted again, in a blending of old and new.

Endnotes

Introduction

1 Isabella Lucy Bird, *The Englishwoman in America* (London: 1856), 17. This volume has been reissued, with a modern introduction, by A. H. Clark (Toronto: 1966).
2 Thomas Raddall, *Halifax, Warden of the North* (Toronto: 1948); a revised edition was issued in 1971.
3 Among the most important and readily accessible books to consult by students of Halifax history are John Bell (ed.), *Halifax: a Literary Portrait* (Halifax: 1990); Brian C. Cuthbertson, *The Loyalist Governor (Sir John Wentworth)*; (Halifax: 1983); J.M. Beck, *Joseph Howe*, 2 vols. (Montreal & Kingston: 1982-83); Judith Fingard, *The Dark Side of Life in Victorian Halifax* (Halifax: 1989); P. B. Waite, *The Lives of Dalhousie*, 2 vols. (Montreal & Kingston: 1994-98), Janet Kitz, *Shattered City: the Halifax Explosion and its Aftermath* (Halifax: 1989); Alan Ruffman and C. D. Howell, *Ground Zero: a reassessment of the 1917 Explosion in Halifax Harbour* (Halifax: 1994); Graham Metson, *An East Coast Port* (Halifax: 1981); Africville Genealogical Society, *The Spirit of Africville* (Halifax: 1992). For article literature, see especially *Acadiensis*, *Collections* of the Nova Scotia Historical Society, and the *Nova Scotia Historical Review* (the latter two now appear as the Nova Scotia Historical Society *Journal*)

Chapter 1

1 Extract from a letter published by the *Gentleman's Magazine*, London, January 1750, found in Adam Shortt (ed.), *Documents Relating to Currency, Exchange and Finance in Nova Scotia* (Ottawa: 1933), 284.
2 The Duke of Bedford to the Board of Trade, London, 6 March 1749. A transcript of this letter can be found in Public Archives of Nova Scotia [PANS], MG100, v. 160, #23.
3 *Ibid*.
4 This is the assessment of Ronald Romkey, *Expeditions of Honour: the Journal of John Salusbury in Halifax, N.S., 1749-53* (London and Toronto: 1982), 18-19.
5 *Ibid.*, 20.
6 Gerard Finn, "Jean Le Loutre," *Dictionary of Canadian Biography*, vol. 4 (Toronto: 1979), 455.
7 *Royal Gazette*, 25 November 1752. What the soldiers had done to warrant death was not reported; what made all this "newsworthy" was the edifying confession of one of the condemned men. See also the issues of this newspaper for 30 March 1752, 30 May 1752 and 8 September 1753.
8 These were the bleak observations of Irishman John Knox, who visited Halifax in 1757, as cited in A. G. Doughty (ed.), *An Historical Journal of the Campaigns in North America* (Toronto: 1914), 3 vols., vol. 1, 32.
9 Letter from Councillor Alex Grant, of Halifax, to the Reverend Ezra Stiles of Boston, May 1760, as cited in George S. Brown, Yarmouth, *Nova Scotia: a Sequel to Campbell's History* (Boston: 1888), 128.
10 These lines were part of a longer poetic condemnation of Halifax written by John Maylen of Boston. This extract comes from Ernest Clarke, *The Siege of Fort Cumberland* (Montreal and Kingston: 1995), 17.
11 An extract from Governor Lawrence's address to the Nova Scotian Assembly in December 1759, as cited by Allan Marble, *Surgeons, Smallpox and the Poor: a History of Medicine and Social Conditions in Nova Scotia, 1749-1799* (Montreal and Kingston: 1993), 64.
12 A. H. Clark, *The Geography of Early Nova Scotia to 1760* (Madison, WI: 1968), 35.
13 T. B. Akins, "History of Halifax City," *Nova Scotia Historical Society Collections*, v. 8 (1892- 94), 73. The problems which plagued Halifax in this era are discussed by Francis A. Coghlan, "Lord William Campbell," " *Dictionary of Canadian Biography*, vol. 4 (Toronto: 1979), 131-132.
14 James S. Macdonald, *Annals, North British Society* Halifax: 1905). The term "North British" reflected Lowland Scottish enthusiasm for the notion that they shared with the English, a common "British" identity; the genesis of this outlook is explored by Linda Colley, *Britons: Forging the Nation* (London: 1992).
15 Observations cited in C. B. Fergusson (ed.), "The Life of Jonathan Scott," *PANS Bulletin* (Halifax, 1960), 43.
16 This paragraph combines local news items from the *Nova Scotia Gazette and Weekly Chronicle* for 31 January 1769, 8 September 1772 and 13 October 1772.
17 Oliver was one of the earliest of American Loyalists to arrive in Halifax; his comments are found in A. W. H. Eaton, "Chapters in the History of Halifax," *Americana*, v. 10 (1915), 777.
18 John Robinson and Thomas Rispin came to Nova Scotia from England to assess the colony's prospects for farming. The report they wrote, entitled *Journey Through Nova Scotia* (York: 1774), has been reproduced in *Report of the Board of Trustees of the Public Archives of Nova Scotia* (Halifax: 1945), 29-57.

Chapter 2

1 J. M. Bumsted, "Francis Legge," *Dictionary of Canadian Biography*, vol. 4 (Toronto: 1979), 449-452.
2 Bailey, a Massachusetts-born Anglican cleric was an early refugee from revolutionary America; he came to Halifax in June, 1779 His observations appear in John Bell (ed.), *Halifax: a Literary Portrait* (Lawrencetown Beach: 1990), 19.
3 Parr's comments appear, among other places, in J M. Beck, *The Government of Nova Scotia* (Toronto: 1957), 14.
4 The debate which swirls around the identity and motivation of Nova Scotia's Loyalists has been explored by Neil Mackinnon, *This Unfriendly Soil* (Montreal and Kingston: 1986)
5 *Ibid*. 75-76.
6 *Ibid*. 75-76.
7 Ann Condon, "Edward Winslow," *Dictionary of Canadian Biography*, vol 5 (Toronto: 1983): 867.
8 Gregory Townsend to David Hubbards, 8 July 1783, as cited in *Catherine S. Crary, The Price of Liberty* (New York: 1973), 399.
9 Edward to Mary Winslow, 25 September 1784, found in W O. Raymond (ed.), *Winslow Papers* (Saint John: 1901), 233.
10 W. M. Brown, "Recollections of Old Halifax," *Nova Scotia Historical Society Collections*, vol. 13 (1908): 75-101.
11 Benigne Charles Fevret de Saint-Mesmin came to Halifax in June 1793; his impressions of the local scene are printed in Public Archives of Canada, *Annual Report* (Ottawa: 1946), xxiv-xxxvii.
12 *Ibid*.
13 James S Macdonald, "Memoir of Governor John Parr," *Nova Scotia Historical Society Collections*, vol. 14 (1910), 41-78. A graphic description of Halifax gentlemen drinking to get drunk in public is found in Reginald W. Jeffery (ed.), *Dyott's Diaries, 1781-1845*, 2 vols. (London: 1907), vol. 1, 46.
14 Joshua Marsden, *The Narrative of a Mission to Nova Scotia* (London: 1827), 7-15. For background on this visitor, see G S. French, "Joshua Marsden," *Dictionary of Canadian Biography*, vol. 7 (Toronto: 1988), 586-588.
15 Marsden, *Narrative*, 17 See also G. A. Burbridge and M. D. Morrison, *Historical Sketches of St. Andrew's Church* (Halifax: 1949), 10.
16 These pithy words came from the Reverend William Black, the leading pioneer of early Nova Scotian Methodism; see R M. Hattie, "Old-time Halifax Churches," *Nova Scotia Historical Society Collections*, vol. 26 (1945), 49.
17 Linda Colley, *Britons: Forging the Nation* (London: 1992), 375
18 These are the comments of William Dyott, who was posted to Halifax in 1787 at the age of 26; see Jeffery, *Dyott's Diaries*, vol 1, 65.
19 J M. Beck, "John Howe," *Dictionary of Canadian Biography*, vol. 6 (Toronto: 1987), 332-335.
20 James S Macdonald, *Annals, North British Society* (Halifax: 1905), 75.
21 Archibald MacMechan, *Old Provincial Tales* (Toronto: 1924), 143-161
22 Judith Fingard, "Sir John Wentworth," *Dictionary of Canadian Biography*, vol 5 (Toronto: 1983), 848-852.
23 *Acadian Recorder* 14 May 1814
24 T B. Akins, "History of Halifax City," *Nova Scotia Historical Society Collections*, vol. 8 (1892-94), 158.
25 Judith Fingard, *Jack in Port* (Toronto: 1982), 135-136
26 Akins, "*Halifax*," 158

Chapter 3

1 John to William Young, 19 February 1815, as cited in P A. Buckner and J. G. Reid, *The Atlantic Region to Confederation* (Toronto and Fredericton: 1994), 241.
2 *Acadian Recorder*, 25 August 1822
3 T C. Haliburton, *History of Nova Scotia*, 2 vols. (Halifax: 1829), vol. 2, 14-15.
4 William Moorson, *Letters from Nova Scotia* (London: 1830), 7
5 John McGregor, *British America*, 2 vols (Edinburgh: 1832), vol. 1, 80.
6 Hugh Murray, *An Historical and Descriptive Account of British America*, 3 vols (Edinburgh: 1839), vol. 2, 157.
7 Audubon acquired fame from his interest in researching and drawing birds; his comments on Halifax are found in Lewis Harrison, "Some Canadian Audubonia," *Canadian Field-Naturalist*, vol 40.
8 *Acadian Recorder*, 6-13 September 1834
9 Advice for August in *Belcher's Farmer's Almanack for 1824* (Halifax: 1823)
10 Margaret to William Stairs, 2 June 1833, as found in W J. Stairs, *Family History, Stairs, Morrow* (Halifax: 1906); see also D. A. Sutherland, "W. M. Stairs," *Dictionary of Canadian Biography*, vol. 9 (Toronto: 1976), 738-739.
11 J F. Fingard, "English Humanitarianism and the Colonial Mind: Walter Bromley in Nova Scotia, 1813-25," *Canadian Historical Review*, LIV (1973), 123-151.
12 William Jackson, *Man of Sorrows* (Baltimore: 1834), 266-312
13 A W. H. Eaton, "Chapters in the History of Halifax," *Americana*, vol. 10 (1915), 841.
14 *Novascotian*, 15 September 1830; *Acadian Recorder*, 18 September 1830
15 *Times*, 24 January 1837. Halifax's first penitentiary was built in 1841 on the shores of the North West Arm; for a description of the corner-stone laying ceremonies, presided over by Alexander Keith, see *Times*, 29 June 1841.
16 These comments were offered in an editorial discussing how new immigrants from Britain and Ireland were being moulded into "Nova Scotians"; see *Novascotian*, 2 January 1840
17 A summary based on the press coverage provided by *Acadian Recorder*, 2 July 1838; *Novascotian*, 5 July 1838; *Times*, 3 July 1838
18 *Ibid*.
19 *Colonial Pearl*, 16 May 1840
20 Based on press coverage of the *Unicorn's* arrival as provided by *Acadian Recorder*, 6 June 1840; *Novascotian*, 4 June 1840; *Times*, 2 June 1840

Chapter 4

1 The Monthly Record of the Church of Scotland in Nova Scotia and the Adjoining Provinces, August 1866, 156-7.
2 Mayor's Report, p.11, in the 1866-67 Annual Report of the City.
3 *Novascotian*, 25 May 1857.
4 *Morning Chronicle*, 2 July 1867.
5 Quoted by P.B. Waite, *The Lives of Dalhousie University, Volume One, 1818-1925: Lord Dalhousie's College* (Montreal & Kingston: 1994), 93.
6 Robert Sedgewick, 'The Proper Sphere and Influence of Women in Christian Society', a lecture given to the Halifax YMCA, November 1856.
7 D.A. Sutherland, "Henry H. Cogswell," *Dictionary of Canadian Biography*, vol.8 (Toronto: 1985), 167-9.
8 *Novascotian*, 7 July 1851.

Chapter 5

1 *Morning Chronicle*, 10 August 1885.
2 City Council Proceedings, *Acadian Recorder*, 13 February, 1909.
3 Mayor's address, p.xli, Annual Report, City of Halifax, 1884-85.
4 City Engineer's Report, p.27, Annual Report, City of Halifax, 1872-73.
5 *Acadian Recorder*, 24 August 1894.
6 Inaugural address of Mayor Alexander Stephen, 12 May 1897, p.18, Annual Report, City of Halifax, 1897-98.

Chapter 6

1 Mayor's Address, April 1908, Annual Report of the City, 1907-08, p.25.
2 City Engineer's Report, pp.183-4, Annual Report of the City of Halifax, 1908-09.
3 Henry Roper, "The Halifax Board of Control: The Failure of Municipal Reform, 1906-1919," *Acadiensis*, XIV, 2 (Spring 1985), 48.
4 *Acadian Recorder*, 20 Sept. 1910.
5 J.H. Hamilton, 'The Factory Girl of Halifax,' unpublished paper, Pine Hill Divinity Hall, 20 March 1912.
6 *Acadian Recorder*, 6 July 1910.
7 *Acadian Recorder*, 31 Aug. 1910.
8 Archibald MacMechan, "The Halifax Disaster", reprinted in *The Halifax Explosion, December 6, 1917* (Toronto: 1978), compiled and edited by Graham Metson, 18.

Chapter 7

1 *Halifax Citizen*, 26 February 1926.
2 *Halifax Citizen*, 23 January 1920.
3 Evelyn Theakston, personal letter. Judith Fingard, Personal Papers.
4 Samuel Henry Prince, *Halifax Housing: A Report* (1932), 3.
5 Hank Snow, the Singing Ranger, with Jack Ownbey and Bob Burris, *The Hank Snow Story*. (Urbana and Chicago: 1994) 141.
6 E.R. Forbes, "Consolidating Disparity: The Maritimes and the Industrialization of Canada during the Second World War," *Challenging the Regional Stereotype: Essays on the 20th Century Maritimes* Fredericton: 1989) 172.

Chapter 8

1 *Halifax Mail*, 10 January 1948.
2 William Kaplan, *Everything that Floats: Pat Sullivan, Hal Banks, and the Seamen's Unions of Canada*. Toronto: 1987), 136.
3 Robert J. McCalla, "Separation and Specialization of Land Uses in Cityport Waterfronts: The Cases of Saint John and Halifax," *Canadian Geographer*, XXVII, 1, 1983: 48-61.
4 NSARM MFM#12451, Halifax City Council Minutes, 21 Jan. 1954.
5 Encounter of Urban Environment, Vol.1. Nova Scotia: Voluntary Economic Planning 1971: 153.
6 J. Brian Hannington, *Every Popish Person: The Story of Roman Catholicism and the Church of Halifax 1604-1984*. (Halifax: 1984), 224.